The Day Aberystwyth Stood Still

MALCOLM PRYCE was born in the UK and has spent much of his life working and travelling abroad. He has been, at various times, a BMW assembly-line worker, a hotel washer-up, a deck hand on a yacht sailing the South Seas, an advertising copywriter and the world's worst aluminium salesman. In 1998 he gave up his day job and booked a passage on a banana boat bound for South America in order to write *Aberystwyth Mon Amour*. He spent the next seven years living in Bangkok, where he wrote three more novels in the series, *Last Tango in Aberystwyth*, *The Unbearable Lightness of Being in Aberystwyth* and *Don't Cry for Me Aberystwyth*. In 2007 he moved back to the UK and now lives in Oxford, where he wrote his most recent novel, *From Aberystwyth with Love*.

THE LOUIE KNIGHT SERIES

The Day Aberystwyth Stood Still

Malcolm Pryce

BLOOMSBURY

LONDON · NEW DELHI · NEW YORK · SYDNEY

First published in Great Britain 2011
This paperback edition published 2012

Bloomsbury Publishing, London, New Delhi, New York and Sydney

50 Bedford Square, London WC1B 3DP

A CIP catalogue record for this book is available from the British Library

ISBN 978 1 4088 2195 4
10 9 8 7 6 5 4 3 2 1

Typeset by Hewer Text UK Ltd, Edinburgh
Printed in Great Britain by Clays Ltd, St Ives plc

MIX
Paper from
responsible sources
FSC® C018072

www.bloomsbury.com/malcolmpryce

SHE WAS just a Baal-worshipping Phoenician princess who got thrown out of a window by her eunuchs and eaten by dogs; could have happened to anyone. All they remember Jezebel for now is painting her face, and for that they call her a tramp. But the one thing they never tell you is the reason she did it: she knew she was about to die. The rouge was scorn thrown into the face of her assassin, whose name was Jehel. He's not remembered for anything much apart from the events of that day. He didn't sack towns, nor take into captivity all the virgin girls; he didn't even hang the king from a tree outside the city gates. In the Old Testament you were nobody if you didn't do that. As kings go, he was a peanut grifter. But thanks to him the flesh of Jezebel was as dung upon the face of the fields. In Aberystwyth they named a club after her, on the caravan park. A quiet place where you could sit late into the night holding the hand of a girl in a stovepipe hat and forget for a while the disenchantments of this world. I met a girl there once, and bought her a drink. It didn't cost much. Just my heart.

Chapter 1

IS NAME was Ercwleff, which is Welsh for Hercules, and he was very big. He kept his trousers held up with packing string, tied in a knot just below his nipples, and wore a dung-stained tie that was never removed and had grown into the flesh of his neck the way wire sometimes cuts into the bark of trees. His head had two indentations where normal people have ears and this was the result, they said, of a clumsy forceps delivery sixty years ago when the doctor performed the operation with coal tongs while drunk. They said he was one of God's children, but in contrast to most of God's children he carried an axe down the front of his trousers, the bright, shiny blade hanging out over the packing-string belt. He also carried a toy rabbit. He was a gelder by trade, and castrated the lambs the old-fashioned way, using his teeth. The axe was for special occasions. He was very big and he was in my office, and, standing next to him, was Preseli Watkins, his brother and the current mayor of Aberystwyth. He wasn't one of God's children. He was about the same age as Ercwleff, early sixties, and wore a midnight-blue, chalk-stripe, hand-tailored mock Italian suit from Swansea, and he explained to me what Ercwleff was going to do.

'He's going to play the chopping game . . . with your desk.'

I nodded. 'All for poking my nose into your affairs.'

'That's right. All for poking your nose in my affairs.'

'Even though I haven't.'

'Even though you haven't; yet. But you will. I'd move back if I were you, and take the rum out of the desk drawer.'

'You know about the rum, huh?'

'I make it my business to know about people who make the mistake of mistaking my business for their business.'

I did as I was told and put the bottle on the windowsill. 'Does he really need to do this? Desks are expensive.'

The mayor gave a sort of apologetic half-grin that suggested the matter was beyond his control.

'I don't mean to cause any trouble,' I said.

'You're a private detective, how could you avoid it?'

'I need my desk.'

'Buy a new one, this one's crap.' He nodded to Ercwleff who handed him the rabbit and pulled the axe out of his trousers. I slid my chair back and stood up. The mayor handed me the rabbit, and for some reason I held it.

Ercwleff swung the axe and brought it down with a crunch. The head sank deep into the cheap, stained wooden surface. A splinter of wood landed at my feet. He wrenched the axe out and lofted the head, then brought it down again in one fluid movement. It was the easy grace of a man who is more at home with an axe than he is with a knife and fork.

'When do you think I will begin poking my nose in your business?'

'Soon.'

'How can you be so sure?'

'My soothsayer told me. He seldom gets it wrong.'

'Trouble is, if the prophecy is right, chopping up my desk won't stop me. And if it isn't, you've chopped it up for nothing.'

'In that case send me the bill.'

Ercwleff kept chopping.

'This won't look good if your brother ever wants to stand for mayor.'

'He is standing for mayor,' said Preseli. 'I step down at the end of summer.'

Crunch. The axe head came down again. Crunch, crunch, crunch.

'We'll be sorry to see you go.'

'Thank you. It has been a privilege serving you. But it's time now, I think, for a fresh perspective.'

Crunch.

Ercwleff began to sweat. It was still only May and quite cool and blustery outside, but Ercwleff was putting his back into his work. The desk itself had been reduced to a pile of wood no longer recognisable as an item of furniture, and now he was picking up the individual pieces and splitting them along the grain to make kindling. He didn't say anything as he worked. He wasn't a big talker.

'What are you going to do with the wood?' I asked.

'Leave it for you. If you keep it dry over the summer it will be good for the fireplace in the winter.'

Ercwleff stopped chopping and straightened up; he placed the axe down by the side of his leg like a sentry with his rifle. He looked across to Preseli. The phone rang amid the bird's nest of splintered timber and we all searched with our eyes. Preseli spotted it and pointed; without needing any further encouragement, Ercwleff kicked the phone free of the debris and smashed it with an axe blow. Glistening splinters of Bakelite skipped across the room. He put the axe back inside his trousers and stood to attention. I handed him the rabbit. They both walked to the door. In the doorway Preseli stopped and turned, as I knew he would; they always do.

'My advice to you is replace the desk but retain the fragments of the old one as a reminder of the fate that awaits you if you don't keep your nose clean.'

'How would it be if I glued it back together?'

He let his gaze rest on me for a beat. As they left, Ercwleff said, 'That was a good game.'

I went to the kitchenette for the dustpan and brush.

Chapter 2

AFTER I'D swept the wood into a neat pile I sat down on my chair and pondered. It's hard to know what to do after a visit like that and for a while I cursed the mayor, but looking back I have to admit he was right; his soothsayer was good. Less than ten minutes later the client who would be responsible for the mess walked in.

He was short: less than five six, and dumpy, wearing a grey flannel suit. His head was bald and pointed, as if his shower-head had been replaced by a pencil sharpener. He walked slowly, breathing heavily and paused at the door to catch his breath. He surveyed the room.

'I tried ringing, but the operator said there was a fault on the line.'

'I had an accident with the phone.'

He looked at the shards of Bakelite and nodded. I invited him in and pointed to the client's chair, which was set opposite me at the distance of a desk. He took a seat. The desk had always presented a barrier that I appreciated between me and the clients and I felt naked in its absence. The movement of air, displaced as he sat down, wafted the faint, cloying scent of Parma Violets. He took a packet from his pocket and removed a sweet from the wrapper with the same intensity that some people show for the ritual of lighting up a cigarette.

'You are Louie Knight, Aberystwyth's only private detective,' he said. He took it for granted that I was and continued. 'My name is Iolo Raspiwtin. I was born in a croft in the district of Pontwerwyd, overlooking the Nant-y-Moch River, in 1931. Nant-y-Moch, as you know, means "river of the pig" in English.'

'How can I help you?'

'I bring you a case, not just any case, but a special case, probably the toughest case you have ever had; possibly the toughest case any private detective has ever had.'

'I'm a tough guy.'

'You'll need to be.'

I let that one ride, leant back in my chair and crossed my legs.

'In view of the difficulties involved, I mean to be generous. I will pay you £200 now, and £200 in the unlikely event that you complete the task.'

I smiled and offered him a glass of rum, which he accepted. I fetched two glasses from the drainer in the kitchenette and poured two measures. We raised our glasses in a silent toast.

'I seek a man. One who I have reason to suspect is either in Aberystwyth now or will arrive very shortly. This man can help me with a project that has preoccupied me most of my life and which is not relevant to your inquiry.'

'In my experience such things are almost always relevant to the inquiry.'

'Not this time.'

'Tell me what makes him difficult to find. I assume he is difficult to find?'

'Absolutely. Why else would I pay you £200? He is difficult to find because he is dead.'

'Dead people are usually quite easy to find because they are kept in the ground.'

'Conventionally, yes, the ground is the appointed storage for our mortal remains.'

'Where did this man's remains end up?'

'On the bus to Aberaeron.'

I gripped my chin gently between thumb and forefinger, pretending to think deeply about the mystery. 'Did he catch the bus himself?'

'Yes.'

'That would imply that he was alive.'

'Precisely. His name was Iestyn Probert. He was hanged at

Aberystwyth gaol in 1965 for his part in the raid on the Coliseum cinema. This raid is quite famous.'

'I've heard of it.'

'Indeed, who hasn't?'

'Do you have any grounds for believing the man who caught the bus was the same as the man who was hanged?'

'The bus driver recognised him from the photos.'

I tried to stifle a mounting sense of irritation. Raspiwtin had a disconcerting way of not quite answering questions. 'Let me put it a different way. How does a dead man perform the act of catching a bus?'

'He was no longer dead. They resurrected him.'

'Who?'

He paused and stared, his eyes boring into mine with an intensity in which hints of fanaticism glinted. I stared back. He walked to the window and closed the curtains before retaking his seat. Then he leaned forward slightly. 'Have you heard of the Ystrad Meurig incident?'

'There have been many incidents at Ystrad Meurig.'

'This one featured a flying saucer. It crashed. They called it the Welsh Roswell.'

'Why did you close the curtains?'

He ignored me. 'I presume you have heard of the Roswell incident?'

'In America?'

'Yes, in New Mexico in 1947. They found saucer debris and exobiological remains that were secretly taken to Area 51.'

'I heard it was just a crashed weather balloon.'

'You wouldn't say that if you had seen the autopsy footage, as I have.'

'How does this relate to the dead man?'

'The raid on the Coliseum cinema took place the same week as the Ystrad Meurig incident. The getaway car drove right through the area cordoned off by the military. For some reason Iestyn Probert was evicted from the car and went on the run. A week or so later he was arrested again. You see?'

'Not really. Don't hanged men get put in a canvas winding sheet and dissolved in quicklime?'

'Normally, yes, hanged men were buried in an unmarked plot inside the walls of Aberystwyth prison; but Iestyn Probert came from the Denunciationist community at Cwmnewidion Isaf, and arrangements were made to return his corpse to them for burial. While his corpse was still in the possession of the prison morgue a most remarkable event occurred. A strange woman turned up and bought the cadaver from the attendant. He described her as elfin with no thumbs and cat-like irises. She paid with a Cantref-y-Gwaelod doubloon. Cantref-y-Gwaelod is the lost Iron Age kingdom that sank beneath the waters of Cardigan Bay after the last ice age.'

'I know. Strange as it may seem, I've had a number of clients with connections to Cantref-y-Gwaelod.'

He smiled, as if this fact lent credence to his tale.

I eyed him over the rim of the rum glass. 'Perhaps you should tell me a bit more about yourself. Your name sounds familiar.'

'You are no doubt thinking of my famous cousin Grigori Yefimovich Rasputin, former Counsellor to Tsar Nicholas II and physic to his son, Alexei. It was my forebear's proud boast that he was able to treat Alexei's haemophilia by telegram. My branch of the family travelled to Wales via the Welsh settlement of Hughesovka in the Ukraine, shortly after the armistice of the Great War. We adopted the Welsh spelling of Raspiwtin to better assimilate.'

'That was a smart move; the Welsh can be suspicious of foreigners.'

He looked pleased. 'Indeed. At the age of six I was sent to live and study with the monks on Caldey Island. I applied myself to my studies with great diligence, and because of my quick wit and piety I was lucky enough to earn, at the age of ten, a scholarship to the Vatican laundry. There, for the next eight years, I passed my time listening, and learning, and attending with great solemnity the Hephaestian fires that burned night and day beneath the great steaming wash pots. I became an expert in the laundering of liturgical vestments: surplices, stoles, albs, chasubles, cinctures, tunicles, copes, maniples, humeral veils, birettas, palliums, fanons, faldas, pontifical gloves and, of course, pontifical underlinen. It was from the latter that I first descried the contradictions – the Janus-faced god-beast that is Man – that would underpin my later *apostasia*. The Vatican laundry is the great university of the human condition, for therein is contained in its entirety the true folly of Man. Gold threads and satin smeared with the pollution that mocks our aspirations to rise beyond the fur that defines us as beasts. Boiled up, distilled through the divine agency of Persil, rising up as a vapour, condensing . . . daily its sweetly perfumed and laundered truth fell as rain upon our eager upturned cherubic faces. I say truly, you can never look at a pope the same way again after you've washed his pants.' He drained his glass and held it out for a refill; I dutifully obliged. 'It was here that the first stage on the slipway to my spiritual disintegration took place, which would eventually bring me to your door.'

I drummed my finger against the tumbler. 'So you seek a man called Iestyn who took part in the famous raid on the Coliseum cinema. For that they hanged him. But you say he was seen alive after they hanged him.'

'Yes.'

'You know, a lot of people would say your story was a load of phooey.'

'I did too. Until I made inquiries regarding this man many years ago and was assured by the authorities that no such person existed.'

'Because he was dead.'

'No, no such person had ever existed.' He paused and looked intensely at me. 'You see?'

'No.'

'What more proof do you need?'

'That he doesn't exist?'

'Evidence of his existence is being suppressed by the authorities.'

'Not necessarily; lots of people don't exist.'

'Name one.'

'Santa Claus.'

'Yes.'

'The Tooth Fairy.'

'OK.'

I paused.

His eyes flashed in expectation of victory.

'Fingal.'

'Who?'

'The giant who owned the cave in Scotland. Someone wrote a symphony about him.'

'See! You struggle after three. Who has heard of this Fingal and his symphony? There is in fact hardly anybody who doesn't exist in this precise manner.'

'Neptune.'

'Yes, I accept that Neptune does not exist.'

'Jack Frost.'

'I concede Jack Frost also.'

'The Jabberwock.'

'You are good at this.'

'Little Miss Muffet.'

He swung an arm out as if catching a fly and clicked his fingers. 'You see? You have already run out. The character of Little Miss Muffet is said by many scholars to be an allegory of Mary, Queen of Scots.' He stood up in triumph and carried the glass over to the windowsill.

'What makes you think Iestyn has come back to town?'

'Two weeks ago there was an alien contact just outside Aberystwyth. A farmer reported seeing a flying saucer land in one of his fields. He was approached by the occupants of the craft, one of whom was an elfin woman with no thumbs and cat-like irises. She told him she wanted to make love to him as her race was dying and she wanted the earth-man's seed to save it. This is a remarkably common feature of accounts of alien contact.'

'Or of fantasies about alien contact.'

'These stories occur too frequently and with too much consistency of detail to be fantasies.'

'You could say the same about people who think they are Napoleon.

The details there are usually pretty consistent: they always stick one hand inside their coat over the heart and claim to have a wife called Josephine.'

'You are too cynical.'

'You really think they need the earth-man's seed? Surely after travelling all that way they could think of an easier way to collect it.'

Raspiwtin gave me the condescending smile such people reserve for those of us who err in darkness. 'You may have a point, but the pertinent thing for our inquiry is this: they also asked for directions to Iestyn Probert's house.' He stood up.

'Is that supposed to prove he is alive?'

'The aliens evidently thought so. Are you saying they are wrong?' He walked to the door, adding, 'I'm staying at the Marine.'

'This would be his old house, I take it?'

'That's right. It seems pretty clear, does it not, that some sort of rendezvous had been arranged.'

'Where is this house?'

'Out at Ystumtuen in the hamlet of Llwynmwyn.'

'How do you spell that?'

'I don't know. You won't find it on a map; it has been effaced.'

'How convenient.'

'You are familiar with the narrow-gauge railway to Devil's Bridge that passes in the valley below Ystumtuen?'

'Sort of.'

'If you sit on the left-hand side of the carriage and look out across the valley just before Rhiwfron, you will note a discoloration in the grass of the distant valley side, caused by seepage from the lead mines; some people think it forms the shape of a duck. Iestyn used to live in a house that stood at the end of what those people would regard as the bill.'

'Talking of the bill,' I said, 'this £200 up front that you mentioned. Up front usually means right now, doesn't it?'

'So you take the case, then?'

'Yes, I take the case.'

Chapter 3

THE MORNING light had the bright lemony sharpness that you get in spring, the sun still in its original wrapping, not yet weighed down with the weary pathos, the sheer pointless repetitiveness of it all. A few people huddled on the beach; dogs chased things we couldn't see; a caravan of donkeys plodded across my field of vision, in sharp silhouette against the sea. The man at the front was my father, Eeyore, wearing an old mac that flapped in the breeze, his outline made jagged by lightning bolts of straw.

At the north end of the Prom, beneath the shadow of Constitution Hill, Sospan was leaning on the counter of his ice-cream kiosk, squinting as he stared out to sea, as if the answer to the mysteries of life were encoded in the hieroglyphical waves. He saw me approach, pushed himself up and turned to the machine that dispensed the nectar that attracted us all to the wooden flower of his kiosk.

'Everything OK?' I asked.

He replied with a noncommittal grimace and handed me the ice cream. 'Had to replace a few timbers in the north-west corner of my kiosk, it gets the brunt of the sea breeze there, you see. It always unnerves me, making repairs. We don't like to be reminded of the advance of decay in our lives, do we?'

I made no answer, but put some change on the countertop with a sharp rattle. He took the money. Out of the corner of my eye I saw a girl appear, walking along the edge of the Prom near the bandstand. She wore jeans and a wind-blown military parka and was taking care not to step on the cracks between the slabs of paving stone. It was Calamity, my partner, who had just come back from a fortnight at Kousin Kevin's Krazy Komedy Kamp in Pwllheli with her aunt. I watched her approach with a quickening sense of delight. Calamity was almost eighteen now and had been my partner for five years. During that time she had become the daughter I had never had. I had felt her absence keenly. She gave up the cracks-in-the-pavement game and ran the last few steps, skipping up to me and kissing me.

'How was Kousin Kevin's?' I asked.

'Great!' A gust of wind blew the hood of her parka up and framed her with a halo of rabbit's fur.

'I sent you a food parcel via the International Red Cross in Geneva.'

'I got it. I shared it out among the other holidaymakers. Did you hear about the flying saucer?' She looked at me with a bright gaze, as pure and unsullied as the spring morning; her eyes shone and in them was an innocence and absence of guile. It was sometimes hard to believe that when I had first discovered her she had been one of those teenage troglodytes who haunted the caverns of the Pier amusement arcade, kids for whom fresh air was chlorine gas. It was a milieu in which slouching, moping and eye-rolling impatience with the manifest stupidity of adults were the lingua franca. In acting as a father figure to her I had acquired the father's secret melancholy: watching her do her best to rush through the years of enchantment in the forlorn belief that adulthood was something worth rushing for.

'I saw a flying saucer. It was silver, with red and green lights flashing round the rim. We saw it out at sea.'

I turned to Sospan. 'Did you hear that? She saw a flying saucer.'

'Loads of people have,' said Sospan. 'Farmer out at Ynys Greigiog —'

'It was in the paper,' said Calamity, assuming possession of the story. 'He was driving home from the Farmer's Co-op in Aber' with some seed in the back of the Land-Rover. The UFO buzzed the car for a while and then landed, filling the valley with a blinding light. Then the bloke found his engine stopped. He got out of the car and was approached by four aliens in silver suits. The lead one was a woman. Face like an elf, blonde hair and four fingers on each hand; probably a Nordic, but it's possible they were Greys, it's hard to tell.'

'Wanted to make love to him,' said Sospan, unable to hold back what for him was the most interesting aspect of the encounter. 'Bold as brass.'

'What language did she speak?' I asked.

'He didn't say.'

'Did they make love, then?' I asked.

'No one knows,' said Calamity. 'He said his memory of the incident was very hazy. Why did you chop up the desk?'

I told her about the visit from Raspiwtin.

Eeyore appeared, leading a train of donkeys. Sospan reached again for the dispenser, but Eeyore stopped him. 'No, Sospan, not the usual. There is an ache in my heart today that vanilla won't expunge. I need something special.'

Sospan adopted the grave mien of the bespoke necromancer. 'What sort of special?'

'These are troubled times,' said Eeyore. He always had a tendency towards melancholy, but this morning the glum tone had a sharper edge. Before becoming the town donkeyman he had been a cop for most of his life and had presided with great distinction over the processing of the town's hoodlums, inhaling them one week, exhaling them the next from the iron lung of Aberystwyth gaol. Now he spent his years cleaning up after the donkeys, doing for them, some said, what for many years he had been doing for the people of this town.

'Everything all right, Pop?' I asked.

He looked at me, still holding the bridle of the lead donkey, Mnemosyne. 'I'm a bit troubled today, son, to be honest.'

Sospan rubbed his chin thoughtfully. 'I might just have a scoop or two left of the Absinthe.'

Eeyore shook his head.

'Or the Ambergris?'

'No.'

'Mescaline?'

Eeyore considered. 'No, not that. Have you got anything to ward off the evil eye?'

The light of understanding entered the ice-cream man's eye. 'I may have some blueberry made with water taken from the shrine at Lourdes. The blue is the colour of the famous stained-glass window in the apse of the chapel in Reims cathedral. That will put you right.'

Eeyore looked unhappy. 'I've heard a troubling rumour.'

We all looked at him expectantly. He sighed. We waited. He shook his head.

'What troubling rumour would that be, then?' asked Sospan.

'I'm not sure if I should say.'

'Of course you should say,' cried Calamity. 'What's the point in mentioning it if you aren't going to say?'

'It's only a rumour,' he said.

'You might as well say it, Dad.'

'Well,' said Eeyore. 'As I said, it's just rumour, but I've heard they've put a Zed Notice on the town.'

There was a moment's silence as we allowed the news to sink in.

'What's a Zed Notice?' asked Sospan.

'I don't know,' said Eeyore. 'All I know is, it's very bad.'

Sospan tut-tutted. 'Who put it on us?'

'I don't know that, either,' said Eeyore. 'The people responsible for Zed Notices conduct their arcane rites in the shadows beyond the reach of the public gaze. Or, at least, that's what this chap told me.'

Even though nobody knew what a Zed Notice was, it was unsettling to discover one had been put on the town.

Sospan broke from his trance. 'I think I know what is needed. Something very, very special. Something from my under-the-counter "Katabasis" range. Of course, it's not literally under the counter, that's a figure of speech. I keep it off site, for obvious reasons.'

'What was it called again?' asked Calamity.

'Katabasis; it's the Greek word to describe a journey to the Underworld and, by extension, any journey through a dystopic realm. It's made from the ayahuasca plant, which is a powerful hallucinogenic plant used by shamans of the Amerindian tribes in Peru, Bolivia and Ecuador. The name translates as "Vine of the Corpse" in their language. It comes highly recommended by Hunter S. Thompson and the Chilean novelist Isabel Allende.'

'What does it do?' asked Eeyore.

'Opens doors.'

'What sort of doors?'

'Of perception, mostly. Look!' Sospan crouched down and rummaged under the counter, then brought out a copy of *National Geographic* magazine. 'This is an account by Kira Salak, an adventurer, of her experience:

> *I will never forget what it was like. The overwhelming misery. The certainty of never-ending suffering. No one to help you, no way to escape. Everywhere I looked: darkness so thick that the idea of light seemed inconceivable.*
>
> *Suddenly, I swirled down a tunnel of fire, wailing figures calling out to me in agony, begging me to save them. Others tried to terrorise me. 'You will never leave here,' they said. 'Never. Never.'*
>
> *I found myself laughing at them. 'I'm not scared of you,' I said. But the darkness became even thicker; the emotional charge of suffering nearly unbearable. I felt as if I would burst from heartbreak – everywhere, I felt the agony of humankind, its tragedies, its hatreds, its sorrows. I reached the bottom of the tunnel and saw three thrones in a black chamber. Three shadowy figures sat in the chairs; in the middle was what I took to be the devil himself.*
>
> *'The darkness will never end,' he said. 'It will never end. You can never escape this place.'*

Sospan looked up as if expecting the sale to have been clinched.

'I think I'll just have a strawberry,' said Eeyore.

Calamity, evidently bored with the Vine of the Corpse, asked Eeyore about the raid on the Coliseum cinema. 'I remember it well,' he said. 'Iestyn Probert and the two Richards brothers from the garage at Llanfarian. A policeman was run over during the chase and they hanged Iestyn for it. Three of them were on the run for a while, out at Ystrad Meurig. For many of us that robbery marked a watershed. I suppose you could describe it as a loss of collective innocence. The takings were especially good because it was the opening week of *The Sound of Music*. The whole town went to see it, literally everyone: the streets were empty like on Christmas Day. They called it the day Aberystwyth stood still. Somehow it seemed below the belt to hit the cinema when Julie Andrews was playing.

Calamity pulled a face and Eeyore put his arm on her shoulder. 'It probably seems daft to you today.'

'I've seen the movie,' said Calamity, 'my aunt watches it every Christmas. Just some kids in Austria singing and then they escape from the Nazis, but no one really tries to stop them.'

'Stated baldly like,' said Eeyore, 'I suppose it doesn't sound like much. Things were different in those days. They didn't have so many explosions and stuff; things were more sedate. The scenery was very beautiful and the singing was nice . . . and . . . you see, Austria was a faraway place, people didn't take foreign holidays or go skiing in the Alps. Just seeing the mountains on the big screen like that was a thrill, and the music . . .' He sang a couple of bars of 'The Lonely Goatherd'.

Calamity said, 'I can't see why they had to escape from the Nazis just for teaching some lousy kids to sing.'

'At the very least,' I said, 'you'd expect Julie Andrews to do some kick-boxing or something.'

'Or dynamite the bridge so no one could follow them,' said Calamity.

Sospan put the magazine back under the counter.

Chapter 4

THE WAITING steam train snorted puffs of strongly perfumed smoke into the blue sky. A man and a boy stood next to the engine, both identically dressed in neatly pressed black trousers and white shirts, open at the collar. The boy was listening to the side of the engine with a stethoscope.

Every railway station has a zone way out beyond the normal hubbub. Most people are too lazy to walk that far, but once you pass a certain point, beyond the front of the longest train, beyond the final pillar where the last awning peters out, the atmosphere changes; noise drops off, a wind that has been absent from the cauldron of the town centre cools your brow. The only sound comes from the soles of your shoes. This is where the narrow-gauge steam train to Devil's Bridge stands awaiting orders.

The boy wrote something down in a notebook.

'I hope she's well enough to travel,' I said with a smile to his father.

'I bring my boy up to be observant,' said the man.

Calamity and the boy stared at each other with the muted suspicion that kids of similar ages feel when a chance encounter brings their parents together.

'Most trainspotters just write down the numbers,' I said.

'We are not trainspotters,' said the man. 'We just like machines.'

'We're not allowed to have them at home,' added the boy.

'Except the plough, and the hair clip and the gallows. Although, of course, in these corrupted times our gallows rot and the hangman's children cry out for hunger in the night.' The man put his hand gently on the back of his son's head. 'To us, a big train like this is almost like pornography.'

'You must be Denunciationists,' I said.

The man smiled.

'Are you Upper or Lower? I can never remember which is which.'

'We're Lower Denunciationist, from Cwmnewidion Isaf; we have no beards because the Lord in his mercy allowed us to use the engine of the scissor. It is those chimp-faced fools from Ynys Greigiog who abjure the very necessary act of grooming.' He reached out a hand to shake. 'I am James the Less.'

'Louie Knight, and this is Calamity.'

The engine wailed its impatience and the guard blew a whistle. I opened a compartment door and allowed the man and his son to enter. We climbed in after them and slammed the door. Calamity pulled a face, as I knew she would, when her bottom hit the hard polished wooden bench.

'Just try and enjoy it,' I said. 'The scenery is nice at least.'

'No upholstery,' she said. Two words that encapsulated an entire world view.

The engine squealed again, and tugged, picking up the slack like the anchor man in a tug-of-war. The carriages groaned like cows calling to be milked; unconsciously we clenched our muscles in sympathy. We began the long, slow trundle to Devil's Bridge.

'The line to Devil's Bridge was built by Chinese immigrant labour between 1865 and 1869,' said the boy.

'And some Irish,' added his father.

'It's like sitting on a roundabout in the park,' said Calamity. 'Even war chariots used to have upholstery; cushions are not a luxury.'

James the Less received that statement with a look of surprise. In Cwmnewidion Isaf cushions were obviously kept on the top shelf at the newsagent's next to the magazines on steam traction engines and those lawnmowers you can sit on.

'Devil's Bridge gets its name from a folk tale about the Devil, who used to exact tolls from travellers wishing to use the bridge across the gorge,' said the boy. 'The Irish navvies resented the Chinese workers, partly because they ate strange food: dried oysters, dried fish, dried abalone, seaweed and dried crackers, all imported from China. And they took baths in empty whisky kegs filled with rainwater, perfumed with flowers.'

'That would offend me, too,' I said.

'Are you on holiday?' said the boy.

'We're looking for the outline of a d . . .' Calamity checked herself and looked at me, unsure whether she should divulge details of our intentions, and aware that it was to me that Raspiwtin had given the information about Iestyn Probert's old house. I grinned and completed her sentence. 'Duck. We're looking for the outline of a duck in the hills, caused, they say, by the run-off from the old lead mines.'

'We're paleo-ornithologists,' said Calamity.

'How fascinating,' said the boy. 'What sort of duck exactly? Dabbling duck, diving duck, eider duck, ferruginous duck, harlequin duck, long-tailed duck, mandarin duck, Muscovy duck, ruddy duck, swallow-tailed duck, tree duck, tufted duck, velvet duck, wood duck . . . ?'

'Just so long as it quacks,' she answered.

'I think there's one by Iestyn Probert's old house, out at Rhiwlas,' said James the Less.

The train moved so slowly across the landscape that its timetable might have been described in geological epochs. Yet for all the languor the engine itself was a source of fury, coughing a series of cumulonimbus clouds into the sky with each chuff, interspersed with wild Cherokee war whoops. The flood plain of the Rheidol passed gently by.

'I met a Deunciationist priest once,' I said. 'He had a red beard.'

'That would be Jude the Schemer. For many years I loved him as a brother and would have laid down my life for him, until the fever seized his brain.'

The boy rested a restraining hand on his father's forearm. 'Do not grieve, Father.' He turned to me. 'My father has taught me to love all God's creatures, with the one exception of Uncle Jude, who is a loath-some heretical swill bucket.'

'It was always the way with Jude,' said the old man. 'He never knew the virtue of moderation. The Lord teaches us that we are all born in corruption and for this we are to be damned to everlasting hellfire. But some there are, one or two lucky blighters, a handful here and there, who through no merit of conduct are to be saved, and this will be made known to them in the privacy of their hearts and this is the true way. But Jude the Schemer, he perverted the words of the Lord and claimed that no one was to be saved. Not a soul! All damned, every last man Jack of us. Such blasphemy! Is God a monster? No, of course not.'

'You see, sir,' said the boy, 'we seek goodness wherever we go and we love God even though the doctrine of eternal depravity has in all likelihood blighted us and condemned us to everlasting hellfire, condemned in the courts of his goodness before the first brick of this prison earth was laid. And for this we love him most of all.'

'How does he feel about machines?'

'The Bible is not clear on this point, but I will bare my back to my father's chastening rod of birch later, and he mine, and thus God will be appeased.'

We were quiet for a while, each enjoying the simple loveliness of the Rheidol valley gliding past. It seemed to gain in splendour through the action of the train's chuffing. A smile spread unbidden across my face, and the boy on seeing this assumed it was addressed to him and smiled in return. I felt touched.

'So, are you going into farming when you grow up?' I asked.

'He hopes to become a forensic linguist,' said the old man.

'What's that?'

'The application of scientific techniques to evaluate the authenticity of documents based on information contained within the document,' said the boy. 'Linguistic and stylistic analysis, stylometrics . . . to help investigators in civil and criminal trials.'

'Poison-pen letters,' added his father, 'and farewell letters from murder victims faked by the murderer; ransom demands . . . he can turn his hand to anything.'

'Principally the assistance of prosecutors and attorneys pursuant to exposing the twisted workings of the criminal heart,' said the boy.

'Where does listening to the train come into it?' I asked.

'I am thinking of expanding the scope to include the characteristic "voice" signature of steam locomotives. In terms of specialisms it's terra incognita.'

'My boy can find out from examining the text whether the cops fabricated a statement,' said James the Less with evident pride.

'He'll find plenty of work in Aberystwyth, then.'

'That's what I told him. A nice steady job with a good future.'

'The technical term is co-authorship,' said the boy.

'Is that so? I hadn't heard it described like that before; most people call it fitting up. Just so long as the cops don't turn honest you'll be a rich man.'

'We have no use for riches,' said his father. 'His purpose is solely the betterment of humankind. He did a project for his school on the confession of Iestyn Probert – he used to be a member of our community – the police claimed it was Iestyn at the wheel of the getaway car in the raid on the Coliseum cinema. A policeman was run over and this was why they hanged him. Iestyn claimed he wasn't driving and the police faked his confession.'

'So far, I have been able to demonstrate certain features of the confession which indicate strong prima facie likelihood of police co-authorship; of particular interest is the non-standard frequency of the word *then*.'

'Non-standard,' said James the Less.

'*Then*?' I said.

'Normally people making statements say "then I", but police diction is notoriously stilted and basically – what is the phrase? Up its own backside, I believe – in police statements there is frequent post-positioning, namely, "I then". I amassed a database of police statements and witness statements for comparison and found "I then" to occur once every 119 words in police statements but not at all in witness statements. Except in the statement of Iestyn Probert, which evinced nineteen occurrences. This was statistically highly significant. I'm hoping to get Iestyn a posthumous pardon, but some rumours that he is still alive render the undertaking problematic.'

'Would he have even known how to drive?' I asked. 'I mean as a Denunciationist . . .'

'That was his tragedy,' said James the Less. 'If he had stayed in his community where he belonged, none of it would have happened. But the fever seized his brain. It always starts in adolescence. You get feelings, we all do, about . . .' – he shot a swift guilty glance at his son – '. . . engines. Motorcars are the worst because you can see them pass by the fields as you till the soil. If only Iestyn had spoken to one of the elders . . .' He shook his head ruefully at the waste of a young life. 'They could have told him, as I tell my boy, how to manage the temptation. But, like so many young men before him, he dreamed of running away to Aberystwyth and becoming a mechanic. I remember him sitting on the hill at the end of each day, staring into the west. It was no surprise when the news came that he had gone.'

After we passed Cwm Rheidol, Calamity began to scan the adjacent valley side with a pair of small binoculars. Just before the station at Rhiwlas we saw the duck-shaped discoloration on the hillside.

'I'd say it was more of a drake,' said the boy.

We left the train at the station and climbed down the steep hillside to the ford at the bottom.

'The sky's always bluer when there are clouds,' said Calamity.

I didn't answer but pondered the phenomenon. She was right; the surrounding sky was bluer because the clouds were brighter, as if illuminated from within.

There was a bridge at the bottom made of slabs of slate laid on stones embedded in the stream. We crossed and climbed over a stile, then began to climb. From the train in the valley below the discoloration in the hillside had, indeed, looked a bit like a duck. But as we climbed towards it, the outline became less and less distinct. The path reached another stile which led onto a rough farm track and we proceeded up what was presumably the duck's leg.

'If you ever have some butter that you don't want to melt,' I said to Calamity as we climbed, 'it might be a good idea to put it in that kid's mouth.'

'Either that or my fist, I can't work out which would be best.'

I laughed. 'I'm just glad you didn't do it there and then.'

'Why do you think the aliens asked about Iestyn Probert?'

I didn't answer.

'I know what you think. There are no aliens.'

'Got it in one.'

'How come they knew his address?'

'Don't you think it's more likely that the farmer invented the whole story?'

'Why would he do that?'

'People are funny.'

'All the same, don't you think it's odd? This Raspiwtin bloke has been looking all his life for Iestyn Probert, and then some aliens turn up looking for him, too.'

'Odd, yes, but not uncanny. My guess is Raspiwtin's story is largely fiction and he got the name from the newspaper on the way to the office.'

'He said we'd find Iestyn's old house by a duck's bill in the hillside, so the story can't be all fiction, can it, because we've found the duck.'

'You think so? Looks more like a drake to me.'

She paused and turned to me with a grin. 'Do you think the duck stain might be deliberate as some sort of a sign to the flying saucers?' asked Calamity.

'No.'

'It would make sense.'

'In your universe perhaps.'

'It happens a lot. Plenty of ancient monuments are laid out in ways that only make sense from the air. In South America there are loads.'

I rolled my eyes.

'Your mind is closed,' said Calamity with amusing pomposity.

'It's not closed, it just has a strict door policy. I don't admit riff-raff.'

'UFOs aren't riff-raff. Loads of people have seen them.'

'Loads of people have seen something they personally weren't able to identify.'

'They can't all be hallucinations.'

'Why not?'

'I saw one in Pwllheli. Are you saying I didn't?'

'You saw a light in the sky; there are lots of things that cause lights in the sky. And because you had read about flying-saucer sightings recently, you interpreted it as one. Five hundred years ago you would have called it an angel or a wheel of fire.'

Calamity made a raspberry sound and then we both suddenly stopped our ascent. The track we had been following ended abruptly in a flat section of ground cut into the hillside; it was overgrown with grass, brambles and gorse, but the rectangular outline signifying the foundations of a house were unmistakable. Lumps of masonry littered the brambles. Two rooms were still standing, open to the sky; slats of wood and bits of plaster lay entangled in the undergrowth like twigs in hair. Off to the right on a raised piece of ground there was a grave. Calamity walked over and knelt down. I joined her. Time and weather had effaced the writing on the simple stone which protruded from the turf like a tooth, but at the foot, encased in a clear plastic sandwich bag taped to the stone, there was a business card. Calamity took it out, read it and handed it up to me. It was for Jezebels, the nightclub at the caravan site. In colours of scarlet, mauve and black the silhouette of a lady in a stovepipe hat raised a leg clad in fishnet stockings; in the foreground was a martini glass. I turned the card over; on the back someone had scribbled in biro, 'Ask for Miaow.'

A voice interrupted our thoughts and we looked up. An old lady, bent at the waist and carrying a basket, hobbled down the hillside towards us. 'Haven't seen any Bishop's Trumpet have you, dears?' she asked. The curvature of her spine forced her thorax forward and she looked sideways and up at us. Strands of silvery hair, pinned in a bun, slipped out and veiled her face, which was ruddy and kindly. Her back was alive with the agitated flapping of some birds trapped in a net slung across her shoulders.

'What's Bishop's Trumpet?' asked Calamity.

'What indeed! You're from the town, I can see.' The woman pushed her basket, laden with freshly plucked roots and leaves, towards us. 'I've got me Foxbright and Marly, me Blue-Dog, Purple Trolls-foot, Night-feather, Trollop-me-Bright, Bog-Grail, Prim Willow, My Lady's Hymen, Fan-white, Silver Milchgrüssel and a pinch of Satanicus, but I'm blessed if I can find any Bishop's Trumpet.'

'We can help you look, if you like,' said Calamity.

'That's very kind of you, but we won't find any today; the spirit of the mountain is being grumpy. But you could help me carry my basket back to my cottage, it's just over the hill. Would you do that?'

I took the basket and we followed her up the hill and then down the other side to a small cottage on the edge of the Forestry Commission plantation. We went through a garden gate and waited while she took the net over to an aviary in which birds of all descriptions fluttered about. The woman released the new birds and took us into her kitchen, where she put the kettle on without asking. 'You will stay for tea, now.'

'We wouldn't want to be any trouble,' I said.

She looked at me in wonder. 'Trouble? To make a little cup of tea for the next mayor of Aberystwyth? How strangely you talk!'

I stifled a startled look and said, 'I think you must be mistaken there. The next mayor of Aberystwyth will probably be Ercwleff.'

'That's what you think, is it?'

'That's what everybody thinks.'

'It's not what my cat thinks.' She sat down with a groan, her rheumatic limbs clearly aching.

'I think you must be feeding her too many kippers.'

'Eightball doesn't eat fish, and she's never wrong about the mayoral elections.'

'What do you do with the birds?' Calamity asked.

'Lots of things. I use the feathers for me cardigans, the feet to scratch me back, but mostly I use the croaks to black me hats.'

'What sort of hats?' asked Calamity.

'Stoveys, of course. Best stovepipe-hat blacker in all of Wales I am. You ask them, they'll tell you, get Auntie Pebim to black your stovey if you want it to stay black.'

'Is it hard to black them?' asked Calamity.

Auntie Pebim scoffed politely and rolled her eyes as she recalled the magnitude of the task. 'It is if you do it properly. The hardest part is not the herbs, of course. If the spirit of the mountain wants to give them to you he will, or if he's being a pest like today, he won't. You also need a Bible that's been used as a pillow on the deathbed of some-one who died of meanness, but they are getting harder to find these days. People are turning away from God.'

'What about the croaks?' I asked. 'How do you collect them.'

Auntie Pebim poured the boiling water into the teapot. 'First you get the birds to build a nest and lay an egg; you can't hurry that, you just have to make the circumstances right and wait for nature to take its course. Then, when the chick is about to hatch you put a bell jar over mother and egg and wait. Soon the chick hatches and the hen fills the bell jar with croaks of love, caw, caw, caw. Then you remove them and fill the jar with oil and from this you can distil out the caws. That's not easy. Eventually you end up with a little drop like quick-silver.' A cloud darkened her brow. 'Of course, that's the light way. There's a darker way, too, where you put a poisonous spider in the jar and it kills the chick. Then you collect the lamentation of the mother, the *Stabat Mater*.' She brought the teacups over to the table.

'We were wondering who the house belonged to back there,' I said.

'Which house?'

'Where we first met you.'

Auntie Pebim thought for a second. 'A house, you say? I suppose it's possible; but I can't say I notice things like that, too quick for my old eyes, you see. One minute here, the next gone. I tend to notice slower things like the rise and fall of the mountains, the changing levels of the sea and the ice ages – things like that. Even the growth of trees is a bit quick for me.'

Calamity and I resisted the temptation to exchange glances. 'That's a shame,' I said. 'It must have been there quite a while; there's lots of masonry lying around.'

Auntie Pebim's voice took on a dismissive tone. 'Masonry! To me stone is no more substantial than the fluff of a dandelion on a windy day.'

'Most people find it quite substantial,' I persisted. 'Enough, at least, to build houses lasting hundreds of years.'

'I wouldn't trust it myself,' she said.

I looked around at her croft, which seemed to have followed convention in being made from stone.

'We heard Iestyn Probert used to live there,' said Calamity.

'Iestyn Probert? Oh yes, so he did. Nice boy. The family moved after they hanged him.' She tutted and opened a packet of digestive biscuits, letting the contents fall onto a plate with plinking sounds like sonar.

'How awful,' said Calamity.

Auntie Pebim peered at her and considered for a while, then said, 'If you have a little bird in a cage and you release the bird, does it matter if you damage the cage?'

'I don't know,' said Calamity. 'Probably not.'

'There you are, then. Iestyn's spirit is free now of the prison of the flesh; it has passed on to the real world. His body was just a broken beaker, no longer needed. I don't imagine he pines too much for a moment's pain when they stretched his neck and made him free. Would you like some jam to take back with you?' She stood up and hobbled over to the pantry and brought back a jar of dark-coloured jam.

'Isn't this the real world?' asked Calamity.

Auntie Pebim smiled indulgently at our spiritual impoverishment. 'Oh Lord, no, who could bear it if it were? The only thing that makes our travail bearable is the knowledge that this – the material world, as you people from the city call it – is a chimera.'

Calamity looked confused. 'I thought the material world had to exist because it's made of . . . material.'

'Is that what they teach you in school these days!' Auntie Pebim turned to me. 'You'll have to do something about these schools when you are mayor.'

'I really have no intention of becoming mayor.'

Auntie Pebim smiled. It was clear that my thoughts on the matter counted little against the opinion of Eightball. She wrapped the gift of jam in some muslin and showed us out. 'You know, it's funny you asking about Iestyn Probert. Some travellers were asking about him last week. They looked Norwegian, with four fingers on each hand. I couldn't tell you much about them – it was Eightball who answered the door.'

Chapter 5

THAT EVENING I went to Jezebels. There was a twinge of melancholy or some other unease in my heart, or wafting on the night breeze, and I struggled to construe it. Spring nights sometimes have this haunting quality, when the brightening day, having promised the joys of summer, still ends shipwrecked on the cold shoals of night. At such times hopes mingle in the soul with old memories of times better forgotten. Unease can stalk the heart. Or perhaps it was just something about this case that seemed out of joint. It appeared to be unfolding according to an unseen script, as if written by somebody who did not have my interests at heart. Two men enter my office and chop up my desk claiming they are punishing me for a case I am about to take on. After they leave, a client turns up with a fantastical story that cannot possibly be true. He offers to pay up front but somehow forgets this vital detail, and it seems to me that his entrance was so neatly timed following the desk-chopping that it seemed part of a double act. He sends me in search of a man called Iestyn Probert, and at Iestyn's old house I find a business card from Jezebels. Ask for Miaow. I could feel the sharp-cornered card snagging the lining of my pocket as I walked. Two days old and already I did not like the taste of this case. If it transpired that Raspiwtin had put the card there, I would not be surprised.

Sospan was closing up as I arrived at the Prom. A hurricane lamp hung from the ceiling inside the kiosk; the sea had that cold spring-evening gleam; the sky above was indigo tinged with lime on the horizon. Sospan greeted me with a wan smile but carried on packing. It seemed that he too was touched by the strange quality of the spring night.

'How are the new timbers holding up?' I asked.

He paused as if considering whether to unburden himself. 'To be honest, I find their presence a touch unsettling.'

'How's that?'

'Pardon me asking, Mr Knight, but do you ever get a strange feeling, as if somehow you are here on this earth without an invitation?'

'Yes, sometimes; we all do.'

'You feel like an uninvited guest?'

'On occasion. But it passes.'

'Any disturbance to the integrity of my box affects me deeply.'

'Wasn't there an ancient Greek who had the same problem with his ship?'

'Theseus, the chap who slew the Minotaur. While replacing every plank of his ship with a new one, he wondered if it was still the same ship. John Locke had a similar issue with the darning of his sock. Talking of the Minotaur, I see your old school games teacher, Herod Jenkins, is standing for high office.'

'How high?'

'Mayor. He's standing against Ercwleff. They're going to have a jamboree to decide the issue, sort of an Aberystwyth version of a presidential debate. They'll be competing in three activities: human cannonball, a drinking game and a fist fight in the pub car park. Ercwleff and Herod Jenkins. The word on the Prom says Ercwleff is going to take a dive in the fifth.'

'Herod Jenkins,' I said softly, as if fearful that he might appear if I spoke too loudly. Even after thirty years the sound of his name made my skin prickle with a hot flush of anxiety. It was during his games lessons that we divined the bitter truths of this world, that suffering was the currency in which we all must trade. Progress through those years was done at a forced march with little time for stragglers, for the weak and infirm. The most infirm of all was my friend Marty, the consumptive schoolboy. Ordinarily that talismanic chit of paper, the note from your mam excusing you from games, should have been enough to save him. But one cold bleak January the note lost its power to charm and Marty was sent out alone, on a cross-country run into a blizzard. For Herod the important thing was to get as many boys across the ice floes of life as fast as possible, regarding it as inevitable that some would be left behind. Who knows how differently things would have turned out if he had been a kind man? Perhaps I would be a plumber now, happy in the docile simplicity of my pipes and spanners. I would not be kept awake at night by the wolves howling in the sewer beneath the city streets, nor by the nameless anxiety that flashed through my heart every time the headlights of a turning car raked the ceiling.

'According to the publicity, it's one of God's children versus the Philosopher King,' Sospan explained. 'Lamb versus Lion.'

'Herod is a philosopher king?'

'He's got lots of ideas.'

'Like putting newborn babies on the roof overnight?'

'Not sure about that.'

'What about Ercwleff? What's his manifesto?'

'A rabbit in every pot.'

'I'll vote for that.'

I walked back to the office to pick up my Wolseley Hornet. I drove out of town, over Trefechan Bridge, and turned at the fire station; the road became a track and the street lights petered out. I slowed to a crawl. The track ran parallel to the sea, which lay to the right, invisible in the darkness. On my left, also invisible, brooded the hill of Pen Dinas and its Iron Age ramparts. Up ahead lights gleamed from the old mansion on a distant hill, Plas Tan-y-Bwlch, which had at various times billeted soldiers, lunatics, military brass, gentry, typhoid sufferers, consumptives and, finally, when all other uses had been exhausted, students. But before you reached it the road passed a straggle of caravans that seemed to have been washed up on the grass by a freak wave. This was Maelor Gawr caravan park. Facilities were minimal: an office and reception, a shower block and Jezebels. It was a simple club for people with uncomplicated desires, lost souls who didn't even have anything to drink to forget. There was a cheap concrete floor, a disco sound system and low-end lighting rig retired from active service at weekly weddings, and a handful of girls in the inevitable stovepipe hats.

I sat at a table and picked up the drinks menu. A stovey girl slinked out from the shadows and stood in my light. I looked up, squinting, and said, 'I'm looking for Miaow.'

'I can purr.'

'So can she. Is she here?'

'Later.'

'I'll have a Jim Beam.'

She paused for a second, pulled a face of mock disappointment and went off to fetch my drink. I waited; there was not much to see. It was early, and these sort of places never get going until midnight, even then nothing happens. My drink appeared and I sipped it slowly.

Half an hour later another stovey girl slipped into the vacant chair opposite me. Her hat loomed over the table like a detonated factory chimney hanging momentarily in the air before it falls.

'I'm Miaow,' she said.

'Louie.' I reached out and shook her hand.

She wore the traditional folk costume of black-and-white checked flannel skirt, a red shawl and a white apron – and, less traditionally, under the apron, a black basque. She reached into the front of it, pulled out a shot glass and put it next to mine. A waitress clubbed the table with a bottle of Jim Beam and Miaow filled the glasses. 'Chin, chin,' she said. We drank. She knocked hers back in one and refilled it. I took mine more gently.

'You're disappointed,' she said.

'About what?'

'Because I'm flat-chested. It runs in the family. This is my gran's corset. It's made from real whalebone. She won a lot of Sunday School attendance medals wearing this.'

'Why don't you invite her over?'

'She's dead, silly. All those hymns wore her out.'

'I bet the hat is hers, too.'

'Of course. It's antique, real beaver. That makes it waterproof.'

'Such a shame to turn beavers into hats – they build excellent dams.'

Miaow rested her chin on her palm and gave me a cool stare. 'I hadn't thought about that. Guess which part of the beaver the Eskimos use.'

'Surprise me.'

'The bollocks.'

'Really?'

'As a painkiller. Beavers chew lots of willow trees, which is where aspirin comes from, isn't it? They store it in their . . . glands.'

'Do they have willow trees at the North Pole?'

Miaow considered the question and frowned slightly as if this rather obvious thought had not occurred to her. 'I'm sure they have trees in Greenland, and that's where Eskimos come from, isn't it?'

'I don't know. I thought in the real world they came from Canada.'

'There you are, then. They've definitely got willow trees in Canada.'

'Maybe they trade seal furs for the willow bark.'

I sipped my Jim Beam and peered in the gloom at her face. The twisting disco ball picked out her cheek's edge with a line of silver; the line moved and shimmered but remained in the same place like the stripes on a barbershop pole or the moonlit sea going in and out but not really going anywhere. The line curved up from her chin with the delicate grace of an Egyptian vase, an amphora, one specially created to hold the frankincense hauled by caravan across the desert from Nubia. Her skin was pale and marked with that barely perceptible dusting of freckles that the Celts left behind along with the grey-green eyes and the sacrificial stones. Her hair was the colour of mahogany, dishevelled not through the absence of a brush but in a different way, the sort acquired from standing in the howling wind on the ramparts waiting for the first sight of a returning sail. She was one of those girls whose loveliness pierces your heart with a strange melancholy. It shone like a star in this sordid club and made me think about the men of the Iron Age hill fort who used to drink their mead here beneath a disco ball of real stars. I understood the source of this melancholy. It was born of the knowledge that in this shabby world we could never hope to be the man at the helm of that returning ship.

'My real name is Penardim, but I think Miaow is much better, don't you?'

'Honestly? No, Penardim is a very beautiful name.'

'I don't like it. I'm a student, from Cwmnewidion Isaf.'

'Are you a Denunciationist?'

'Sort of, I guess. Not any more.'

'What are you studying?'

'Anthropology. Kinship rituals along the upper Rheidol.'

'So what's it like growing up among the Denunciationists?'

'OK, I suppose. It's not as bad as people think. I had a doll and a doll's house just like other little girls, I just wasn't allowed to have a washing machine or hoover for it.'

'Didn't you meet other girls from outside the community?'

'Sometimes, but they thought we were the lucky ones because we had horses. And besides, a lot of the things we couldn't have are not so great. When I was small, we thought the people of Aberystwyth must be so wonderful because they ate food from tins, but now that's all I ever eat. It's not so great; our food was much better. I know you think I'm old-fashioned.'

'No, I don't.'

'You can't buy me, I'm sorry. I don't do that.'

'Nor do I.'

'I'm a virgin. Do you believe that?'

'Yes.'

'Are you staying at the camp?'

'No.'

'You're lucky, it's crap! I'll get the sack if you tell them I said that.'

'I'd better not tell them, then.'

'Maelor Gawr. What sort of name is that for a caravan park?'

'I expect all the good ones were taken.'

'He was a giant who lived up on Pen Dinas, did you know that?'

'No, I thought I knew everything about Aberystwyth, but I didn't know that.'

'He founded the town.'

'Are you sure?'

She looked confused and put her glass next to mine and chinked. 'I think so. If he didn't, who did?'

'I don't know that either.'

'Don't know much, do you?'

'Do towns always have to be founded? Can't they just spring up?'

'Not this one. He had a son called Bwbbwg. He's the patron saint of Scrabble players with lousy tiles.' She giggled and so did I, like a teenage boy on a date. 'It's not my joke,' she added. 'I stole it.'

'Why confess? I would never have known.'

'I wouldn't want to give you the impression that I was funny. I wouldn't want to mislead you.'

'I think you are funny.'

'You see!'

'I promise not to complain if I find out I am wrong.'

More people began to arrive. One of them was Raspiwtin. He glanced at Miaow as he passed and she returned his gaze, and it seemed to me that a glance of recognition passed between them, but I could not be sure.

'Do you know that man?' I asked.

She asked, 'Who?' in a way that lent support to my suspicion because it was hardly possible that she didn't know which man I meant. He was shown to a table towards the back where the two disks of his spectacles caught the spotlight and shone like silver pennies stuck in his face. A girl went to sit with him, but seemingly without much enthusiasm. She sat with her body twisted away, her chin resting on the back of her hand as she stared into the middle distance in an attitude of exaggerated petulance. Raspiwtin stared the whole time at Miaow.

'Which is your favourite girl?'

I pulled a face.

'You're looking around; if you point out which one you like, I can get her to sit with you. There are lots of pretty girls here.'

'No, there aren't.'

'Prettier than me.'

'That's not true either.'

'You're only saying that. What sort of girls do you go for?'

'I'm looking for the sort of girl who stands on the battlements scanning the horizon for the return of my ship.'

'What is she wearing?'

'She is wrapped in a cloak of wool dyed with herbs she picked from the woods; the cloak is clasped at her throat with a silver brooch of intricate Celtic design. Her hair is a thousand shades of chestnuts like yours and on top sits a genuine antique beaver stovepipe hat.'

'I wear a cream-coloured mac and a school satchel when I'm not working.'

'So does she, sometimes.'

'Tell me more about her; she sounds nice. Isn't it cold up on that battlement?'

'Of course, but that's why I love her; her love is pure and her heart steadfast. She's there in all weathers, standing still as a statue: in winter when the howling wind drives the sleet against her cheek, and in spring when the apple blossom dapples it with pale green snow.'

'Your ship is late.'

'All the best ships are.'

'Don't other men try to tempt her away?'

'Yes, but they mean nothing to her.'

'I wish I was her.'

'You are her.'

'Do you have a boat?'

'I could organise one.'

'I'd like that. We could sail away.'

'We could.'

'To the land where the bong tree grows.'

'Orchards full of them; we would take a basket and collect the bongs to make jam.'

Miaow leaned forward, staring at me but really looking through and beyond. 'It sounds so lovely.' A shadow passed over her brow. 'But then it will all go sour when you find out I'm not her.'

'Not who?'

'The girl you are looking for.'

'Aren't you Miaow?'

'Yes, and you asked for me like you knew me, but we've never met.'

'I was looking for you. I wanted to ask you about Iestyn.'

'Who's Iestyn?'

I picked up the bottle and refilled the glasses. 'Nobody important.'

'You're different to the other men who come here.'

'Thanks.'

'I say that to all the customers.'

'I know.'

'I have to say it.'

'That's all right, the one thing all men in places like this have in common is they think they are different.'

'In one respect you are like all the rest.'

'And what's that?'

'Sweet-talking me, saying you'd take me to the land where the bong trees grow.'

'I meant it.'

'Really?'

'When's your day off?'

'The day after tomorrow.'

'I'll pick you up at 9.00.'

She narrowed her eyes slightly and tilted her head. 'You serious?'

'Of course. If you want.'

She didn't speak immediately, but watched me closely for signs that I might be joking. 'Do you know what I really want? You'll laugh at me if I tell you but I don't care, I'm going to tell you anyway. Even though I know you'll laugh. Will you laugh?'

'How can I tell? It sounds like I might.'

'If I tell you, it will confirm all your prejudices about girls from Cwmnewidion Isaf.'

'If you are going to tell me you want to go on the Devil's Bridge train it won't shock me.'

'Worse than that. Promise you won't laugh.'

'I promise.'

'I want to go on an escalator.'

Chapter 6

THE NEXT morning was damp and grey – chilly. On such days, the Prom never looked more forlorn. The only hint of colour was the glossy scarlet tube of the human cannonball they were erecting, pointing like a finger at God. This was how we chose our mayors: on the premise that public men may lie, but you can't fake flying through the air.

Calamity was sitting on the floor of the office, amid photocopies of newspaper cuttings, and an OS map of the area spread on her knees like a blanket. She looked up and smiled. I went into the kitchenette, put the kettle on and returned to sink down to the floor opposite her. I did so without the easy grace that Calamity displayed.

'We must get a table,' she said.

'Yes, the room looks bare without it.'

'I've been checking out the *Cambrian News* archives about the night they raided the Coliseum cinema.'

'Found anything interesting?'

'Loads. There were three perps: two brothers called Richards from Llanfarian, and Iestyn. There was a lot of bad feeling about the case; a cop got run over in the chase. They pinned that on Iestyn. The Richards brothers each got twenty-five. I'm still trying to find out what became of them.'

'What about the hangman? If we are investigating the claim that a hanged man might still be alive, he would be a good place to start.'

'Died ten years ago, but I've found the doctor who presided at executions; he lives at the top of town in Laura Place.'

'We'll have to pay him a visit. Ask him if he might have made a mistake about the hanged man being dead.'

'Stop making fun!' said Calamity. 'Here's something else. The cop who arrested them turns out to be our old friend Preseli Watkins, the mayor.' She let her gaze linger on me for a second. She knew this was significant.

'So the mayor claims to have a premonition that I will be poking my nose into his business and chops up my desk to teach me a lesson. The very same day a man walks in with a case involving Iestyn and two crooks who robbed a cinema twenty-five years ago. The cop who arrested them just happens to be the mayor. Sounds like he has a good soothsayer. Or he knew Raspiwtin was coming to see us.'

'Isn't that the same thing?'

I formed my hand into a mock pistol and shot her. She grinned, then smiled shyly and said in a small voice, 'There's something else. Something you . . . you won't like.' She placed the palm of her hand down on a cutting and twisted it round. The headline read, 'MORE STRANGE LIGHTS IN CARDIGANSHIRE SKIES'.

'Don't get angry.'

'I won't get angry.'

'It's the Ystrad Meurig incident – the Welsh Roswell. Just like Raspiwtin said.'

'I told him Roswell was just a crashed weather balloon.'

'That's ridiculous.'

'It's what the US Air Force said.'

Calamity rolled her eyes. 'What do you expect them to say?' Her tone suggested that she expected better of me than to fall for the official narrative. 'They performed autopsies on three aliens; that was *some* weather balloon.'

'We don't know that.'

'We do! I've seen the footage.'

'So have I – on a documentary once. But I don't understand – how come the footage is so shaky and grainy?'

'Because they . . . they're shooting covertly.'

'But the cameraman must have been in the same room as the medics.

You can't hide in an autopsy room, so why not just use a proper camera and a tripod and shoot a proper film?'

'I don't know . . . loads of reasons.'

Calamity's spirits began to sink under the weight of my obtuse refusal to see the dark truths of this world. I backed off.

'Tell me about the Welsh Roswell.'

'It took place the same week as the raid on the Coliseum cinema; it happened in a wood outside Ystrad Meurig. There had been a number of flying-saucer sightings in the days leading up to it, and then, so the story goes, a saucer crashed and the military sealed off the area. They found wreckage and dead aliens in silver suits. Some say there were three, others five. Some say they were still alive.' She looked at me, not crestfallen but fully expecting the eventuality. 'I know you don't believe this stuff.'

'I don't want to be a killjoy, but aliens in silver suits? Looking humanoid? Why would they look like us if they were from a different star system?'

'I don't know. Maybe they just disguise themselves to look like us so as not to frighten us, the same way people who shoot ducks have whistles that sound like duck calls.'

'Don't you think it's odd, though, that these super-advanced beings from another star system keep crashing their saucers?'

She began to lose patience with me. 'They don't *keep* crashing –'

'Yes, they do! It seems to happen a lot. How can they master the intricacies of inter-stellar flight and then hit a tree?'

'You're making assumptions.'

'Yes, I'm assuming there is probably a simpler explanation located in the realm of human psychology. People have been seeing strange visions throughout history; once upon a time they attributed it to the Devil or his works; now we live in a more rational scientific age and people are embarrassed to profess belief in the Devil –'

'Not in Ystrad Meurig, they aren't.'

'Most people are, so they find a more scientific explanation. I'm not saying they are lying; I'm sure they genuinely experience the hallucination and their mind provides an interpretation with which they can feel comfortable.'

'You could be right, but there's one sure-fire way to find out, isn't there?'

There was a pause. I gave her a quizzical stare. 'Is there?'

'Of course. Men in Black.'

'Who are they?'

Calamity pulled a library book from under the pile of clippings. 'I've been looking through Project Blue Book, the official US Air Force investigation into the flying-saucer phenomenon in the '50s. Judging from the newspaper report, it sounds like the aliens from the Ystrad Meurig incident were Nordics, whereas the ones from Roswell were Greys. Greys are malign and are known to say the thing which is not.'

'Not what?'

'Just "not". They say it, whereas the Nordics are more spiritually advanced. Some people call them Pleiadeans because they come from the Pleiades star cluster.'

'How do you know the difference between a Nordic and a Grey, apart from saying the thing which is not?'

'Nordics are very attractive and look like Scandinavians. They are tall and statuesque and have pale skin and blonde or white hair. They admire the human race.'

'Are you sure? That sounds like the thing which is not.'

Calamity ignored the jocular tone and continued with earnest mien. 'Nordics never say the thing which is not. Maybe "admire" is the wrong word. They take a close interest in our spiritual development.'

'And what about Greys?'

'They are short and stumpy and grey. They have big almond-shaped, slanted eyes that go round the sides of their heads, like a praying mantis. They also have no irises or . . .' – she consulted her notes – 'Sclerae.'

'What does that mean?'

'I don't know; I think it means the white of the eye. They mean us harm.'

'They are not great admirers of the human race, then?'

'No, they are malign.'

'So is it just those two races?'

'Of course not! There are loads of exobiological entities visiting us.' She counted them off on the fingers of her hand: 'Reptilians, Sirians, Tall Whites, Hairy Dwarfs, the Hopkinsville Goblin, Dropa, Andromedans and the Flatwoods Monster. But the interesting thing is this: in all the celebrated cases, the contactees received visits shortly after from mysterious strangers dressed all in black. The first was the Maury Island incident. Harold A. Dahl was scavenging with his dog for some logs on Puget Sound in Washington State in 1947. He saw six flying doughnut-shaped craft and one of them seemed to be in trouble; it started ejecting debris which fell on his dog and killed it. A few days later he got a visit from the Men in Black; they seemed to know everything about what had happened and told him not to talk about it. Men in Black always turn up in a black '47 Buick. They claim to be from the Government, usually the Air Force, and give names and stuff, but when their IDs are checked it turns out that either they don't exist or are the names of dead people. Men in Black act strange; sometimes they giggle and seem unfamiliar with Earth customs.'

'I think I saw a film about them once.'

Calamity looked irritated.

'What's wrong?'

'I'm being serious.'

'I know. So am I.'

'The films are . . . films like that just make jokes of it, but the Men in Black are a very real and mysterious phenomenon attached to early flying-saucer contact reports.'

'OK, forget the movie. Who do they work for?'

'Some people say they are G-men, but my money's on them being aliens. They turn up afterwards to silence witnesses.'

'If they are aliens and they don't want people to talk, why do they abduct people and make love to them in flying saucers?'

'When they do that they wipe the memory, it only comes out later under hypnosis.'

'You mean they dream it.'

'It's different.'

'It seems awfully similar to me.'

'They report details under hypnosis that they couldn't possibly have known.'

'Like what?'

'Like the map of Zeta Reticuli. In 1961 Barney and Betty Hill were taken aboard a saucer and saw a map on the wall. They drew it under hypnosis. It had stars on it that hadn't been discovered yet.'

I stood up and went over to the kitchenette. 'You really think they have maps of the stars pinned to the wall of their flying saucers? It seems a bit primitive.'

She followed me, not willing to let the subject drop. 'Why not? You've got a map in the glove compartment of your car. What's the difference? It had lines connecting the stars; the aliens said they were trade routes.'

'I can't believe that if there really are such things as flying saucers the skipper needs a star map to avoid getting lost.'

'How else can they find their way? There are more stars in the Milky Way than grains of sand on the whole of Planet Earth.'

I filled the kettle and shouted over the sound of gushing water. 'But there are no corners in space, there's nothing for the stars to hide behind. You just work out which star you want and head for it. You don't need a load of lines on a chart. What for?'

'We'll see, then, won't we?' said Calamity. To disguise her growing irritation she began to help me; she swirled hot water round in the teapot to warm it and then put three tea bags in. 'The black '47 Buick is the nutcracker; this is what we use to crack open the case.'

'You're about to unveil one of your schemes, aren't you?'

Calamity pulled two mugs down from the cupboard and carried on as if she hadn't heard me. 'The way I see it, the aliens are not likely to carry the Buick in the saucer all the way from Zeta Reticuli, are they?'

'It would seem an extravagant thing to do, although of course people often tow boats behind their cars when they go on holiday, so it's not out of the question.'

'I'm going to assume they don't do that; in which case they must get them when they arrive. And that is how we trap them.'

'Don't forget that the most likely possibility is this whole Raspiwtin story is moonshine.'

She carried on doggedly. 'We don't know why the aliens insist on black '47 Buicks, but the evidence is clear. Back in the '50s, that wasn't a difficult item to get hold of, but here, now, in Aberystwyth, there aren't any. So what do they do?'

'Look in the classifieds.'

'Exactly.'

'I was joking.'

'I'm not. We advertise a second-hand black '47 Buick in the *Cambrian News* classifieds section. If anyone rings up we can count them as a possible alien, or an intermediary representing their interests.'

'Nothing I say will stop you, will it?'

'It's worth a try.'

'Is it? Of all the wildest goose chases you've ever proposed, this . . . this takes the biscuit.'

'How can a goose chase take a biscuit?'

'You know what I mean. We're looking for a chap called Iestyn who robbed a cinema in 1965 and was hanged; but for some reason as yet unexplained he is still alive. Allegedly.'

'Looking for a dead man is also a wild goose chase. If you are allowed then so am I. What's sauce for the goose is sauce for the gander.'

I looked at her in surprise. She grinned. 'Point is, we are not the only ones looking for him. If the farmer is to be believed, so are the aliens. Raspiwtin says they had a rendezvous arranged. So we find out what their connection is. That way we find Iestyn.'

'Assuming the farmer can be believed. My guess is, he dreamed the whole thing up.'

'Why would he do that?'

'I don't know. We'll ask him. Get his address.'

'Already have. He lives out at Ynys Greigiog.'

I filled the teapot with hot water and carried the tray over to where we once had a desk. 'We'll go and see him.'

'Sure, but we also do the ad.' She picked up a sheet of paper torn from an exercise book and read. 'For Sale. Secondhand 1947 Buick, black. One careful lady owner, 27,000 miles on the clock. Must be seen to be believed.' She looked up grinning. 'I've already placed it.'

I put my hat on.

'Where are you going?'

'I'm going to see the mayor and ask for the address of his soothsayer.'

It was raining on the Prom but not heavily – a drizzle. Dark rags of cloud scudded across the blue sky and turned the world to silver and anthracite. The pale blue wooden benches misted over; the charcoal grit that passed for sand on the beach darkened; there were no bathers to disturb, just dog-walkers who didn't care, and a few students defiantly sitting on the pebbles, dressed in that strange amalgam of charity shop and high street, a sort of Dickensian-New Aquarian oddness. It probably wasn't a good idea to see the mayor, but that was often the trouble with being a private eye: most of the good ideas were simultaneously bad ones.

I cut through the public shelter to South Road. The town hall was up ahead on the left; the mayor held an afternoon surgery every Wednesday. I entered a small anteroom and approached a counter. I gave my name and told the clerk I wished to speak to the mayor about the arrest of Iestyn Probert in 1965. Then I took a seat. There was one other person waiting. He was staring at me with a venomous intensity. It was Meici Jones.

'I thought it was you,' he said.

Meici was a spinning-wheel salesman I had encountered on a previous case. He was one of life's misfits who had lived with his mum till the age of thirty-five and still wore short trousers on her orders. As a consequence of that case – indirectly, although I was sure he didn't see it that way – his mum had been sent to jail for murder. At the time of the trial I had wondered how he would cope on his own, and the image that presented itself to me in the mayor's anteroom suggested not all that well. He was wearing long trousers now, but they were ragged and crumpled. His white shirt was grey and blotched, though he had managed to wear a tie. His hair was badly in need of a cut.

'Hi Meici.'

'I saw you come in. I was here first.'

'How have you been keeping?'

'To tell you the truth, Lou, things have been pretty difficult. I'm on my own, did you know that?'

'Yes, I . . . assumed . . . at the trial I –'

'I wash my own clothes and stuff now, and I get my own food. Mum used to be quite hard sometimes, but . . . it's funny . . . now she's not there . . . no one's there . . .' He didn't finish the sentence, but shook his head disconsolately. People like Meici have something painful about them. An earnest, bovine simplicity, a gaucheness and the air of a soul not at home in the world and easily wounded. These traits constitute the cheese in the jaws of a psychological mousetrap that snaps shut the moment you begin to feel sympathy.

'That's tough,' I said. 'Living alone isn't easy if you aren't used to it.'

'She got fifteen years, did you know that? She doesn't find it easy either, Lou.'

I prickled with shame.

'I died, did you hear about it?'

I turned to give him a puzzled look.

'When they sentenced her, I was in court. I collapsed and my heart stopped beating. They put me in an ambulance. I had one of those near-death experiences, have you heard about them?'

'No, Meici.'

'I was in a tunnel of light, Lou, climbing towards a really bright light, like the sun. I could hear singing up ahead and then there was a gate and an angel with a clipboard. He said, "Meici Jones, you're not due today." I looked over his shoulder and I saw Esau – you remember me telling you about my little brother Esau who died when I was five?'

'Yes, I remember.'

'He was sitting in an orchard and he waved. I was going to say something but the angel said, "You have to go back, your task is not completed." Then I felt a sucking force behind me, dragging me back. It got stronger and stronger, and I felt myself being pulled back and back, down the tunnel, and the light dimmed. I opened my eyes and found myself in the ambulance staring up at the medic. He was playing cards on my chest. He looked quite shocked and said, "Oh, sorry mate." ' Meici turned to me and gave me an intense gaze. 'He made me promise not to tell anyone he had been playing cards on me. What do you think of that?'

'That's a pretty amazing story, Meici.'

'My task isn't finished, Lou. I've always sort of known I was put on this earth for a reason. That's partly why I am here today. I'm applying for the human cannonball, I hear there's a vacancy.' He opened his fist and revealed a crumpled newspaper advert, roughly torn out. 'It's for the election, Ercwleff is looking for . . . for . . .'

I peered at the advertisement. 'A surrogate?'

'Yes. I could do that.'

'What happened to the other guy?'

'He hit a wall.'

'Doesn't that put you off?'

'I'm ready for it. Marathon runners get the same problem, don't they? Something to do with carbohydrates. You have to eat spaghetti. I love spaghetti hoops.'

Soon after that he was called in and I didn't see him again that afternoon. There must have been another way out. I was next in the mayor's private office. He had a client's chair, like mine only grander and made from mahogany treble clefs. It was the sort of client's chair Queen Anne used to favour before she got out of the gumshoe business. The desk was also mahogany with a glass top on which were arranged a telephone blotter and a pen holder, both even cornier than the chairs. I sat down and smiled.

The mayor removed a cigar from a box on the desk, took pains not to offer me one and spent a long time retrieving a device from the inside breast pocket of his jacket. With this he sliced off the end of the cigar. Then he belaboured the ritual of lighting it and taking the first draw, still affecting not to notice me. I made a few half-hearted snoring noises. Finally, once his cigar was satisfactorily alight, he positioned it in his cocked index finger, across the top of his other four knuckles, and aimed it at me.

'Where have I seen you before?' he asked.

'Damned if I know.'

'I'm usually pretty good with faces.'

'You mean rearranging them.'

'Wisecracker, eh?'

'It was a clue to my profession. I thought it might help you place me.'

He nodded slowly. 'In my experience, only two professions are distinguished by a predisposition for the wisecrack. Cops and peepers. You're not a cop.'

'This is where you do the phoney act of dawning realisation. But you can spare me that one; not even the mayor of Aberystwyth is so busy he can't remember the face of a man whose desk he chopped up two days ago.'

'I must admit I wasn't expecting to see you again so soon.'

'I've come about the human-cannonball job.'

'You're too tall. You would stick out too far from the end of the barrel.'

'Why do you need a surrogate anyway? I thought the candidates were supposed to do it themselves.'

'Delegation. The ability to find the right man for the right job. It's an essential requirement in a mayor. You are not the right man, I'm afraid. We're looking for someone with a better knowledge of semiotics. That's the study of signs and meaning.'

'I know what it is.'

'There are a lot of danger signals involved in a job like that, red flags. You strike me as someone who ignores red flags.'

'You shouldn't rush to judgement; I got map-reading and signals intelligence badges in the Cub Scouts.'

'The last thing I want to do is prejudge you unfairly. How would it be if I gave you a little aptitude test?'

'Fire away.'

He observed me through narrowed eyes and stroked his chin. 'Well, using all your skills and wide knowledge of semiotics, which we have both agreed is the study of signs and meaning, tell me how you would read the following situation. A man walks into your office and chops your desk up with an axe.'

I scratched my head. 'That's a tough one.'

'Any red flags there you can see?'

'This is pretty advanced semiotics.'

He put the cigar down on a vulgar onyx ashtray. Then took out a semi-automatic pistol, pointed it at the ceiling and made a clicking sound in the back of his throat. 'Walther PPK, my favourite, the one favoured by James Bond –'

'There are not many mayors who can say that.'

'Adolf Hitler shot himself in the bunker with one, too. What do you think the PPK stands for?'

I shrugged.

'*Polizeipistole Kriminalmodell* or *Polizeipistole Kurz?*'

'You got me there.'

He looked unhappy. He put the gun down on the desk and swivelled it round to point at me. 'Why have you come to see me?'

'It's about your soothsayer. I need to know how good he is. You told me that I would soon be poking my nose into your affairs and for that reason you were taking the precaution of chopping up my desk in advance. Then shortly after you left, a man entered my office with a case that may or may not constitute poking my nose into your affairs, but I need to know.'

'Who was this man?'

'I'm afraid that information is protected by client privilege.'

'It was that fool Raspiwtin.'

'I can't confirm or deny.'

'You don't need to. My soothsayer gives very detailed prophecies.'

'Maybe you should let me have his card. I like to have my fortune told.'

'I don't think you would like what's in store for you.'

'I need to know if I had a client who wanted me to ask questions about say, for the sake of argument, a man called Iestyn Probert, would that be OK?'

He narrowed his eyes slightly and you could see he was debating whether the forced politeness was worth the effort any longer. The debate went on for a long while. Eventually he said, 'Mr Knight, I'm afraid I haven't been entirely frank with you. I don't have a soothsayer. When I referred to my soothsayer I was being . . . I was just . . .'

'Cracking wise?'

'Call it a figure of speech. You see, Raspiwtin is a man with whom I have had some dealings in the past. Word reached me that he was in town and that he had been asking for your office. How do I know this? Because I am the mayor and I get to hear about things. I am well informed: I know where he stays and what pyjamas he wears. I know what brand of toothpaste he uses and what he has on his breakfast toast. I know because I know. Unfortunately Mr Raspiwtin is unwell in the head, and in that head there is an obsession with matters from the past that I wish to remain private. But there is no soothsayer, just a prediction that your fate will mirror that of your desk if you decide to oblige Mr Raspiwtin.'

He glanced for effect at his watch. 'Goodbye, Mr Knight. Your time, I'm afraid, is up, both here in this office and in the wider context of life in Aberystwyth. I gave you fair warning; let's hope I haven't wasted my time. The mayor of Aberystwyth is not a guy who likes to have his time wasted; he's not the sort of guy who likes to give duplicate warnings, it's wasteful.' He reached forward and pressed a buzzer that indicated the interview was over.

It was just after midnight, maybe 1.00 or 2.00 in the morning. I lay asleep in my caravan in Ynyslas. The far-off susurration of the waves was barely audible, but the wind coming in off the sea cuffed the caravan like the hand of a giant schoolteacher and made the metal fabric sing. There is something deeply comforting about that sensation, of feeling protected and cocooned in warmth and yet aware, too, of the proximity of the ocean. Ynyslas is 6 miles north of Aberystwyth and lies hidden from the world in a corner of sand adjacent to the estuary. During the day in summer nothing moves here except tide and cloud and, occasionally, across the estuary on the distant hill, two carriages of a toy train going north.

There was a noise. Close. I opened my eyes, knowing without knowing how that there were people inside. The deepest, darkest fear of every householder in the night. The one that has never changed throughout time. The moment when you come face to face with your own mortality. Someone shone a flashlight into my face; someone put a gloved hand over my mouth; someone pressed the barrel of a gun into my eye. I was ordered to dress, and a hessian sack was placed over my head. I was pushed out into the cold night and into a car. We drove off. Fifteen minutes later the chimes of the station clock striking 2.00 told me we were passing through Aberystwyth.

When the hood was removed, I was sitting in a hard-backed chair facing four men across a desk in a dingy room. It felt like a basement but there were no clues for thinking this. Just the conviction that the business to be transacted was probably going to be hidden from the world. An Anglepoise lamp was trained on my face. After the darkness of the hood it was unbearable. I pushed the lamp down to cast its beam on the desk. One of the men was an officer in the military, wearing combat fatigues; he had silver hair, closely cropped, and his face was red. One was dressed in the neat, sober and expensive suit of a Whitehall mandarin in his sixties, with the pallor of a snail, the

Man from the Ministry but not one you can find in the telephone directory. The third had cop written all over him: standard-issue crumpled suit, police hair grease, truncheon-battered ear – he was eating an ice cream. Next to him, doing his best to counterfeit a kindly face, was a military chaplain. The brass hat looked to the mandarin for a cue regarding the lamp. The mandarin nodded acceptance. His shirt was crisply ironed, the tie knot small and rammed home without compromise. He looked tired, his face lined and pallid with the air of one used to dispensing authority in rooms that seldom saw daylight. The cop simply stared at me with a look that might have been bored contempt or maybe amusement. The brass hat spoke first.

'Thank you for coming.'

'No problem, I was passing anyway.'

He looked round to the mandarin, as if unsure how to react and needing a cue. The mandarin made an impatient grimace and said, 'We want you to help us.'

I smiled.

'If it was up to me,' the brass hat added, 'I'd have you flogged.'

'What a shame it's not up to you; you look like you'd enjoy it.'

'Don't get funny. It doesn't mean I can't have you flogged, or that I won't. It's just not in our best interests at the moment.'

'Or mine.'

His face turned a deeper shade of red. 'Look here you –'

The mandarin placed his hand on the officer's forearm. 'Let's not get distracted.'

'How can I help you?' I asked.

'We want you to betray someone,' said the mandarin.

'Who do you want me to betray?'

'The man calling himself Raspiwtin,' he said.

'What do *you* call him?'

The mandarin sighed. 'Please don't keep asking impertinent questions. We're not here to negotiate. We're offering you a deal you can't refuse.'

'It's not a deal then, is it?'

He raised his head slightly and looked over my shoulder. He nodded. Four strong, hard hands grabbed me from behind, hoisted me clear of the chair and dragged me across the room. In one fluid movement they twisted me round and slammed me into the wall. Then they did it again and put me back in the chair. My nostrils began to clog with blood which frothed and bubbled. I could feel it trickling across my upper lip. Drops fell and spattered the tabletop. My interlocutors gave no hint of having noticed.

'You will observe, Mr Knight,' said the mandarin in a tone that suggested my being thrown into the wall had somehow tried his patience to the limit, 'that the wall is made of brick.'

'What is it you want?' I asked.

'Raspiwtin has been to see you.'

I shrugged.

'What for?'

'I can't remember.'

'We already know what for.'

'Who are you? And don't say, "We ask the questions".'

There was the sound of movement behind me and I braced. I was thrown into the wall again. When I was back in my chair, he said, 'Our organisation is a secret subsection of the Welsh office known as the Aviary.'

'Which branch?'

There was a moment's silence.

'Look, snooper,' said the cop, 'quit the comedy. We could rub you out now. Not just here, everywhere. We could make it so you never existed. We could remove every record of you. We'd change the hospital records to say stillborn. We'd arrange a fire in the church where you were baptised. Anyone who claimed to remember you, we'd convince them they didn't. We can do that. The ones who stubbornly clung to your memory, we'd have them sectioned. We do it all the time; it would be like swatting a fly to us.'

'Is that what you did to Iestyn Probert?'

None of the assembled faces showed a sign of recognising the name, but this stony absence of a reaction was in its own way a reaction, as was the slight but palpable increase in tension. The cop spoke too quickly. 'We'll keep you in a cell and send you the tapes of your father going to the police station to report a missing person. "What missing person?" they'd ask him. "There's no record of such a person ever having existed. Go back to your donkeys, you silly old fool." For a long time he wouldn't believe it; he'd cling to the belief he once had a son, but he'd get used to it. We'd put him in the cell next to yours so you could hear him crying in the night. You could tap out messages to him on the plumbing, saying, "Hey, it's me, Louie." And he'd tap back, "Louie who?"' He stopped and for a moment there was silence. 'We can do that,' he said.

'Who is Raspiwtin?' I asked.

'He's not who he says he is,' said the mandarin.

'That's who he isn't, not who he is.'

'You need to know who the man is before you betray him?'

'I've never betrayed anybody before.'

'I'm sorry, we don't work for the Boy Scouts, Mr Knight. We have issues of grave national security at play here; sentiment doesn't come into it. We could do this other ways, we have plenty of options; you have none. We could get the information a dozen other ways, but for reasons it is not necessary to disclose to you, this avenue of approach appears the least problematic.'

'You'd be helping your country,' said the chaplain.

'My country can go to hell and so can you.'

The hands grabbed me again and slammed me against the wall before returning me to my seat. This time I sat hunched forward, in pain, without the strength to right myself. There was silence for a while and then the mandarin said, 'It makes no difference to us. We can arrange for your mangled corpse to be found in the wreck of a stolen car, wrapped round a tree somewhere. We will do it tonight. It makes no difference to us.'

I pulled myself up. 'Please don't.'

The chaplain smiled as if he hadn't noticed what they did to me.

'Raspiwtin is looking for someone. When he finds this someone, you tell us. That's all you have to do.'

'Just tell you?'

'Then you walk away a free man. There will be no repercussions. No one has been hurt yet, just think of that. It really is an excellent time to walk away from the table.'

'Who is the man he is looking for?'

'You don't need to know that,' said the brass hat.

'How will I know when he finds him?'

'You don't need to know –'

The mandarin raised a hand to silence him. 'Of course, it's Iestyn Probert. There is no need to pretend. We know Raspiwtin has you looking for him. He believes some nonsense about Iestyn having a rendezvous with some aliens from a UFO. All you have to do is let us know if you find him. That way you don't crash into a tree.'

'I thought they hanged him.'

'Well, they obviously didn't make a very good job of it, did they now,' said the brass hat.

'There is nothing to deliberate about,' said the mandarin. 'The arrangement is so obviously to your advantage that you can't be stupid enough to turn it down.'

The army chaplain took a scrap of paper out of his pocket and slid it across the desk.

'This is a number you can call if you need to contact us. Just call and hang up, we'll find you.'

I stared at the slip of paper, not making a move.

'It's just a number,' said the chaplain, 'it won't bite.'

I paused and regarded him. 'I knew an RAF pilot, once,' I said. 'He served during the Second World War; he said the chaplain told them God approved of their bombing, but woe betide them if they slept with the girls in the town.'

He forced a chuckle, trying to be my friend. 'I've heard that story, too. It's very funny.'

'I always find it strange seeing a man who works for Jesus dressed as a soldier.'

'Oh yes, why's that?'

'Jesus was a subversive. Are you?'

'I like to think so –'

The mandarin slapped the table and made an impatient gesture to the men behind me.

'We didn't come here to discuss theology. The interview is over.'

I picked up the scrap of paper. The hands reached out again and lifted me to my feet.

'You'll be dropped back at your caravan,' said the mandarin. 'It's a crap caravan where you live a life of squalid desperation. But I understand it's all you've got. If you don't want to lose it, I advise you to take the proceedings of this evening very seriously.'

Chapter 7

CALAMITY AND I sat stiff-backed on a bottle-green chesterfield next to a Georgian window overlooking Laura Place. It wasn't much of a 'Place' really, any smaller and it would have been called Laura Mews. But it possessed an air of modest affluence. It was the sort of square where you might expect to come across a film crew and a horse and carriage clip-clopping across the cobbles; just the sort of address, in fact, to which country doctors retired. We stared at a mantelpiece crowded with knick-knacks – framed photos, china figurines, a Toby jug holding letters from abroad, a brass shell case acting the part of a vase for dried flowers, a brass bowl containing hairpins, matches and a bottle of eye ointment.

'I'm not sure I'd like to be treated by a doctor who moonlights at executions,' said Calamity.

'I know what you mean, but it's not really moonlighting. It was a serious duty. If you are going to hang people, it stands to reason you need a doctor in attendance to certify the death and things.'

'It doesn't seem right for a doctor. Don't they swear some sort of oath to preserve life?'

'People thought differently about such things back then; they weren't so squeamish. I'm sure he probably can hardly believe it himself, looking back.'

'Still, it's a bit ghoulish.'

'You're the one who dug up his name from the *Cambrian News* . . .'

'Yes, I know. We have to ask him. Iestyn Probert. That's quite a common name. They might have executed more than one. Maybe he's forgotten.'

'I'm sure he will remember the Iestyn Probert who took part in the raid on the Coliseum cinema; everyone else seems to.'

'I'll let the doctor know you are here,' said Mrs Lewis, his housekeeper, from the doorway.

The gloom in the sitting room was as palpable as plasticine; you felt you could grab it from the air and mould it into shapes. Heavy velvet curtains, kept in check by sashes of braided gold, hung from curtain rails; closely packed lumps of mahogany furniture pressed down on the spirit; a grandfather clock stood sentinel and delivered tocks like water dropping in a cave. The tops of all the chests and cabinets were arranged with black-and-white photos, pictures of frozen happiness from the '50s. A car, an Austin perhaps, with shiny chrome trim, amid the tufts of marram grass overlooking a beach. Caravans were discarded on the dunes like children's blocks; a woman in a headscarf and sunglasses sat amid a picnic and gazed at the camera; from her expression, the mixture of tenderness and gentle reproach, it was possible to imagine the photographer peering inexpertly into the viewfinder of a Rolleiflex camera, giving instructions. Who was she?

'You promise we're going to see the farmer who saw the flying saucer after this,' said Calamity.

'I promise, even though I would like to put it on record that I think it's an unpromising avenue of inquiry, although not as unpromising as advertising a black 1948 Buick in the *Cambrian News*.'

'It's a '47, not a '48.'

Mrs Lewis showed us up. The door was ajar at the top of the stairs and darkness seeped out, perfumed with the faint smell of formaldehyde that clings to the lives of old doctors. We walked in; there was a rustle of sheet; two ferret-bright eyes shone from amid the shadows.

'Good morning,' he whispered.

'We're sorry to disturb you . . .' I began.

'I wasn't doing anything – apart from dying. Come into the light. It's nice to see you whoever you are. I don't get many patients these days; they don't like my bedside manner. Isn't that what they told you?'

'They told us you were a fine doctor,' I said.

'They told you I was an awful doctor.' He put on a cartoon voice: "*I sent my little boy to him with tonsillitis and the damned fool told the boy he was dying*". Isn't that how it goes? Well, I make no apologies for not sugar-coating the truth.'

'You told a little boy he was dying?' asked Calamity.

'I tell all my patients they are dying; it's the only diagnosis I can make with any certainty. You'd think they would be grateful. Set against the implacable fact of their mortality, what does a cold or case of tonsillitis matter? It's all too trivial for words.'

'Ultimately, yes,' I said. 'But it's not trivial at the time.'

'Tell me, do you follow the latest scientific developments?'

'Not too closely.'

'Just as well; you'd stick a paperknife into your heart if you did.' He raised a feeble finger and pointed at Calamity. 'Tell me, little girl, do you like flowers?'

'They're OK.'

'Of course you do. You like bright colours, too, eh? All little girls do –'

'She's not so little.'

'The soft peacock of the hills and sky; the deep, coagulated carmine of the rose; the custardy yellow of the daisy's face, fringed with those perfect spears of white that yet somehow contain within their lucence a hint of the sky's azure . . . You like colours, don't you?'

'Maybe.'

'They are lies, all lies. Tricks and falsehoods, more deceiving than a lover's tongue.'

'I don't believe you. How can colours be lies?'

'Because you see, little girl, they are not properties belonging to the things we see, not intrinsically; they are fictions invented in our own heads. Yes, there is no doubt of it. Outside our bodies, beyond our skin, there is just electromagnetic radiation – radio waves that have no brightness nor colour. Ask yourself, where are these colours? If you chase them down the rabbit hole of the eyes, along the paths of nerves to their home in that porridge we call the mind, what do you find? Nothing but palpitating lumps of goo and slime.' He swept his arm up and pointed through the window to his garden and, beyond it, the universe. 'Everything we love about this world, all the beautiful things, are fictions our mind invents to conceal from us the insupportable truth: that the world is a colourless, seething quantum soup wrapped in endless night. Tree and flowers are just outlines we draw on to the darkness.'

'If I felt like that I would find it hard to get out of bed in the morning,' I said.

'Do you think staying in bed would change anything? Mrs Lewis tells me you want to know about Iestyn Probert.'

'You remember the case?'

'Vaguely. He was lucky enough to be hanged young.'

'Most people wouldn't call it lucky.'

'Of course not, but most people are fools who are scared of the dark and so persuade themselves that this torrent of empty days that we call life is preferable to the darkness that awaits them.'

'We heard you certified his . . . er . . .' Calamity paused.

'Death? Can't you say it? Are you frightened of a word? You poor, feeble, mouse-hearted things. Death is our friend, the only friend who keeps his appointment, who never lets us down. Death the lover who never forgets our birthday, who never jilts us for another, gentle death . . .'

'Have you always been so unhappy?' asked Calamity.

'What makes you think I am unhappy?'

'You hate flowers.'

'No, you are wrong. I don't. There is nothing to hate. It is not the flower's fault. A flower has no intention, no more than a rock has. A flower is just a little machine that blind chance over endless geological epochs has contrived into an arrangement that produces copies of itself. What is there to hate? The only hateful thing is the myth of the flower that we create for ourselves.'

'But have you always felt like that?'

He made a bitter smile and paused. 'No, there was a time when I loved flowers too, when the colours of which we spoke brought the same uncomplicated joy to me as to the rest of my fellow herd.' He reached across and picked up a photo from the bedside cabinet. 'I keep a picture of Rhiannon to remind me of my conversion from that happy state. She left me, you see, when the world was young and we bestrode the sun-burned dunes like gods. We were betrothed and thus immortal like all young people, invincible, at least for an hour. She left me at the acme of my earthly bliss, beached on an Ararat of woe.'

'Why did she leave?' asked Calamity.

'Who knows? They never tell you the true reason, do they? They think they want to spare you, but really they want to spare themselves. Suffice to say, for a season we played in our own walled garden of delight, and then autumn came and she was gone. Anon, the park keeper locked the gate and melted down the key.' The muscles of his shoulders relaxed, he exhaled slowly, as if released from the grip of the memory. 'Iestyn was nothing. A cheap crook who pulled off a cheap raid on a cheap fleapit of a cinema and somehow stupidly contrived to kill the poor policeman who gave chase. For this the boy was hanged. He was dead. They generally are once you've dropped them from the end of a string.'

Calamity looked disappointed. 'You couldn't be mistaken? We heard . . .'

He snorted. 'You heard? You heard he was still alive? You heard perhaps the story of a strange alien-looking woman who bought his cadaver, paid for it with some antique coin, and lo! a week later, like Jesus, he walked among us again. You prefer such nonsense to the sober, evidence-based professional opinion of the physician who presided at his hanging, who noted, and marked it down on his report, that the fifth cervical vertebra had been snapped by the force of the drop, as indeed was inevitable. This doctor who in all his years never saw or heard of a case in which a hanged man with a broken neck came back to life. What contemptible superstitious nonsense you bring to my bedside.' He put the photo back and turned it to face away. 'You are worse than that imbecilic housekeeper of mine who no doubt at this precise moment has her ear pressed to the keyhole. They said I'd done my fiancée in, you know, those shrew-faced gossips from the village. Said she was buried in Tregaron Bog. How their pointy tongues wagged until the following spring when Rhiannon came back for a week. That wiped the smile off their faces. That's the one thing they never forgive, letting them down like that. You can see it in their eyes, the look of reproach. How could you! How could you make us believe we had a murderer in our midst and then spoil it all like this? That's the great paradox upon whose meat I daily feast: they cast me out, not because I murdered my fiancée, but because I didn't.'

A man sat on the bench in that section of the castle that projects out into the sea. He was reading the Bible and waiting for me. He had called me the previous week and I had put the meeting off a number of times. The breeze flicked his thin, sandy hair into his eyes and made the collar of his tan-coloured mackintosh slap his face. I knew he had noticed my approach but he affected not to. He was the president of the remembrance society that had been formed to remember Marty, who had died on the cross-country run when we were in school. I sat down next to him and stared out to sea. It looked like porridge.

'Funny thing about ruined castles,' I said. 'They always fill up with earth. Where does it come from?'

He said nothing.

'It's always cold up here, isn't it? Do you ever wonder what it must have been like, standing on the tower wearing iron clothes?'

Glyn gently closed the Bible and said, 'I didn't come here today to talk about castles.'

'What did you come for?'

'You never come to our meetings.'

'I don't see the point.'

'Only because you refuse to look for it. One evening two or three times a year, how much of a sacrifice is that?'

'Why should I have to make a sacrifice?'

'We all have to make a sacrifice. The world isn't a theme park. We were put here for a purpose, even if we are but dimly aware of what it might be.'

'That's your opinion.'

'It's the Lord's opinion.'

'Marty was fifteen and had tuberculosis but no one knew. The inquiry cleared Herod Jenkins. I loved Marty and grieved for him, but I can't hate. It just won't come. I guess I'm not a good Christian.'

'Don't insult my religion.'

'You are the one insulting it. Didn't Jesus preach forgiveness?'

Glyn turned to me, his face strangely impassive. 'Where? Where does he preach that?'

'Forgiving those who trespass against us and stuff.'

'He clearly didn't mean it to apply equally in all cases. And besides, our community is not about forgiving, or blaming, it is about remembering and celebrating Marty's short life. If you came along once in a while, you would know that.'

'Didn't Jesus also say something about worrying about the living, not the dead?'

'He said the Lord our God is a God of the living, not the dead. But we are not Gods. You presume too much.'

'You twist my words; what do you want?'

Glyn held the Bible up between his palms as if drawing inspiration from it. 'You heard that Herod Jenkins is standing for mayor?'

'Yes.'

'A monster.'

'So don't vote for him. Vote for Ercwleff. One of God's children, your ideal candidate.'

'He's a simpleton. A choice between a fool and a monster is no choice. We need a proper candidate, the town needs a proper candidate.' He deliberated for a few seconds. 'We want you to stand.'

The hairs on the back of my neck stood on end. 'That's absurd.'

'Why is it absurd?'

'I have no interest in politics.'

'That is a recommendation.'

'I already have a job.'

'It need only be for a year.'

'There are hundreds of reasons. I don't want to.'

'No doubt, but sometimes our desires and our duty do not coincide and in such cases a man, a real man, knows which is more important.'

'I couldn't do the human cannonball bit. I'm too tall.'

'You think Ercwleff is doing it himself? We can supply a surrogate; that part is easy.'

'And what about the fist fight in the pub car park?'

'Ercwleff is going to take a dive in the fifth. That makes Herod the winner; you only have him to beat. Think of it! Think how old he is now, while you are young and in your prime.'

'He would tear me limb from limb. Age has nothing to do with it; he's my former games teacher. It doesn't matter how old or frail or infirm he is, he will always be tougher than the boys he taught. That's how it works. I would rather fight an anaconda.'

'Do me a favour, Louie, think about it. For Marty . . . no, not for Marty, for Aberystwyth; do it for your beloved town.'

'It's not my beloved town. Where do you get that idea from?'

Glyn put the Bible up to his chin and pondered.

'Anyway, what's wrong with Ercwleff for mayor?'

He tried a different tack. 'Have you never wondered why Preseli wants to elect his idiot brother as mayor?'

'Yes.'

'And what answer did you arrive at?'

'None.'

'He's doing it to pay us back. For the humiliations they suffered as children. When Ercwleff was born, his father was too drunk to help and his mother sent Preseli to fetch the doctor. He was drunk, too, so drunk he could hardly see. He used the coal tongs as forceps and deformed Ercwleff's skull. The mother died, but not before naming him Ercwleff and making Preseli promise to watch over him all his life. Preseli promised her he would, and throughout school he was his brother's protector. They had a school rabbit and one day

Ercwleff accidentally broke its neck, he wouldn't stop hugging it, you see; even as a kid he was very strong. They made him spend the rest of the term in a dog kennel at the back of the class. Imagine the mockery. You know how cruel children can be – they discovered a wonderful trick for making Ercwleff cry. All they had to do was say the police were coming to take him away. The threat must have seemed very real to him because even by the age of nine or ten he had seen two uncles and a cousin depart the district in this manner. They teased Ercwleff relentlessly, and Preseli would get into fights protecting him; but he always seemed to be the one who got blamed for starting the trouble. You know what teachers are like in situations like that: they assume as a matter of routine that the boy from the bad family started the trouble. Such ignorant, unthinking dolts . . . so blinded by their own prejudice . . . They don't see how by singling the child out, and treating him as a black-hearted good-for-nothing, they create the very thing they condemn. When the four o'clock bell rings, the teacher has forgotten all about the casually dispensed retribution earlier in the day, but the child remembers. Nothing festers in the heart more than such injustice meted out by adults, those towering figures who are forever declaiming their own moral infallibility. Yes, the child remembers.'

'How did Preseli get to be mayor?'

'After National Service he went abroad and was away for a long time. He came back a different man; educated, worldly, sophisticated to a certain degree; and he had money. Joined the police out at Ystrad Meurig. He did quite well, made a name for himself clearing up crimes, usually by fitting people up. Then his career got a boost for catching the gang that robbed the Coliseum cinema; went into politics. No one knows where he went when he was abroad; he just incubated his revenge.'

'So this is it? His revenge? He comes back like some Welsh Heathcliff and makes Ercwleff mayor?'

'That is my opinion, yes. This way he pays back all the teachers who punished him and all the kids who mocked his brother.'

I cast a glance at Glyn, who stared straight ahead, out to sea. He talked of adults declaiming their own moral infallibility, but I never met a man more richly deserving of that description than him. I stood up. 'A man who hugs a rabbit to death would make a pretty good mayor.'

'Nothing's ever serious for you, is it?'

'Ercwleff would make a better mayor than me.'

He stood up and faced me, placing himself between me and the sun. 'For sure. They say he saw an angel once, so he's got the right connections. All I can say is, it must have been a pretty bloody stupid angel. Just think about it, that's all I ask. Think about it.'

He strode off into the grey wall of sky, dwarfed by the borderless expanse. The intensity of purpose was painful to behold; he was like a needle in the celestial sewing machine, darting here and there, up and down the town, leaving incomprehensible tracks sewn into the ground.

There was a fair being set up on the Prom at the junction with Terrace Road, as part of the mayoral election. The human-cannonball barrel, resembling the scarlet horn of a mythical beast, was anchored in front of the bandstand and pointed towards Constitution Hill; the catching net was just before the shelter by the wishing well. The other stalls consisted of a tombola and white elephant, Punch and Judy, and a permanent donkey-ride base. Meici Jones was striding around with his head held high, his bearing almost military. He chatted with holidaymakers in a manner which even at a distance struck one as expansive; a girl accompanied him and occasionally handed him leaflets which he signed and passed out to onlookers.

When Meici spotted me, he broke away and marched over.

'Louie, excellent of you to come,' he snapped in the manner of one who has just inherited the Prom and decided to open it to the public. He grabbed my hand and pumped it.

'You got the job then? Congratulations.'

'Thank you, Louie. Your support means a lot to me.'

'When's your first flight?'

'Mission, Lou', we call them missions. I'm still training at the moment, down on the recreation field at Plas Crug. I hope to be operational in about three weeks. Come, you must meet Chastity.' He grabbed my tricep and propelled me across to meet the girl.

She looked about nineteen or twenty and wore a knitted two-piece mouse-coloured outfit and had a supernumerary arm, about the size of a wooden spoon. Meici excused himself to go off and sign autographs and discuss ballistics with some tourists. Chastity watched him go with a longing that suggested he was going off to battle.

'Isn't he amazing?' she said.

'Yes,' I said, 'there's no one quite like Meici.'

'I've always wanted to fly, ever since I was a little girl.'

'Are you on holiday?' I asked.

'Yes, we're from Shawbury in Shropshire; I'm here for the summer with my aunt. We're staying at the caravan park in Clarach, do you know it?'

'Clarach, yes . . . an interesting place.'

'I think it's dreamy.' She was young but had a quality that made her seem much older, as if she had spent the past hundred years imprisoned in an enchanted wood; maybe it was the clothes – the knitted suit, the fawn socks and sensible, round-toed brown leather shoes – it all evoked a claustrophobic, walled-in upbringing. You could trace the hand of someone much older directing events. If you asked her the name of a pop star you knew she would cite enthusiastically an old crooner – Sinatra or Dean Martin – derived from a stack of worn LPs that her auntie played on Sunday evenings after church.

'Some people find Clarach a bit quiet,' I said.

'Aunt Marjorie and I chose it for precisely that reason. The doctors told her to go somewhere quiet for her nerves. She has terrible problems with her nerves. I had to give up learning the harp because of them.'

'In which case I would say she has made an excellent choice in Clarach. There isn't a single incident mentioned in the records dating back to 1734 of a visitor to Clarach getting overexcited.'

Chastity's eyes flashed. 'Goodness!' She reached into a pocket in her cardigan and pulled out a notepad and pen. 'I must make a note of that. Aunt Marjorie will be pleased. I forget so easily, you see.' She opened the notebook with her right hand and pulled the cap off her pen with the little wooden-spoon arm and held it in her little hand like a lobster pincer and wrote, 'Records date back 1734 no overexcite'.

'What exactly is wrong with her nerves?'

'We don't know. Fuss upsets her. That's why we had to get out of Shawbury. It wasn't easy finding somewhere with less fuss than Shawbury.'

'I can imagine.'

'It was my job, really; that's why I'm glad to have the facts at my disposal. The one about 1734 is excellent.'

'I can give you some more if you like. Before the last Ice Age, Clarach was the gateway to the legendary kingdom of Cantref-y-Gwaelod, which now lies sunken beneath the waters of Cardigan Bay.'

Chastity opened her mouth in goldfish-like wonder. 'A sunken kingdom! How thrilling!'

'According to popular belief, you can hear the bells of Cantref-y-Gwaelod ringing out on moonlit nights, although perhaps you had better not tell your auntie that.'

'No, no, I won't; she'd be a bag of nerves if she found out there was a sunken kingdom on her doorstep, ringing bells at all hours.'

'But that's ancient history; it's very quiet now. Archaeologists tell us that the Pleistocene age is the last recorded instance of there being more than five people on the beach at Clarach at the same time.'

'Golly!'

'Have you walked the other way, to Borth?'

'Not yet, but we are planning to. There's just so much to do. Meici says he will show us the way if he can get some time off from flight school.'

'It's not really hard, you just follow the path up the coast.'

'I'd feel safer if Meici was with us, we might fall among thieves.' Chastity's gaze flicked away, over my shoulder. 'He looks so strong in his space suit, it must be wonderful to fly through the air like that.'

'The journeys are quite short, though.'

'I've never met anyone like Meici before. He's the only person I know who has read *Pollyanna* more times than me. I've read it fifteen and I'm going to start again in August. Have you read it?'

'I think I saw the movie with Hayley Mills.'

'The book is better. Hayley Mills is too pretty, she would have had lots of friends and nice things in school. I never did. Meici and I play the Glad Game sometimes. He's much better at it than me, though. Yesterday he said he was sad that he had no friends at school but he was glad because it meant he knew what it must have been like for me.'

'That's very touching.' I noticed Meici had stopped signing autographs and was staring at me with what appeared to be irritation.

'Yes he's wonderful. You must be very proud to have him as a friend. He's so philosophical. He told me yesterday that when he's flying and looking down on the people on the Prom, they all look so tiny, like ants, and he says all our problems look tiny too.'

I said goodbye and as I wandered off I was aware of Meici watching me through narrowed eyes.

We drove out to Borth against the incoming tide of lunch-time traffic. Huw Pugh, the farmer who claimed to have witnessed the alien visitation, lived out at Ynys Greigiog, along the shores of the estuary. You could get there directly by going inland, but to drive that way without making a needless detour through Borth would be to display the wrong attitude to life, the attitude evinced by those who are too busy to stop and admire the view, unaware that this is largely what life is for. It's just a simple road, ruler straight for 3 miles, between the railway line and the shore, parallel to each; a few shops; a railway station whose primitive simplicity evokes those halts in the Wild West where the gunslingers wait three days for the train and shoot the only man to step off the train. The road and houses, beads on a string, are a single thread thinner than a tripwire. Borth is a cheerful haven of demotic pleasure. The land between the railway and the sea is scrub, like a tramp's coat – weather-stained and trimmed at the cuffs with marram grass. In winter everything is closed and the shutters squeak.

But in summer, everything is bright, silver and blue. Dark spots dance before your eyes from the endless brightness. It is a vinyl-scented trove of rubber rings, spade, buckets and mats. The eyes ache from squinting and the distant roar of the churning water has the effect of muffling all sound, near or far. Sand gets in your eyes and between your teeth; in the milk and the butter, in your bed and in your tooth-paste. And every evening, inflatable rubber dinghies wildly unsuited to the sea transport children like little Hansels and Gretels over the horizon to Greenland.

Mrs Pugh opened the door to the farmhouse and feigned delight. She looked like a mouse in a bonnet. We told her we were old friends of Farmer Pugh and had come to offer our sympathy following his recent close encounter of the third kind. She led us into the kitchen where she put the kettle on and then took us upstairs. Huw Pugh lay beached on the big pillows of a big bed. The room had bare stone walls and funereal black oak furniture. He stared at the ceiling with the intensity of an Old Testament prophet.

'I've got someone to see you,' said Mrs Pugh. 'Isn't that nice, an old friend from long ago.' She made a few cosmetic changes to the arrange-ment of the bedclothes and then hobbled past us out of the room.

There was a pause. We stood in the doorway, hesitant to enter the room of a stranger. He moved his head and stared at us, narrowing his eyes as he tried to focus.

'Rhys? Is it you?'

We shuffled our feet.

'No, no, it can't be . . .'

'Good afternoon, Huw,' I said.

'Rhys? No . . . it's . . . it's not possible. Not after all these years, not after all that's been said.'

I looked at Calamity. Her face blazed with silent imperative, urging me to act the rôle of the mysterious Rhys.

'Nothing's impossible, Huw, for a man whose heart is strong.'

'But . . . you . . . oh dear Lord! Come closer!'

I walked over to the bed. 'You're looking well, Huw.'

He continued to stare at the ceiling, but reached out with his hand and grabbed my sleeve. 'Promise me you'll do it quickly . . . no . . . no . . . I have no right to ask such a thing; did I promise an easy deliverance to our sweet brother? No. But at least show me mercy, permit me to say one small prayer first. Just the one to the Lord Jesus.'

'No, Huw.'

'No? You'd slay me without more ado? You, who had half a lifetime to savour this act of fratricide; only now do you make haste to fulfil the vow you made? Do you think Ifan would object to a little prayer? Gentle Ifan —'

'No, Huw, I come not to kill you.'

'Not?'

'Not.'

Confusion creased his features. 'And the vow you made to our dying mother?'

'They lied to you, Huw, I never made such a vow. She went to her grave not knowing; I thought it best to spare her.'

'You have a big heart, Rhys Pugh.'

'What good would it have done to tell her?'

'It would have broken her in two. You did the right thing.'

'Only me and you know.'

'And Sioned.'

'Oh . . . er . . . yes and Sioned.'

'If it hadn't been for her, none of this would have happened, would it? When she told me what he'd been doing to her — his own flesh and blood! His own sister! Well . . . you know what happened. Who could have stayed his hand on hearing such things?'

'Who indeed!'

'Still, it was wrong. To kill a brother . . . I deserved your curse.'

'No longer. I come to embrace you and beg forgiveness for the years I cast you out from my heart.'

Tears filled his eyes and overflowed, big drops fell down the sides of his face and thudded the counterpane. 'Oh Lord! Quick, pass me my specs – they're on the table somewhere.'

I looked at them lying on the bedside table. Calamity picked them up and hid them behind a flower vase.

'I can't see them, Huw.'

'Is there someone else there? I sense a presence.'

'My daughter Eluned. I never told you.'

'A daughter!'

'Yes.'

'Wonder of wonders! How old? No, not you. Let me hear her speak.'

'I'm eighteen, Uncle Huw,' said Calamity.

'She sounds just like you. Quick, dear niece, hold your uncle's hand.'

Calamity pulled a face and placed her hand in his. 'I've prayed for this reconciliation every day,' she said.

'She's studying Law now,' I said. 'At Bangor.'

'My oh my! A Pugh at university, who'd have thought it! Makes a change from the debtors' prison.'

Mrs Pugh brought in the tea and left without a word. We drank politely, trying to change the subject.

'We read about you in the papers,' I said.

Huw Pugh nodded and answered dreamily. 'Yes, it was a great strain; having to tell all those lies, having to pretend all the time about Ifan. I had to keep making phone calls to relatives and folk, asking if they'd seen him, even though I knew he was dead in the cellar. "We think he might have lost his memory," I'd say. "He might be wandering around all lost. You will look out for him, won't you?" And I'd say to mam, "See? He'll be back next week, you mark my words. He won't be able to keep away from your home cooking much longer, not if I know old Ifan." ' Huw Pugh wiped his eyes with the sleeve of his nightshirt. 'You remember Old Gelert the dog? He used to bark at the cellar door, and scratch at it. And if I went near him, his hackles would rise and he would snarl. If I put food out, he wouldn't eat it. I told mam it was just a reaction to losing Ifan and she would say, "But what's that got to do with the cellar? Ifan used to be scared of the cellar; he never went near it." Eventually I decided the only thing to do was get rid of the dog. Smash his head in with a brick, I thought. But he was a clever bugger, that dog – he knew, you see. He knew what I was thinking. It's funny how they can tell, isn't it? I spent a whole month trying to catch him and all the time when my back was turned he'd be there whining and scratching at the cellar door. It was doing my head in. Then I had an idea. I dressed up in Ifan's clothes and came back down the lane like he always used to. Well, I tell you, that fooled him, he came bounding up the lane, barking and yapping with joy until he was about 5 foot away, then he screeched to a halt like they do in the cartoons; amazing it was, he left skid marks in the dirt; you wouldn't think a dog could do that, would you? But I tell you, he did. It was too late, though, I had him by the collar so there was nothing he could do. Bashed him in good and proper, although he fought like a tiger. Then I left him in the road so it would look like he'd been hit by a car. I was almost high and dry until mam came back from the shops early whooping with joy, saying she'd seen Ifan in the lane with Gelert. "He's back!" she cried, "he's back!" She wouldn't be persuaded neither; she went round telling everyone in the village she'd seen him. That's why they had to commit her. After that, I waited a while, then moved the body to Tregaron Bog.'

'Let's not dwell on the past,' I said.

'No, you're right,' he said.

'Now we need to get you well again. Tell us about the flying saucer.'

'Oh that,' he said without interest. 'First, come and give your brother a hug and let him feel your love.' He reached his arms out.

I looked at Calamity. Her expression said plainly that here was a challenge that could not be ducked. I leant forward into his embrace and dug my arms under him, clasping him in a bear hug. He squeezed. 'Oh Rhys,' he croaked. 'Rhys, Rhys, Rhys.' The bristles of his unshaven chin, hot with tears, rasped against my cheek. 'Oh Rhys bach . . .'

I let my hug go limp but waited patiently to be released.

'Sometimes I used to stand on the railway line and think, Welshpool is only an hour away. I am no more than an hour from the love of the brother I have wronged. But really I knew the distance between us was unbridgeable, or so I thought until the Lord blessed this day.'

I extricated myself and stood up. 'Tell us about the alien, we're all agog. Is it true she wanted to make love to you?'

'She did, but I'm afraid she was in for a bit of a disappointment.' He stared up with a sheepish look. 'You know how it is first time with a girl. We all brag about it down the pub, don't we? But when it comes down to brass tacks . . . well, it's not the same. Especially if the girl is experienced. To tell you the truth, Rhys, I can't do it unless I'm pissed. It's different then, isn't it? And then doing it on a table inside the saucer . . . it felt all wrong, sort of clinical. She was ever so nice about it, she said I shouldn't worry because she'd done this loads of times, but that's what worries you, isn't it? I mean, I wasn't expecting her to tell me I was the first, but we like our little illusions, don't we? And there was another thing: the table was in the centre of the room and there were two other blokes, aliens like, operating a console set against the wall and looking over their shoulders at us and then flicking buttons and levers on the console, and it was almost like she was responding to their inputs. She said, "Please don't worry, earth-man, your semen will be safe with me." And then she looked confused and asked what was wrong, and I asked, like, if she had any music and she said she would sing to me and bugger me if she didn't! "Myfanwy" she sang. Quite good, too, but it wasn't what I had in mind. The mood was all wrong, you see. Then the blokes on the console pressed a red button and she told me she loved me and couldn't bear to be apart from me. It still didn't do any good and so then she cried and said this had never happened to her before. Then I woke up sitting in the car, and twelve hours had passed.'

'In the papers it says you couldn't remember much about it,' said Calamity.

'I told the press I couldn't, but I was lying wasn't I? I'm hardly going to tell them the truth now, am I? It's bad enough all me mates laughing down the pub as it is. Imagine it if I told them I couldn't perform!'

'We heard they asked about Iestyn Probert,' I said.

'They did, and I told them the Proberts are not from round here, they used to live over at Ystumtuen, but they've moved. I didn't say they hanged Iestyn because it didn't seem nice if they were friends of his.'

'Maybe they told you lots of interesting things but you can't remember them,' said Calamity hopefully.

'Maybe they did, but if I can't remember them, they're not much use to me, are they?'

'We were wondering, maybe you should be hypnotised to stop you getting nightmares.'

'I'm not getting nightmares.'

'But you will,' lied Calamity. 'They always do. We could arrange a hypnotism session to straighten you out. You know Mrs Bwlchgwallter from Ginger Nutters? She could do it. I mean, you must be curious to find out what happened.'

'Not really, to tell you the truth.'

Chapter 8

REFUGEES FROM caravan sites shuffled through the town, glistening and torpid in the wet, not so much a drizzle as a tingling miasma of rain. The damp seeped up through my bones and made the climb up the stairs to the office feel more difficult, as if gravity had increased.

The window had been left ajar and rain formed a pool on the windowsill. Calamity had put newspaper down to soak up the puddle. The rooftops of the town looked like they had been varnished. The phone had been replaced and was ringing as I entered. I picked it up.

'This is Mrs Lewis.'

'Hello Mrs Lewis.'

'You remember me? From Laura Place.'

'The doctor's housekeeper! How is he today?'

'Never mind that. I have something that might interest you.'

'Really?'

'Information that might be useful to your case.'

'What case is this?'

'Don't get fresh with me, Mr Knight. The whole town knows you are a private detective.'

'I expect they do; it's not a secret.'

'I haven't got much time; the doctor is taking his afternoon nap but he is easily roused. Listen very carefully. The price will be £25. Cash would be preferable, but I will accept a personal cheque drawn on an account bearing your name.'

'What about a postal order?'

She hesitated. 'That's a bit troublesome, but I expect . . . oh I see.

That was a wisecrack, wasn't it? I was warned to expect this sort of flippancy.'

'I'm not sure if it counts as a wisecrack.'

'Mr Knight, do you want the information or not?'

'Tell me what it is.'

'You must think I'm daft. If I tell you what it is you won't have to pay for it.'

'But how can I pay for it if I don't know what it is?'

I could sense a growing exasperation. 'B . . . but you . . . you always pay for your information, don't you?'

'Not always. Sometimes people give it to me for free, although that happens less and less these days. Usually when I pay it's for something I want and I know the party has but doesn't want to give me.'

'But that's me.'

'Yes, but I don't know what you've got.'

'It's about the matter you were discussing with the doctor.'

'And what was that?'

'As if you didn't know.'

'Oh, I know all right; I was just wondering how you knew. You weren't there.'

'It's possible I may have overheard some of your conversation with your girl while I was waiting for the kettle to boil.'

'That can happen.'

'Sometimes words carry –'

'I've noticed that. Especially through keyholes. It's something to do with the acoustics in old houses . . . Aberystwyth is famous for it.'

'Such impertinence!'

'Just tell me what you've got, and I can warn you now it won't be worth £25. Maybe a tenner if it's really good.'

'Fifteen pounds is my final offer.'

'OK, twelve if I really like it. That's *my* final offer.'

'It's about someone called Iestyn Probert.'

'What about him?'

'He came to see the doctor the night the boys robbed the Coliseum cinema.'

I tightened my grip on the phone; it was almost as if she had sent an electric jolt along the line. Mrs Lewis cackled like a witch discussing holiday plans with her familiar. 'Ha ha! You're not so cocky now, are you, Mr Big Shot Wise-Cracking Snooper.'

I said nothing, waited for the moment of cheap triumphalism to pass. It took a while.

'Oh yes, not so cocky now, are we?'

'That's very interesting.'

'More than interesting, I'd say, wouldn't you? I was surprised, you see, they never mentioned it in the papers.'

'Yes, I can see why that would surprise you.'

'Fifteen pound.'

'It's not that interesting,' I lied.

'Don't play games with me, Mr Knight, I heard you gasp from here. And that was just the starter, that's nothing compared to what else I know.'

'Mrs Lewis —'

'I've got to go, I can hear him stirring. Meet me at the community singing at Castle Point tonight at 9.00.'

There was a pause.

'Well?' she said.

'I was just waiting for you to say, "No police and no funny stuff".'

'I won't rise to your bait. Bring £15 and make sure you are not followed. Castle Point community singing, at the back.' She hung up.

Calamity having divined that the call had taken me aback, stared at my face for clues.

'Whose turn is it to make the tea?' I asked.

Before she could answer there came the sound of singing from the stairwell, a strange mixture of giggling and wailing. A man appeared in the doorway, dressed — except for a white shirt — entirely in black. Black suit, black tie, black silk handkerchief peeping out of his jacket pocket, black pigskin gloves, black shoes. He carried a charcoal fedora with a black band and wore a black flower in his buttonhole. He also carried a folded newspaper. His face was old and wrinkled like a prune but surmounted by a perfectly smooth bald dome of a head which was entirely clear of wrinkles. It made him look ancient and alien like a goblin foetus. His eyes were piercing arctic blue and he smiled.

'I've come about the car,' he said.

Calamity and I glanced at each other.

He held out the newspaper. 'Black 1947 Buick, one careful lady owner.'

'Oh!' said Calamity. 'They put the advert in a week early. Oh no.'

The man looked up and around at the room. 'Wow, a real private detective's office. I wasn't lucky enough to see one on my last visit to Earth. My sister was so disappointed.' A tiny frown flitted across his face and a look of concentration formed. 'But there is a feature, common to all such places, that is missing.' He looked up and clicked his fingers. 'The desk!'

I clicked my fingers too. 'Why don't you take a seat, Mr . . .'

'Joe, my name's Joe. With an H.'

'Where does the H go?'

'Where do they usually go?'

'Usually they don't go anywhere; most people spell Joe without an H.'

His face fell. 'Really?'

'It's an old Earth custom.'

'After the J is probably best,' said Calamity.

'After the J, yes, that sounds like a good place.'

'Jhoe it is then,' I said.

'So you've come about the car,' said Calamity.

'Yes, can I see it now?'

'I'm afraid not,' said Calamity. 'It's still stuck at Customs.'

'Oh, I see. Maybe in that case you can tell me the price; your newspaper advertisement failed to mention it.'

'We were thinking of offers in the region of £25,000 weren't we, Louie?'

I avoided her gaze and stared instead at my shoes.

Jhoe looked surprised. 'They've gone up. My last one was $126.42.'

'That must have been some time ago,' said Calamity.

'Yes, it was. My first was in 1947, my second in 1965. I drove the length of Route 66, Chicago to LA. I remember all the Burma-Shave signs.'

> *Don't stick your elbow out so far*
> *It might go home in another car*
> *Burma-Shave*

'That's very good,' said Calamity.

> *My job is keeping faces clean*
> *And nobody knows de stubble I've seen*
> *Burma-Shave*

'Yes, well, these cars are collectors' items now,' I said. 'They command a premium price.'

'Oh dear. This news ingroks me terribly.' It was as if a light behind his cheeks had been switched off.

'I'm sorry,' said Calamity.

'Perhaps we could trade,' said Jhoe. 'I could give you my hat.'

Calamity threw me a look of appeal.

'Hats on Earth don't generally fetch more than £75,' I said.

'Oh, I see. On Noö they are worth more.'

'So it's a Noö hat? Why didn't you say! On Earth a Noö hat generally goes for about a hundred.'

'But not £25,000,' said Calamity. 'I'm sorry.'

'How are things on Noö these days?'

'Much the same as ever, really,' said Jhoe. He looked glum. 'Still raining.'

'Does it have to be a Buick?' Calamity asked.

Jhoe seemed thrown by the question. He frowned.

'I mean,' she said hurriedly, 'how would it be if you bought a car that . . . that wasn't a black '47 Buick?'

Jhoe looked baffled, like one of those hunter-gatherers who have no word for numbers greater than three when the TV interviewer asks what two and two make. He pulled his forearms close in front of his chest and hid his face behind his fists. 'This question completely ingroks me,' he said.

'Please don't be ingrokked,' said Calamity.

'Now look what you've done with your horseplay,' I said. 'She was just joking.'

Jhoe pulled his hands away. 'Really?'

'Of course!' said Calamity.

'I am relieved,' said Jhoe. 'Your bizarre question came close to expressing the thing which is not. And yet you seem such a lovely girl, I couldn't believe you would say the thing which is not.'

Calamity looked pleased.

'She used to skip school,' I said, 'but she never says the thing which is not.'

'Would you like a cup of tea?' asked Calamity.

He gave her a querying look.

'She means the hot infusion of oriental leaves, not the letter of the alphabet.'

Jhoe brightened. 'A cup of tea.'

'It's made with water,' added Calamity. She fetched a cup of water from the kitchenette and held it out. He looked at it in wonder. 'I am honoured. You offer me the water ritual.' He dipped the tip of his index finger on the surface and then licked his finger in solemn reverence. He looked at Calamity and she did the same. She brought the cup over to me and I followed suit.

'Now we are water brothers,' said Jhoe.

I left Calamity to give Jhoe a tour of Aberystwyth and help him send some postcards back to the folks on Noö. I decided to drive home for lunch at my caravan in Ynyslas and perhaps take a swim. The drizzle had stopped and the sky had become blue again with that hard mineral clarity of a spring sky after rain; the few white dots were those a fawn loses before the end of summer. As I left the office someone ran into me. It was Chastity, the girl I had last seen on the Prom casting admiring glances at Meici Jones. Not many girls had ever done that, just as not many had forsaken Shawbury for Clarach in the hope that it would be quieter. 'I have to go and tell my aunt,' she said in a breathless rush. 'He's bought me a handkerchief, can you believe it!' She waved the handkerchief. It was a small, white cotton thing with some mauve and pale green stitching at each corner and the initial C. 'Am I blushing? I'm blushing, aren't I? Don't deny it, I know I am.'

'Maybe a little,' I said.

'Goodness knows I've never had anything like this before. He says he got it from a catalogue.' She made a shocked expression. 'He's such a scoundrel!'

I gave her a lift to Clarach and she spent the time extolling the quality of the handkerchief's workmanship. 'I think it's Egyptian cotton, but I'm not 100 per cent. I expect so, that's the best isn't it, Egyptian?'

I pursed my lips to indicate that I really couldn't say.

'It's certainly very fine. I haven't seen one as good as this for a long while.' She held the little square up to the light and then painstakingly folded it. She placed the neatly folded hanky on her knee and leaned back in the seat to admire it. After a while she exclaimed, 'My word it's hot today!' She picked up the hanky and dabbed the sweat from her brow.

'Open a window,' I said.

'No, no! There's no need, really.'

We passed a farmer and his dog walking along the side of the road. Chastity waved the handkerchief at them, perhaps the first person ever to do such a thing along that road.

'Be careful you don't wear it out,' I said.

She look concerned. 'Do you think I might?'

'It's a possibility.'

'Yes, you are right. I'll put it away . . . no I'll just put it down here where it's still handy in case I need it.'

We passed over the hump-backed bridge by the church and turned left. As we pulled into Clarach an ice-cream van was turning on the stones above the beach, preparing to leave. Streams of children radiated outwards like the crowd dispersing after a football match. Chastity gasped, 'Quick! Let me out, he's leaving.' I pulled up sharply. She leaned over, kissed me on the cheek, then jumped out and darted towards the van, waving to the driver to make him wait. I drove back to the junction and turned left onto the slow road to Borth, with an exultation in my heart like a dog who hears his master fetch the lead. The track rises and dips, rises and dips, and the bonnet of the car points skyward for a while, like the prow of a fishing boat, before plunging into the enveloping abyss of green. The succession of hills and dales across which cows wander like currants in a cake acquires a rhythm, and like a musical passage it builds with a sense of expectancy until reaching a crescendo. Everyone who knows this road knows the crescendo: that moment when you clear the brow of the final hill and the coast for the next 50 miles flashes into view. It doesn't matter how often you have seen it, you are always taken aback by the piercing, glittering beauty. I pulled over onto the verge and leant across to get some sunglasses from the glove compartment. As I did, I noticed Chastity's handkerchief lying in the footwell. I put it in the glove compartment and made a note to return it before the day was out.

My caravan was on the landward side of the dunes and enjoyed a view over the top of the other caravans through the netting of TV aerials to the Dovey Estuary. When you die, if you have enough clout to get in the VIP seats, this estuary is what you look at. I turned into the main compound and passed a giant silver sweet wrapper discarded at the side of the road, as if a fairy-tale ogre had been dropping litter. When I rounded the bend by the shop and my caravan came into view I realised the giant was Ercwleff and the sweet wrapper was my door.

I climbed wearily out of the car. Ercwleff and Preseli were sitting at my camping table on my folding chairs drinking tea from my pot, invigorated with rum from my bottle. They were eating sandwiches made from bread that looked like it was mine, spread with my Shipham's crab paste, and drinking straight from my carton of homogenised milk. They weren't wearing my pyjamas but probably because it wasn't time yet.

They squinted up at me as I approached. 'We started without you,' said Preseli. Ercwleff smiled and lifted the sandwich upwards in the way people do to convey appreciation when their mouths are too full.

'You didn't have to break the door. The key is under the mat.'

'Where's the fun in that?' asked Preseli.

'Looks like I'll have to replace the door now.'

'Looks like it,' said Preseli with a full mouth.

'Doors are expensive.'

'Good ones are.'

'To tell you the truth, I'm getting tired of you destroying my property.'

'Your problem, peeper, is, you don't listen. I told you not to go poking your nose in my affairs but you carried on anyway. That desk was a gentle warning, a way of telling you this is what happens to your face when you cross paths with Preseli Watkins. I hear you went to see Doc Digwyl. What for?'

'Chilblains.'

'Always cracking wise, eh?'

'What business is it of yours what I go to see a doctor about?'

'If you want time off sick I can arrange that.'

'Is that what you did to Iestyn Probert?'

He carried on chomping nonchalantly, giving no indication of recognising the name. 'There is no such person.'

'Maybe not any more.'

'And there was no such person. There was never anyone by that name.'

'I heard he took part in the raid on the Coliseum cinema; I heard you were the cop who arrested him.'

'I arrested the two Richards brothers, who each did a twenty-five year stretch. There was no one else.'

'That's not what I heard.'

'Your informant is delusional.'

'My informant was Doc Digwyl.'

He gave a fake laugh. 'You'll have to do better than that. Apart from the fact that Iestyn Probert never existed, I happen to know that the old doc would never tell you a damn thing about him if he did exist. He's too busy moping about that woman who walked out on him.' He threw a crust over his shoulder. 'I also hear you've been friendly with Meici Jones, my new human cannonball. That has to stop, too.'

'Why would you care about these people?'

'If I told you that, you wouldn't have to go round bothering them.'

'So tell me.'

'No need because you're not going to go round bothering them anyway.' He peeled a triangle of processed cheese and smeared it on a cream cracker. 'Your food really stinks. Get some Stilton in next time.'

I said nothing but thought about ways to make him go; I let my gaze wander to the shovel lying discarded under the caravan. It wasn't far away.

Preseli picked up a red triangle of paper napkin and dabbed his fat lips. 'I don't want you talking about me or my affairs to the doctor, butcher, baker or candlestick maker, or for that matter my human cannonball. Otherwise I might have to take that job away from him. He likes that job.'

'None of that means a damn to me. I don't care about Meici.'

'So maybe I need to have a conversation with someone you do care about, that little girl for example, the one who works with you. I could give her to Ercwleff to play with; he likes little girls.'

Ercwleff smiled and chomped like the fat kid at your seventh birthday party.

'I hear he likes rabbits, too.'

Ercwleff beamed. 'I like rabbits.'

The mayor looked irritated.

'Hugged one so hard it couldn't breathe, is that right? Spent the rest of term in a dog kennel?' It was my turn to smile, the smile of a man pulling the tiger's tail.

'That's not a subject I care to have aired,' said Preseli. 'It's painful for my brother.'

'Those are the sorts of subject I make my living from.'

'You just don't get it, do you?' said Preseli with mounting anger. 'You're just too stupid. You'd think having your desk chopped up might be a clue, but it just wasn't obvious enough for you.'

The breeze whispered past the caravans; the sun flashed on the chrome bumpers and aluminium trim of the caravan and the tubes of the deckchairs. It was beautiful. I kicked the picnic table and it slammed against the side of the caravan spilling sandwiches over the laps of them both. Preseli jumped up; Ercwleff bent down to retrieve the sandwich he had been eating. I picked up the shovel and brought the thin edge of the blade down the back of his skull. It sounded like a stonemason chiselling rock. Preseli stared at me in astonishment and fear as I raised the shovel again. Ercwleff was frozen on the ground, his rear end jutting like a badger in trousers.

'That's what will happen to you if you ever touch Calamity. Your tame bear won't be enough to protect you. Now get out.'

The blow would have killed most men, but Ercwleff just looked drunk. He climbed unsteadily to his feet and Preseli helped him back to the car. As they drove off, he said through the window, 'You've just started something you can't finish.'

I knew he was right.

I put the door inside the caravan, removed my shoes and socks, and headed towards the sea. I climbed the mane of marram grass to the crest where the breeze was stronger and made the sharp stalks of grass quiver and spin; as I stumbled down the face of the dune the world became silent except for the soft pat of bare sole on hot, dry sand. And then I found a gap in the wall of dune and was assailed by the distant rumble of the sea. The tide was out, and the sea far off, separated by a long walk across ribbed sand that held quivering pools of hot, sparkling water. Across the sea, the peaceful town of Aberdovey glinted; little white specks signified houses like teeth in the smile of a cartoon giant. Five minutes by boat, but an hour or more by car or train. The estuarial waters moved back and forth, like waters to and from the heart. Glass flashed on the hillside, and the train to Pwllheli moved slowly across the green backdrop with the speed of a bubble rising in a glass of water or a satellite moving across the night sky. Given the choice, it was a wonder anybody opted for burial on land, dropped into a muddy hole, soil in your nostrils and worms in your mouth, to engage in decomposition, a word uncomfortably close to compost. In the sea, down on the ocean floor among impervious fish, you didn't disintegrate into mulch for the garden, you were purified. You became part of the heartbeat that draws the waters back and forth; you dissolved into that main, the constantly self-renewing, gleaming, pulsing body of salty loveliness.

Chapter 9

SOSPAN RAN a damp cloth along the counter and talked of escape. I lifted my elbow to let the cloth pass. 'Everything is prepared, ready for the moment should it ever come,' he said. 'An ice-cream van, anonymous and untraceable, secreted in a lock-up garage in Bow Street. Behind the row of council flats, with the red door. The key is hanging from a string taped to the water pipe at the rear. There is ice cream, money, food and clothing in the van. Enough to last a month or more.'

'What are you expecting to happen? Armageddon?'

'You mock, perhaps, but my family came to this country after the St Bartholomew's Day Massacre. We lost a lot of customers during that dark period. An experience like that makes an impression that lasts for many generations. It's like people who knew starvation during the war; they never forget it, do they? Always haunted by the fear that such a time might come again. They can't even throw away a crumb of bread.'

'Are you really worried you might be massacred in your beds?'

'I worry about the unforeseen and make what allowances I can. No one knows what lies in store, no one can predict. The wise man prepares.' He wrung out the cloth and put it away. He leaned forward onto the counter, supporting his face with his hands. 'But to tell you the truth, physical escape is the easy part, isn't it?'

'What other types are there?'

'I mean relocation of the physical body makes little difference if the soul is in prison, does it?'

'I guess that's true. Is your soul in prison?'

'None of us are truly free. At least, not until we have slain the dragon that lives in all our hearts. You remember me mentioning a special ice cream to you before. The one I keep off-site. The ice-cream man's Katabasis.'

'I remember.'

'This ice cream facilitates escape via the inner route. Not the road of the flesh, across mountain ranges and deserts, but a journey of the spirit, inward and downward.'

'It sounds . . . interesting.'

'There is nothing quite like it. I can let you have a scoop if you like, by appointment of course.'

'Perhaps not today.'

'Most people who take it describe a vision of a journey into a giant's castle, I don't know why.'

'Aren't you tempted to take it yourself?'

'I did once, many years ago, when I was young and frightened and going through a period of great emotional turmoil. I too sought the way of the giant's castle. What happened? A curious thing. I met a lady at the door to the castle who sent me back. She said, "No, Sospan, you are not ready for the way of the giant's castle, this route is barred to you. We have other things in mind. You must return to the surface, return to Aberystwyth. There, on that frontier between the world of flesh and that kingdom of salt beyond the Prom, ruled over by my cousin Pluto, you must pitch your tent, a little wooden pillbox. From there you shall cast forth your wares, principally cold sticky sweetmeats perfumed with vanilla, emblem of paradise and the Lotus Isles, and with this will you ensnare the hearts of men and make them whole with your ministry of love. And for those whose wounds are too grievous, that cannot so easily be remedied, you will send them here to the Giant's Castle, and we will minister to their heart's ache." So I came back.'

'What was it called again?'

'Katabasis. £1.25 a scoop. By appointment only.'

'Do you get a flake?'

'It can be arranged, but I consider it gilding the lily. It's got green ripple.'

A new customer arrived and Sospan changed the subject. 'Mr Raspiwtin! Lovely evening.'

Raspiwtin gave me a sheepish nod and ordered a choc ice.

'Mr Raspiwtin was explaining earlier today that the world is an illusion.'

'If it is, it's a convincing one,' I said.

'Every day we have to invent it afresh,' said Sospan. 'That's what you said, isn't it? Every morning when you awake you groan in torment.'

Raspiwtin's voice took on a wistful tone. 'Ah yes! How I crave that exquisite annihilation of the ego we call sleep. But I wake instead and begin once more the terrible Sisyphean labour of fabricating a universe. But once, many years ago, I saw the world as it really was. A series of mornings lasting perhaps a year or more when the trick by which one resurrects the façade failed and my soul was naked before the darkness as a tortoise who has lost his shell. I shudder still to recall it, although, truth be told, it was principally that experience that brought me to these shores, and to this fine meeting with a hero such as you, Mr Sospan.'

'I think you may be overstating it a bit there,' said Sospan, turning aside the extravagant compliment. 'Me a hero?'

'Not at all! I look at you opening your kiosk every day, feeding the insatiable maw; like a fat sow you parade your teats to the biting snouts of your litter; you suffer in silence, performing the essential sacrament of your trade. The day wanes and you close. The sun sets and you are miserable once more, you who were formerly so glorious are now dross; pathetic. A contemptible jester, nothing more. But for a while – temporarily, yes; provisionally, indeed; fragmentarily, of course! – for a while you created your own meaning. You transcended your fate. You were a hero. Truly you, Mr Sospan, are an Absurd man.' Raspiwtin made a small flourish with the choc ice and walked off chuckling with the light heart of a man who believes himself to be on the verge of discovering the truth that eluded him all his life.

A squeal erupted from the beach. It was Chastity running across the sands, chased by a man in a space cadet's outfit. 'No, Meici, no,' she squealed in mock terror. Two young lovers playing the game that all young lovers play in the days before their minds are informed of what their hearts have decided. Too early to acknowledge their love, they express it obliquely through rough-and-tumble games that serve as disguised caresses. The sight was as familiar on this beach as a dog stealing a toddler's ice cream, but it had more poignancy here because the two actors, Meici and Chastity, would no doubt be appalled if you had made explicit to them the truths embodied in their chase. Chastity was a hopeless runner, and Meici, though not much better, gained on her easily. When she reached the water's edge she found, like many people before her, that her fleeing feet had betrayed her; there was nowhere left to run. She stopped and huddled; Meici caught up and stopped, unsure what to do next. 'No, Meici,' she squealed. As if remembering the rest of the role, Meici grabbed her and began to tickle her. 'No, no, no, stop it, no, don't hit me,' she squealed in play, unaware, as were we all, that one day she would say it in truth.

The Pier began to blink with light; to ping and ding and tinkle; to emit the hot smell of scorched ozone, which mingled on the night breeze with the heavier reek of fried onion and grease-encrusted hot-dog van. Under the Pier, hidden in the gloomy forest of ironmongery, roosting starlings emitted a collective mutter. I walked up the Prom in search of Raspiwtin and found him playing crazy golf. Of all the rituals of the seaside holiday it must be the emptiest. It isn't crazy; not really. Despite the discordant primary colours painted on the concrete, it isn't zany or madcap or subversive or anarchic; it doesn't encroach upon the line separating genius and madness. It is simply dull. The grass is made of cement, which gives no purchase to the ball, and therefore it is impossible to aim with any precision. The ritual survives for one reason only: in our hearts we notice a subtle resonance with our own fates. We too careen around a concrete rink for a while, ping from side to side across a garishly painted world the colours of which betoken fake joys, driven by insane forces, subject to incomprehensible laws and rules in which merit plays no part; eventually, once chance and Brownian motion have exhausted all other possibilities, we drop into a hole and have to hand our putter back to a bearded loon in a kiosk. He ticks a cheap pink scorecard. There is no bar afterwards.

Raspiwtin bent over his putter and lined up his shot with needless precision.

'Who do you work for?' I asked.

'No one any more.'

'Who did you used to work for?'

'An organisation.'

'In what capacity?'

'In many capacities.'

'How about naming one?'

'I have been many things in my time: healer, mystic, prophet, mendicant, heretic, counsellor.' He stood up and walked towards the hole. 'If we cannot help one another on our journey through this dark night they call life, what good are we?' He prepared to putt again.

I grabbed the club and wrenched it out of his surprised hands. I threw it across the concrete floor. 'Look here, you infuriating mystic in flannel. Since you walked into my life I've lost a desk and a door and been thrown violently against a wall by a group of people claiming to be the Aviary. Does that mean anything to you?'

'Naturally, I have heard of the Aviary.'

'Who are they?'

'They are part of the Welsh Office.'

'That tells me nothing.'

Without the golf club to hold, his hands twittered with uncertainty; he reached into his pocket and brought out a pack of Parma Violets. 'I'm not sure if information regarding the Aviary is relevant to your inquiry.'

'You don't get to decide what is and what isn't. When someone throws me against the wall and threatens much worse, it's my decision. Either that or there is no inquiry.'

'If you cancel our arrangement now, you won't get the £200 back.'

'And that's another thing – you haven't paid me yet.'

'I haven't?'

'You know damn well you haven't.'

Raspiwtin smiled.

'Just start talking. What are you doing in Aberystwyth?'

'I told you, looking for Iestyn Probert.'

'He's dead.'

'I have grounds to believe he is still alive, having been resurrected by aliens, and that he will return to this area for a rendezvous with them.'

'So far you have produced no grounds whatsoever apart from a load of gossip and rumour.'

'I have more substantial grounds –'

'Where are they?'

'In my pocket.'

I blinked. 'In your pocket? Perhaps you might like to take them out.'

'I do not think the grounds –'

I slapped the pack of Parma Violets out of his hands. He looked taken aback by the sudden violence.

'Look,' I said. 'Either you start co-operating a bit or I play crazy golf with your head.'

He stared at me in fear or wonder and reached into his jacket pocket. He brought out an envelope and handed it to me. 'Be very careful with this. It is a top secret interdepartmental memo from the Aviary dated 1966 detailing the conclusions of their investigations into the Iestyn Probert case. Do not ask how I came to have it in my possession.'

I waved the envelope. 'But this, you say, is about Iestyn Probert. Back there at Sospan's you said something different.'

'I did?'

'You know damn well you did. Some cock-and-bull story about resurrecting the universe every morning –'

'Hardly cock-and-bull –'

'You have two stories, one cock, one bull. They can't both be true.'

'Of course they can. It all has to do with what we call proximate and ultimate causes. If I tell you I am hungry and you ask why, I could give two different but not contradictory explanations. I could say, "Because I haven't eaten since breakfast." Or I could say, "I am prey to a bodily discomfort resulting from fluctuating levels of the hormones leptin and ghrelin," and I might add that, in truth, my hunger was the result of an evolutionary survival strategy developed to ensure that this particular agglomeration of self-replicating molecules called a human being acquired sufficient fuel to continue the chain of replication. That would be the ultimate as opposed to the proximate cause of my hunger.'

'Why stop there? Why not go back to the Big Bang?'

'Because I don't want to try your patience. I merely wanted to explain that, yes, I am here because I seek Iestyn Probert, but above and beyond that desire lies the landscape of my spiritual desolation, which plays a major role in this particular desire. What I referred to back there at Sospan's was my *apostasia* – the fall from the grace of belief that resulted in my conviction that the redemption I sought could only be supplied by Iestyn Probert. My *apostasia* had many stages.'

'Start with the first.'

'The first . . . the first . . .' his words trailed off, it seemed that a thought that caused him pain had slid into his consciousness. 'I guess you could say I am here because of a girl, a love affair that ended tragically, as do they all, I am told.'

'Finally you make sense.'

'It may please you to think so, but in truth the fate of this girl was an early chapter in that book whose summation was that nothing makes sense. She was Burmese. I was working among the Karen refugees on the Thai border. She was perhaps fourteen or fifteen years old, working as a maid in a household where we can be sure maids from Burma were not treated very well. I used to see her occasionally around the village. There was no one lower on the social ladder than this girl, and yet she smiled often and seemed to me to embody in its purest form the simple piety and meekness that we were told characterised that carpenter's son from Nazareth. She was not a special girl, there were thousands like her living similar lives of sheer hopelessness, and yet for me at that time she became special. I confess I developed a passion for her that went beyond mere wonder at her simple piety. In truth, she ravished my soul. I flattered myself she found my attentions not unwelcome, and, though not a word had ever passed between us, I fancied that a secret accord had arisen between us, a bond of love silent, unvoiced, but burning in each breast. I arranged for a message to be passed to her, assuring her of my earnest in this matter and sounding her out. She did not reply in kind, for to do so would have been too indiscreet, but the day after she gave me an even more beautiful smile than any she had given before and I knew then my cause was not hopeless. The next day she left town and it was communicated to me that she had gone to visit her parents in Hpasawng to ask their permission in this matter. It was a day's trek to the border, which was nothing unusual, and she set off at first light carrying with her the money she had earned through six months' toil. To us it would have been a miserable pittance, perhaps as much as £50, maybe a bit more. Possibly even less. By evening she had arrived at the border post, where the captain of the Burmese guard called her into his office and took her money away. Then he raped her and shot her.' Raspiwtin paused and dabbed his eye with the knuckle of his index finger. 'Of course, nobody cared, apart from the peasants who were powerless to do anything. The captain was not even disciplined. But I cared. When the news of what had happened filtered back to my mission, I held out the cross which was attached by a chain to my neck and spat on it. And nothing happened. That's when I knew: He didn't care.' He rubbed his sleeve across his face; he was crying openly. 'I'm so sorry,' he said. 'I'm so terribly sorry. Forgive me. When I think of that poor girl, it is too much, too much.' He turned his back and walked off towards the castle.

I picked up the putter and ball and returned them to the kiosk. I read the document. It was a fragment, a mimeographed mimeograph of a typewritten carbon copy, covered in marks and obscure annotations and signatures next to meaningless numbers and letters. *TOP SECRET/AVIARY EYES ONLY*. It described the interrogation of the woman who had laid out the body of Iestyn. She admitted handing over the cadaver to a tall blonde Scandinavian-looking woman with four fingers and piercing blue eyes with catlike irises. The woman paid her with an Iron Age coin. The document looked authentic enough, but how would you know? I walked back to the office and left it for Calamity to read.

A distant clock struck 9.00 and the sound of Welsh hymn-singing drifted across on the night breeze: '*Nid wy'n gofyn bywyd moethus.*' The words of the old hymn '*Calon Lân*', which I had sung in school with only a vague idea of what the words meant. Something about a pure heart being worth more than gold or pearls. Mrs Lewis would be singing it tonight while awaiting her bribe, unaware of the irony.

The crowd gathered to sing every night at the public shelter that cut into the face of the hill beneath the castle. Except for the front few rows, it was open to the skies, and the water slapping against the rocks across the road provided a gentle percussion section in accompaniment. When it rained the singers got wet, but this didn't seem to diminish their ardour. I joined the back of the throng and stood erect with the self-consciousness one feels as an outsider among the faithful. Mrs Lewis sidled up to me, nudged my elbow and indicated I should follow. She crossed the road and walked up to the railings where they formed a sharp angle and from where you could see both sections of the Prom in their entirety. The tide was in and the sea gently butting the wall gave off a fine aerosol which puffed across the town like the fluid a gardener uses to spray aphids; it fizzed orange round the street light and collected on Mrs Lewis's spectacles.

'Did you bring the money?' she asked.

'I brought the money. Tell me what you've got.'

'Let me see it first.'

I dug into my pocket and scooped out a fistful of screwed-up five-pound notes. She peered at them longer than I thought necessary, her tongue flicking in and out like a lizard's; she nodded. I stuffed them into the breast pocket of her coat. She cast a glance around us even though it was clear no one was within earshot and took a step closer.

'It was the night of the robbery,' she said. 'Whole county was looking for them. We heard it on the radio in the kitchen; they said the robbers were armed and dangerous, and had been spotted heading east towards Ystrad Meurig. There we were, huddled round that radio, gripped with fear when there was a knock on the door. Of course, it could have been anybody, but we all jumped. We knew straightaway it must be the robbers. The doctor told me to wait in the kitchen while he fetched his gun. Then he opened the door. On the step was this Iestyn Probert and this other chap. Iestyn Probert said there had been a car accident and his friend needed help. The friend was a strange-looking fellah. Not very tall, no more than 5 foot, if that, with a pretty, boyish face, more like a girl, and blonde hair to his shoulders. His eyes were piercing blue and his ears seemed slightly pointy. He looked frightened. The doctor told me to phone Preseli Watkins at the police station. They took the boy upstairs and put him in the guest bedroom. I made some hot soup and took it up to them. Iestyn Probert was very hungry and wolfed it down. He was not much more than a boy himself; so young and scared. And his friend, there was something very uncanny about him.' She stopped talking and stared at me intensely. I noticed her hand was held out, palm upwards. I dug out a handful of coins and placed them on her outstretched palm. She continued with the story with the seamless automaticity of a laughing-policeman machine.

'He was wearing a strange metallic suit – covered him from toe to neck – and we couldn't get it off, so the doctor couldn't examine him. He looked so lost and frightened. The doctor asked him where he was from and he wouldn't answer. Iestyn said he was called Skweeple and was from somewhere called Noö. Skweeple was watching us with fear in his eyes like a timid deer. Then, all of a sudden, he cried out – more of a shriek really, just once. Iestyn Probert must have guessed straightaway that this meant danger, so he made a run for it, leaving the boy with us. Immediately after that we heard the sound of a car pulling up outside. Preseli came straight in through the door while Iestyn was still climbing through the bathroom window. He escaped over the garage roof.'

'What happened to the boy in the silver suit?'

'Preseli took him away. He said he would find a way to make him talk.' She stopped and looked out across the sea. She shook her head. 'I knew what he meant. Violence. I could never abide it. Not then, not now.' She paused and licked her lips, then said in a whisper, 'For another £3 I'll tell you about the lady from the sweet shop in Ystrad Meurig.'

I made a look of slightly bored inquiry. She pinched my lapel between index finger and thumb and hissed, 'They disappeared her!'

'Disappeared?'

In answer, she gave me the sort of emphatic nod gossips deploy to indicate that the information, though it sounds far-fetched, is nonetheless true. 'Off the face of the earth.' She pushed her upturned hand towards me and I deposited three pound coins in her cupped palm.

'Story was, they found exo-biological remains at the crash site, and alien debris which was taken to the RAF base at Aberporth. They said it was a weather balloon, but since when do you need an armed escort for a balloon? The lady from the sweet shop found a bit of the saucer in her garden and used it as a doorstop. It was some sort of black volcanic glass, like obsidian, inscribed with markings reminiscent of the Assyro-Babylonian cuneiform scripts dating from around 2800 BC, and it hummed like the fridge. Two days later they came and took her away, doorstop and all.'

'Who did?'

'The Aviary.'

'The Aviary?'

'Two men dressed all in black, driving a black '47 Buick.' She turned away from me and leaned on the railings, looking into the blackness where slept the sea. 'I've never spoken about this. Even though I knew it was wrong. I'm not a brave woman, Mr Knight.'

'Didn't you ask the doctor about it?'

'I didn't dare. Not long after that they caught the two Richards brothers, and a week later they caught Iestyn. I read about it in the papers, but there was no mention of the boy in the silver suit. Then the doctor received a visit from the men in black. It was a private meeting and I don't know what they discussed. But after they left he was trembling, and his face was white. And then when Nora Dettol disappeared, I knew better than to open my mouth.'

'Who's Nora?'

'She was the cleaner at the base. She was hoovering and walked by accident into a room that should have been locked. It was like a hospital room. There was a chap in there wearing olive-green military pyjamas. He had a bulbous head and big almond-shaped eyes. She said he looked so sad and lonely. She said she startled him and made him jump. "I'm so sorry," she said, "I thought the room was empty." Then he stared at her and it was as if he was looking straight through her and into her soul, and burrowing down through the layers of the past searching for something. All of a sudden she saw a vision of her mother's face and an overwhelming sensation of peace and loving kindness flooded her being; she heard the voice of her mother, who had been dead for many years, saying, "Please do not be afraid, Daughter of Earth. We bring you love." ' She stopped and folded her arms aggressively saying, 'You'll never guess what he said next. It'll cost another quid.'

Mesmerised, I handed over a pound.

'He said, "Can you take a message to your president?" '

Chapter 10

I HAD said I would pick Miaow up at 9.00 for our trip to the escalators of Shrewsbury, but like a kid on his first date I was early. I
parked outside the shop at the caravan site and waited. Then I grew
impatient and walked across to the office. A fat man sat wedged behind
the reception desk, eating a bacon sandwich. The grease that dribbled
over his knuckles glistened in the sharp morning light. The expression
on his face said that, whatever it was I needed, he probably had it but
couldn't be bothered to go and get it. It was the face of someone whose
synapses sparked at a slower speed than other people's. The face a
tortoise wears the first morning after hibernation as he walks downstairs
to collect the post from the mat. It was the face of a man who doesn't
care less and has made it his specialist subject; everyone needs something
they can be proud of. I told him I was looking for the caravan of Miaow
and his face betrayed no sign that the question meant anything at all.
Maelor Gawr was the caravan park at the world's end.

I took a deep breath and said, 'You know, my friend, to look at
your face you probably wouldn't believe this, but you are a lucky
man. Yes, you are. This may come as a surprise. All your life you
have gone to bed at night convinced that nothing good ever happens
to you and yet here am I claiming you are lucky. Why? How can a
man like you be lucky? I'll tell you. Because on any normal day I
would now grab your tie and stick it into the roller of that typewriter
you are busy dripping bacon fat onto. Then I would give the barrel
a violent twist and keep turning until your nose was touching the keys.
Then I would type out a letter to the *Cambrian News*. That's what I
would normally do. But today I have a date beneath a pellucid May
sky with a girl whose eyes are so beautiful that they elevate this day

so far above the common herd of days that it would be a shame to write a letter. But that doesn't mean I won't come back sometime when it is raining and the wonder of this day is but a poignant memory, do you understand?'

'You want a caravan?'

Before I could answer, she appeared in the doorway.

'Sorry I'm late; I couldn't decide which hat to wear.'

'You're not late and you are not wearing a hat, but you can tell me about it in the car.'

She was wearing a cream cardigan over a simple cotton frock patterned with tiny lemon flowers. It was belted at the waist and reached demurely to just below that most underrated bone, the patella. She was wearing cream sandals and carried a cream handbag. Her hair was kept away from her face with a cream hairband. She was also holding a plastic Co-op bag which I knew contained our picnic. We drove in my Wolseley Hornet over Trefechan Bridge and turned right towards the station.

As traffic slowed on the approach to the roundabout I turned to her and said, 'You look lovely.'

Instead of denying it or accusing me of saying it to all the girls, she smiled and said, 'No one's ever said that to me before.'

In the slightly awkward pause that followed, I patted my coat pocket and said, 'I've got the tickets.'

'You must tell me how much I owe you.'

'Don't be silly, it's my treat.'

'How many rides do you get?'

'What do you mean?'

'On the escalator.'

'As many as you like.'

'Really?'

'The tickets are for the train.'

'Oh!'

'You get a special day return to Shrewsbury and it includes unlimited rides on the escalators.'

It is no coincidence that train windows are shaped like the celluloid frames of a movie. All rail journeys are adventure stories, which is why fate reserves her grandest statements for them. Without this tendril of steel linking us to Vladivostok and all stations between, Aberystwyth would be bereft: no Pier, no camera obscura, few hotels, and the tourist information office would almost certainly have been deprived of its proudest boast, namely that on 7 May 1904 Buffalo Bill came to town.

Miaow kept her nose pressed to the window for most of the journey and stared with a sense of wonder that made me regret I could never again take this journey for the first time. As we glided into Shrewsbury the track curved gently round the main signal box; once, no doubt, the red bricks and white-painted window frames would have gleamed like a mansion on a chocolate box, and an entire extended hierarchy of workers would have beavered away at the clockwork intricacies of directing trains. Today it stood in chest-high weeds like an abandoned house in an abandoned field; as with most businesses that have seen their best days, the first to go is always the guy who cuts the lawn. There is still a man up there, moving behind the filmy grey glass, drinking tea and reading the paper resting against rows of levers that don't work. He doesn't know the war is over.

The tracks converged onto a bridge across the river before the entrance to the station, and two buildings, one of pink Shropshire sandstone, the other of red Victorian brick, stood sentinel. Miaow pointed, but didn't speak.

'Guess what those buildings are,' I said. 'Home to two branches of the same family.'

Miaow gave me a look of inquiry.

'Both been in business a long time, the same business in fact, although it goes by different names. The people from the one on the left quite often go and stay with the ones on the right, but it seldom happens the other way round.'

'OK, I give up.'

'That one is the castle, that one is the prison.'

'That's silly, the people in prison are thieves and murderers.'

'So are the ones in the castle. How else do you get to own a castle?'

'No!'

'If you steal small things, you get a room on the right with a view of the river and the railway station. If you steal big things – like counties – you get a room on the left also with a view of the river and the railway station. The room is bigger, and the food is better. You have about as equal a chance of having your throat slit while you sleep.'

'The people in the castle are lords and ladies with coats of arms and pointy Rapunzel hats. All through my childhood I dreamed of wearing one of those pointy hats.'

'Trust me, the pointy hats are all stolen.'

'How can you say that?'

'Along with ermine stoles, gold-painted furniture, pheasants and oil paintings. Do you think they worked for it?'

'Didn't they?'

'No, they were just smarter than the rest of us, or meaner. The way I see it, they are just descended from the better armed robbers. It's like a great Welshman once said: "Who made ten thousand people owners of the soil and the rest of us trespassers in the land of our birth?" '

She pulled a face. 'So why didn't anyone complain?'

'The pointy-hats were smart. They invented the priesthood to preach to the multitude the great spiritual benefits of being penniless; they taught them not only to accept their misery but to love it, and to regard it as evidence of their spiritual superiority. In addition, for those who found themselves unconvinced by these fine sentiments, they had a rather persuasive complaints office in the basement of the castle.'

'That's what they teach us in the Denunciationists as well – to regard poverty as evidence of our spiritual superiority. Are we wrong?'

I smiled and pulled her closer. 'No, of course not.'

* * *

Where do you take a girl for her first ride on an escalator? Marks and Spencers, Boots, Woolies? We did all three. We went up and down ten times in Boots, Miaow clutching the moving handrail with a grip slightly too tight, pausing too long each time before she stepped on. When the security guard asked us if everything was all right, we moved on to the other shops, and so threaded our way down town towards the river and the park along its banks. We chose a tree to sit under and began to unpack the picnic, but then Miaow changed her mind and we tried two more trees until we found one that satisfied.

'I hope it's OK, I've never made a picnic before. Back in Cwmnewidion Isaf such things are considered frivolous.'

'It's perfect.'

'Don't tease me.'

'I'm not. You have every detail right. The thermos flask should always be tartan, the tea should be stewed and the plates bright yellow plastic. Sandwiches can be jam or on special occasions you can use that paste they sell in little glass jars, the one that smells like the harbour and has the texture of wet newspaper.'

'I don't know that one.'

'They grind it up from the bits of the fish the glue factory rejects.'

For a while everything was still save the soft movements of our jaws, the quivering grass and the shadow of a cloud drifting across the lawn. The cloud revealed the sun and the heightened brightness caused an instant upsurge in my breast. A rowing team from the local boys' school slid past.

'Tell me about being a private eye.'

I leant back and spoke to the sky. 'You get hit on the head a lot; it's boring; there's no money. Clients walk into my office clutching the pieces of their lives like the fragments of a broken vase. They expect me to fix it, but normally I can't. This is usually their first introduction to the strange notion that the world is unfair. They think that by paying for a few hours of my time they will be able to buy some sort of redress; the amount they pay me is trivial, I can barely survive on it, but to the people who sit in my client's chair it's a fortune they resent parting with. Sometimes they want me to make everything all right, but most of the time they don't even want that; they just want the world to take cognizance, they want to tell someone about the bad thing that has happened to them. They always think they are the first person since the Garden of Eden to have a bad thing happen to them.'

'What's the point of telling you if you can't fix it?'

'Telling me is the point. It's like telling tales to a teacher at school. They say, look what happened to me, that's not right. And I agree, yeah, that's not right. But in my heart I think, so what? These things happen. There's no reason for it, no intent, the universe didn't set out to upset you; but neither did it set out not to; it doesn't greatly care. The universe is like the rest of us, it just gets on with the business of whatever it is it does, slowly winding down, I guess, increasing entropy, and it just so happens that your suffering is a side-effect of that process, like the squeak of a rocking chair. They want me to oil the universe.'

'I don't see what satisfaction there is in just telling.'

'It's the most fundamental human need of all, the act of bearing witness. Think of all the people in history who have been massacred. The bad guys drive into the village and round everybody up. They load them onto the back of a truck. They drive off into the forest and stop at a clearing. The villagers are forced to dig graves. They do it because they know there is no redemption. They listen to the scrape of the shovel on dirt, the birds calling in the woods, then straighten up at last from the digging, aware of the puzzling paradox that they are proud of having done a good job of the hole, and then the crack of rifle shots sends the startled birds flapping into the air. What is the last thing the poor victims think before tumbling down? They hope someone from the village escaped and will tell the world what happened. Even though that knowledge, that acknowledgement, won't make any difference to them, won't save them and won't make their deaths easier, it is still the last hope. They couldn't bear for the world to never hear of it, the terrible way they died.'

'So are you a Christian?'

'No, but I admire Christ. Even though he did his best to put me out of a job.'

A park keeper walked past. Miaow reached into her handbag, took out a camera and rushed over to the man. He took the camera and peered through the viewfinder. Miaow sat down again but this time nestled her head onto my shoulder and we both squinted into the blue sky. The man clicked the shutter and brought the camera back, but, seeing or sensing that now was not the time for Miaow to move from her position, head pressed to mine, he bent down shyly and put the camera on the tartan rug. It was like watching someone place an offering at a shrine. It was a simple Instamatic camera, without adjustments except for the shutter press. But this meant that, paradoxically, it was the acme of the camera-maker's art, because the inevitable fuzziness of the image would perfectly mimic the effects of memory.

'What brought you to Aberystwyth?' I asked.

'Do I need a reason?'

'No.'

'I told you, I'm studying.'

'I thought you might be looking for Iestyn Probert.'

'I've never heard of him.'

'I found your card in the ruins of Iestyn's house. You'd written "Ask for Miaow" on it.'

'Someone else must have done it, not me. It could have been anyone, couldn't it?'

'Yes,' I said. 'I suppose it could.'

It was evening by the time we got back to Aberystwyth. It had grown chilly and the streets were empty, the damp tarmac gleaming beneath the street lights. We walked along Terrace Road towards the sea, without thinking about it. The same invisible force that sucked the water back from the land pulled at us too. The sound of a public speaker drifted over from the Prom, getting louder as we walked. Miaow slipped her hand in mine. On the Prom the emptiness became less stark, couples walked past holding hands, and a group was gathered round a man on a small raised platform who was addressing them with a microphone. He was short and squat with arms that seemed disproportionately long for his torso. A quiver ran involuntarily through my loins, it was Herod Jenkins, my old school games teacher. Miaow turned sharply.

'Louie, what is it?'

'Nothing.'

'You're squeezing my hand so hard . . .'

'It's Herod Jenkins, he used to teach me games.'

'He can't hurt you now, silly.'

'I know, I know. It's . . . it's like a dog that was beaten once long ago who sees his old master in the street again. Even if he saw his old master in a coffin being lowered into the ground he would still tremble. It's involuntary.'

His words reached us; he was talking about the New Sparta he would build in the ruins of Aberystwyth once elected. Did we need one? The original Sparta didn't sound very attractive.

Miaow frowned, sensing that something about the mood had changed, as if it was our wedding day and someone had reported seeing the Ancient Mariner at the bar. I turned and smiled. 'On our first day at big school he gave us a talk about how it was going to be. He called us all milksops and pansies and told us we had had it too good for too long but things were going to change. He offered us a choice: shape up or ship out. We were eleven.'

'They always make that speech, Louie.'

'On that first day at school he said there would be no more free rides, those who lagged behind would be left behind. One boy put his hand up to ask if this applied to him because he suffered from asthma. He said he had a note from his mum.' I peered into her eyes as if my words contained an urgent revelation. 'Herod pretended to be sympathetic and related a story of his time as a prisoner of war in Patagonia. He told how one morning the commandant called the prisoners together and appealed to them for help. He said a number of llamas had died in the night and they didn't have enough to pull the plough so they were appealing for volunteers. He said it would be a great help to them and also a nice day out on the farm, but if they didn't fancy it or were too busy he would understand and would make sure the table-tennis room was left open back at the camp for them to amuse themselves.

' "You, boy, no talking at the back!" Herod called out to me; heads turned to look.

' "If you've got something to say," he said, "perhaps you'd like to share it with the rest of us."

' "Mr Jenkins, I just wanted to ask, in this New Sparta you describe, will there be room for everyone, the weak as well as the strong?"

'He peered at me over the heads of the throng. People began to mutter, as if my question had chimed with their own misgivings. Herod Jenkins raised his arm and swung it across, appealing for calm. He paused for effect, then said, "There is no such thing as weakness." The muttering started again. "Weakness is a state of mind, born of sloth and idleness. Those who truly want to be strong will be strong. And those who can't be bothered, who prefer to sit on their backsides and shirk their duty, they will be weak. But it is their choice."

' "What about sick people?" I asked. "Are they sick because they are too lazy to get well?"

'He stepped towards the edge of the podium and screwed his eyes up. He nodded as he recognised me.

' "It's you, isn't it? Louie Knight. I remember you. The trouble-maker. Of all the milksops that ever crossed my path, you were the worst. Yes, I accept some are too sick to play their part. But you? Louie Knight? What excuse do you have for standing on the sidelines and mocking? Oh yes, I remember you well. You were not sick or halt or in any way infirm. The Lord blessed you with healthy thews. And yet you refused to take part. What excuse do you have?"

' "Quite often I was sick, I had a note excusing me from games, but you mocked me for it. What right did you have? Are you a doctor?"

'He flashed with indignation. "A note from your mum, you say? Let me tell you the truth of this world, boy. If you take a lion cub and separate it from the pride and bring it up in a marble palace, if you feed it milk and dainty roasted goat flesh each day of its life such that it never learns to hunt, is that a kindness? No! And if you then turn it loose into the wild, having no comprehension of the struggle that awaits it, will it survive, do you think? Has your kindness, your diet of milk and kid, helped the lion to make its way in the world? Just so does it come to pass with men. When I was fighting in Patagonia, I learned that on the field of battle, which is but a metaphor for life, there is no note from your mum!"

' "But this is Aberystwyth," I shouted. "We're miles away from Patagonia!"

' "There is no distinction in the geography of the soul. All places are one. In Patagonia when I thirsted I drank the tears of the penguin; when I felt the ravening pains in my belly I chewed on the tapir's foot. When I was weary I did not take the chinchilla for my pillow, but the armadillo! Not once did I cry out in the night for a note from my mum. When I fell into captivity I did not waste time cursing my fate, my thoughts were only for escape. I did not petition the commandant with notes from my mum! You know what would have happened if I had done that? You know what he would have said?" Herod Jenkins sneered and shouted, "You want to know what a note from your mum got in Patagonia? This!" And he ripped his shirt off to show us the stripes on his back.'

We wandered down to the wooden steps where they post the tide tables. Out in the darkness the end of the Pier hung over the water, studded with lights like an ocean liner. Is there any sight more calculated to thrill the heart than a big ship at night? There is something deeply affecting about those lights floating over the watery wilderness. Maybe it is the contrast, the interface of two worlds separated by a membrane of painted steel. Outside salt, and flung spume, endlessly dark, an abyss so profound it would take you twenty minutes to reach the bottom. On the other side of the steel, men and women in evening dress, warmth and light and a theatre performance in which they act out the play called *Don't*

Mention the Iceberg. We carried on walking until the harbour. The jetty brooded and the beacon standing proud at the end flashed like the light of an angler fish. The symmetry of the concrete was broken by the silhouettes of two fishermen, a man and a boy; the dark lines of their rods waved like the whiskers of a dim-bodied crustacean. A breeze rose, fish-scented, from the water and raised goose bumps on Miaow's arm. She shivered and pressed herself against me. I linked my arms behind her and she turned to look up at me.

'Do you know why they call me Miaow?'

'No.'

'Because of my green eyes.'

'They're nothing like a cat's eyes.'

'Why not?'

'The green is the wrong shade. Cats' are more like the digits on a luminous watch.'

'What are mine like, then?'

'Do you really want to know?'

'Of course!'

I pushed a filament of hair away from her cheek as if it were blocking my view and stared intently into her eyes. 'The green is paler, like a phial of seawater held up to the light, and there are flecks of grey radiating like the striations in a slice of lime. At the rim of the iris there is a thin dark band that acts as a frame around a grey-green disk . . . it's like watching the full moon through a bottle of absinthe.'

'Do you want me to cry tears of absinthe?'

I shook my head. In the black waters of the harbour the town lay inverted like a nebula; skeins of shining gas hung like a necklace from the street lamps of the Prom. It was beautiful. Miaow peered into my face, her hair drawing forward like curtains to block out the world. She kissed me lightly on the lips. 'I won't let Herod Jenkins hurt you.'

Chapter 11

I SLEPT badly and arrived late at the office next morning. The new desk had been delivered. It was already installed, and a man, who probably hadn't been delivered with it, sat on the client's chair with his feet on the desk. His shoes were black leather, badly scuffed, his trousers turned up and shiny with age. He wore a mackintosh that looked like it had spent six months tightly rolled up at the bottom of a packing case; his thin brown hair was congealed in a slick of police-issue hair cream. It was the cop who had sat sneering in the interrogation room the night I was taken to see the Aviary. He was eating an ice cream.

I slapped his feet off the desk. They fell to the floor with a thump.

He grinned. 'I knew I wasn't wrong about you.'

'I like to be introduced before I let a man put his feet on my desk.'

The grin widened. 'You can call me Sauerkopp.' He raised a foot and crossed his leg. 'They say the chief of police has a good relationship with you. That's always a mistake in my book.'

'Mistake for who?'

'Everyone.'

'And what makes you think I give a damn what's in your book?'

The phone rang. The visitor picked up the phone, listened and said, 'It's a girl, wants you to find her lost handkerchief.' He spoke to the receiver. 'Sorry lady, he's a dick, not a Boy Scout.' He hung up and smiled. 'Another big case slips through your fingers.'

'Did you come for a reason or were you just passing?'

He reached into his jacket pocket and took out a Polaroid. He threw it towards me. I picked it up. It was the corpse of a woman, hair wet, face bloated.

'Recognise the party?'

'It's Mrs Lewis.'

'Someone tied her to one of the supports under the pier night before last, just before the tide came in. Ain't that a shame!'

Something clenched in my loins, it was like an angry baby kicking against the wall of its womb; I didn't let evidence of it reach my face. 'She should have known better, the tide tables are clearly posted. Where did you get the snap?'

'From my camera.'

'Am I a suspect?'

'I would say so, wouldn't you?'

'Are you arresting me?'

'Why would I want to do that?'

'You look the type that might enjoy it.'

He made a sour grin. 'Not really. Arresting people is boring. It looks fun in the TV cop shows, but in real life it's just paperwork and spending a lot of what the Americans call quality time with people who don't wash very often. Sometimes they try and bite you. They never show that on TV, but that's what it often comes down to. Being bitten by a fully grown man is a very unpleasant experience. Sometimes they struggle in such a way that they threaten to injure themselves. That's not necessarily a big deal, but it means more paperwork, so you have to spray a little something in their eyes; nothing calms a man down faster than a little something in his eyes. Trouble is, it makes them produce a lot of mucus – from their eyes, their nose, out of the mouth. You'd be surprised how much the body can pump out in a situation like that. Believe me, grappling with a man producing loads of mucus isn't fun. I don't arrest people, I get the flatfoots to do it.'

'You can arrest me, I wash every day.'

He smiled. 'You are forgetting one thing: I like you. How are you getting on with Raspiwtin? Anything you want to tell me?'

'There's nothing I want to tell you.'

He threw another photo down on top of the first. It showed me and Mrs Lewis talking on the Prom. 'Looks like you had a date the night she died. As far as I can tell, the cops don't know about it. They're not as quick on their feet or as well informed as old Sauerkopp. But it could change. If something happens that might interest us and you are tempted to forget to tell us, I could forget not to show them the photo.'

I picked up the photo and stared at it while my heart tumbled slowly down the stairs.

'Don't look so sad, it's not as bad as it seems. I know what you are thinking: you don't photograph too well these days. It's the light; sodium lighting is very harsh; it gives a greenish cast. I should have used a filter but I can never remember which one to use. Orange, I think.' He took the photo out of my hand and walked out, saying, 'Pack a toothbrush just in case.'

I loosened my tie, leant back and closed my eyes. Cops and ex-cops have a routine disdain for private operatives, and I don't blame them. I would feel the same too if I were a cop. They know if they want to use testimony in court it helps if it comes voluntarily. When they arrive at a crime scene the first thing they have to do is seal it off, record everything in detail and take great care not to contaminate it with stuff from somewhere else. Not because they care about justice and fairness and due process but because they have learned through bitter experience that all their hard work will end up wasted if they don't follow the rules. The first thing a private operative does when arriving at the scene of a crime is walk all over it looking for significant stuff before the cops come. He doesn't care about contaminating it; let someone else worry, he doesn't have the time. On occasion he will rearrange it, sometimes to eliminate his own presence, at others to try and effect a rough natural justice he has no right attempting but he does anyway. Sometimes he will wipe a murder weapon of prints or put someone else's on it. Sometime he simply takes a key piece of evidence and throws it in the river, leaving a crime scene like a jigsaw puzzle missing a piece. I know the private operative does all these things because I have done them, and the cops know it too. In fact, if they know someone like me is sniffing around they assume the worst right from the start, and this often results in the private operative taking a tumble down the police-station steps.

I made a call to Meirion, a friend of mine on the crime desk at the *Cambrian News*. I asked him what he knew about the Mrs Lewis case. He didn't know anything and so I told him to forget I'd even asked. Calamity walked in and I told her what had happened.

She put on a deep frown. 'Who do you think did it?'

I shrugged. 'I don't know. The mayor, maybe.'

'Or the doctor.'

I nodded.

'Do you think it's connected to us?'

'What do you think?'

She thought for a while. 'Iestyn and Skweeple turn up at the doctor's surgery. They call Preseli. When he comes, Iestyn escapes, so he takes Skweeple away. That's the last we hear of him. A week later Iestyn is caught and hanged. The papers don't mention Skweeple. Something must have happened to him while in Preseli's custody. The doc knows about it too. They're both in on it.'

'Why kill Mrs Lewis; she doesn't know what happened.'

'Maybe she does know, or maybe they think she knows. Or maybe just knowing that Preseli took him is enough.' She stood up. 'I think it is definitely time to try the Barney and Betty Hill routine.'

'I'll probably regret this, but what is that?'

'Barney and Betty Hill are one of the most famous contactee cases of all time, from 1961. They were driving home through New Hampshire after a vacation in Quebec and they saw a bright light in the sky . . .' She stopped.

I looked at her sourly. 'You might as well go on, although try and keep in mind that someone I spoke to the day before yesterday has been murdered and I was probably one of the last to see her. Presumably it won't be long before the cops find out.'

'Fine,' said Calamity. 'We don't do the Barney and Betty Hill.'

'I didn't say that.'

'You didn't have to.'

'You might as well finish it.'

'What's the point, you are going to think it's dumb.'

'OK. I promise to try not to. Tell me in the car.'

'Where are we going?'

'Remember James the Less and his son the forensic linguist?'

'The kid who knows more types of duck than you've had hot dinners.'

'I thought we could go and show him the letter Raspiwtin gave me.'

We set off for Cwmnewidion Isaf and Calamity told me about Barney and Betty Hill.

'They were driving home one night,' she began, 'and they saw a bright light. They stopped and got out to take a look. Then somehow they found themselves at home and six hours had passed which they couldn't account for. After that they started getting nightmares. Eventually they were questioned by the military and offered hypnotism, and it all came out. How they'd been abducted aboard the saucer and given medical examinations and stuff. The aliens were baffled by Barney's false teeth.'

'This was 1961?'

'Yes. In America.'

'Were they Greys or Nordics?'

'Greys.'

We drove south out of town and turned off the main road at Rhydyfelin.

'Mrs Bwlchgwallter from the gingerbread shop does hypnotism. I thought we could get her to hypnotise the farmer.'

'What do you expect to learn?'

'I don't know. My hunch is they are looking for Skweeple. They asked for Iestyn because they think he can tell them what happened to Skweeple. What do you make of Jhoe?'

'Three possibilities,' I said.

'Number one,' said Calamity, 'he's from the star system Noö.'

'That's number three. Between number two and number three there is a wide gap.'

'What's number two, then?'

'He could be an actor sent by the Aviary, or some other body, to bamboozle us.'

'I thought about that, but why?'

'I really don't know. Disinfo, I suppose.'

'Buying a Buick is disinfo?'

'He's not really buying it, is he? You haven't got one to sell. He's just posing as a buyer. Maybe whichever organisation he works for wants to sound you out, see what your game is. Who knows? Did Barney and Betty Hill drive a Buick?'

'No, a '57 Chevrolet Bel Air. Do you really think he works for an organisation?'

'The alternative is . . .'

'Number one: he's a loony.'

'That's not an expression I would use. But I think we should consider the possibility that he may, I don't know, he may have absented himself from the secure wing of a psychiatric hospital.'

'Mmm.'

'In fact, I think you should ring a few when we get back and make some discreet enquiries, see if someone who sounds like Jhoe has gone missing.'

'You really think so?'

'It's up to you, but you did place the ad, and I think that gives you a certain responsibility.'

'Thing is, I think I like Jhoe.'

'All the more reason.'

Cwmnewidion Isaf was a small village where the inhabitants took refuge from the twentieth century, preferring to hearken back to a lost idyll in that land of the golden past that probably never existed. They still fetched water from the well and farmed using only the natural fertiliser their animals provided; theirs was one of the few communities left in West Wales where they preserved the ancient custom according to which you could ask people directions without having to pay them. We did this, and were pointed in the direction of a barn, but first we stopped off at the village shop and bought a bottle of dandelion and burdock. It was carbonated, which technically made it proscribed technology, but the shopkeeper explained with a wink that if the carbonation process took place a long way away where you couldn't see it, one could turn a blind eye. As bribes go, it was a lot cheaper than the ones used in Aberystwyth. James the Less and his son were grooming a horse inside the barn and beamed with pleasure to see us. Their eyes locked on to the fizzy drink with barely concealed lust.

'We thought you might like a little drink,' said Calamity. 'It must be thirsty work living in a world without machines.'

'How thoughtful of you,' said James the Less. 'Samson, go and fetch some cups. It is so nice of you to come and visit. Most people shun us for our alien ways, even though our lives are not so very different from the ones their forebears would have lived.'

'That's very true,' I said.

'If they only cared to wish us good day or engage us in conversation, they would discover the same heart beats in our breasts as in everyone else's.' He sat on a bale of hay. 'Yes, it is so nice of you to come out all this way just to say hello to some strangers you met on the train.'

'To be honest,' I said, prickling with guilt, 'it would be wrong of us to mislead you into the belief that we came here solely to say hello.'

Samson returned with some unglazed earthernware mugs. Calamity poured the drinks. We raised mugs and wished each other good health. But instead of drinking, James the Less hesitated, then said, 'You . . . you haven't got anything stronger, have you?'

A glance of complicity passed between us.

'Does a still count as a machine?' I asked.

James the Less smiled sheepishly. 'On this particular issue the scriptures are far from clear.'

I took out my hip flask of rum and unscrewed the cap. 'In that case, at least until the scholars reach a consensus, it would be best to proceed on the assumption that a still is not a machine.'

Like a dog who keeps dancing and jumping up to your hands while you're still opening the tin of dog food, James the Less struggled to maintain a dignified reserve in the face of mounting excitement. 'It would be impertinent to argue with such a learned man,' he said and threw the dandelion and burdock onto the floor with a surprising lack of ceremony. He held out his mug. I gave him a generous measure and took one for myself. James the Less took a deep gulp, coughed, swallowed, coughed, swallowed harder and finally looked up with the air of one electrocuted. 'Wow!' he said. 'That hit the spot! Now, what was it you wanted to see us about?'

I handed him the top-secret Aviary document. As I did so, a chit of paper fell out and James the Less picked it up and gave it to me. It was a newspaper cutting, a report, a few lines amounting to a fragment of column space that detailed an atrocity on the Thai–Burmese border. It was one of those stories that are terrible but not deemed newsworthy and serve only to provide copy to fill an empty inch. I wondered: did the story describe the tragedy in which Raspiwtin had been involved? Or did he just read about it and pretend it had happened to him?

James the Less gave the Aviary document to Samson, much like a proud parent cajoles his son to play the recorder for a visitor.

'Interesting case,' the boy said earnestly. 'The story about the alien woman buying the cadaver of Iestyn Probert is widely circulated. I'd never paid much attention to it and had assumed it to be the invention of superstitious fools. This puts a different complexion on the matter.' He brought out a jeweller's loupe and screwed it into his eye. We all held our breath as he pored over the document. He began to mutter to himself as if not pleased with what he was seeing. Calamity looked at me and pointedly rolled her eyes. Finally the boy looked up and removed the loupe.

'The Documents appear to be of dubious provenance,' he said. 'The stamp *TOP SECRET/AVIARY EYES ONLY* appears to be one of those stamps with changeable letters – see, the V and the Y are slightly out of line – this is wrong; official Aviary stamps have always been solid rubber specific to the purpose. Similarly, there are references to the necessity to conceal events from the media; in 1965 this word would not have been current, and the more usual "press" would have been used, or "newspapers". By the same token, the document refers to extraterrestrials instead of aliens, again not current in the 1960s. The typefaces are anachronistic – Helvetica subheads and Times for the body – these would not have been used in Aviary documents until the late '70s and the advent of IBM Golfball electronic typewriters. In the '60s all such documentation would have been produced on Smith Coronas with Prestige Elite fonts. And this is a carbon copy but has been folded. This is unusual: carbon copies were for filing only. I regret to say that my initial examination forces me to conclude that the item is a forgery. Although do not discount the possibility that the source of the forgery may, paradoxically, be the Aviary itself. Sometimes they forge the truth in order to discredit it.'

James the Less clapped his hands. 'Bravo!'

'Could you repeat the last bit?' I asked.

'These people are not acquainted with your advanced theories,' said James the Less. 'You must be patient.'

The boy made a great play of summoning patience.

'As you know,' he said loftily, 'the Aviary exists in the main to suppress truth and keep the masses docile and unsuspecting, happy with their lives of meaningless and unending tedium. No doubt you have observed them yourself: walking up and down Aberystwyth Prom each day, dispensing the requisite oohs and ahs at the sunset each evening, unaware that it is not significantly different from the one they praised the evening before. Taking an ice cream and exchanging tittle-tattle with the lowly stall-holder . . .'

I saw myself doing exactly as the boy described. Admiring the sunset, taking an ice cream at Sospan's the same time each day. Was it unendingly tedious? I quite liked it.

The boy continued. 'A time-honoured technique for suppressing the truth, for getting the self-satisfied burghers of Aberystwyth to ignore the truth before their eyes, is to discredit that truth, to make a mockery of it. It is my belief, derived from my researches into the works of those cunning artificers of invented testimony the Aberystwyth police, that many of the more bizarre accounts of alien contact reveal the hand of the authorities at work. By inventing a story that contains the truth but which is demonstrably absurd, they in effect undermine any credence that might attach to it. The famous flying-saucer abduction account of Barney and Betty Hill from 1961 is a case in point. Most of it came out under hypnotism. We must ask ourselves who supplied the hypnotist. The answer? The military supplied the hypnotist. I leave you to draw your own conclusions from that.'

A rain cloud followed us back to town. It was roughly puma-shaped and had the same deep, lustrous colouring of blue-black silk that glistened and glinted.

'It's gaining on us,' said Calamity, who had her own small cloud left in place by the boy's speech.

'Cheer up,' I said.

'I'm fine, really I am. The kid obviously doesn't know the first thing about the Barney and Betty Hill case.'

It sounded to me like he knew quite a lot about it, but sometimes you need to help your partner just as there will be times when your partner needs to raise you from the trough. That's what partners are for.

'No,' I said. 'He was talking through his hat. We'll definitely go and see Mrs Bwlchgwallter and get her to hypnotise the farmer.'

Calamity grinned.

The cloud overtook us on the long straight down into town at Penparcau and was already in place on the Prom when we reached the bandstand. Mrs Bwlchgwallter moonlighted here in the afternoons from her rôle as official maker of gingerbread to the town. She stood on stage, clutching the mike and backed by her three cousins, the Gingernutjobs. The arrival of the rain threatened to bring an end to the gig. The audience consisted of a coach party of pensioners who moved and acted as a single organism, like a colony of bees or a shoal of fish responding to some unseen, unvoiced communication, telepathic perhaps, or pheromonic. As soon as the first raindrop registered its presence on the spectacle lens of one person, this information was communicated to the colony. They leapt up in unison from their deckchairs, perfectly synchronised, and began the intricate reverse-origami of unpacking pac-a-mac coats. We stood entranced by the spectacle. Their hands worked feverishly like the mandibles of leaf-cutter ants sawing away at a cellophane rose. All of a sudden the bond which held the rose closed was broken, whereupon something even more extraordinary happened: a huge science-fiction dragonfly of polythene squirted upwards and attacked them. Gauzy wings caught the breeze and fanned out enveloping the pensioners in plumes of gossamer. Mrs Bwlchgwallter, in a bid to win back the crowd's attention, launched into a rousing version of her trademark song, 'Blue Suede Orthopaedic Boots':

> *You can burn my house, you can steal my car*
> *Drink my liquor from an old fruit jar*
> *But don't you step on my blue suede 'paedies . . .*

The pensioners completed their pac-a-mac dance and the crisis passed as soon as it had begun. A shaft of sunlight broke through the cloud and spattered the Prom with molten solder. The audience turned once again towards the stage, everything was as it had been, and yet they were all now mummified, side by side like giant moth pupae, shimmering with iridescent colour from the blue end of the spectrum: cobalt, ultramarine, mauve, electric blue. On their wet faces the spectacles glinted like slices of cucumber.

We caught up with Mrs Bwlchgwallter in the dressing room after the performance. She sat before the horseshoe of light bulbs around the mirror, pulled off a wig to reveal her own hair matted down underneath a close-fitting net. She tore off the fake eyebrows and picked up a tissue to wipe away the caked-on greasepaint. 'If you want me to sign something, you'll have to wait a mo,' she said to our reflections in the mirror. We had already decided to give her the good agent/bad agent treatment. It was Calamity's turn to be bad.

'The only thing we want to sign is your contract for the Shrewsbury Palladium,' I said.

She stopped wiping her face. 'What was that?'

'That's if you want to be famous. Not everyone does.'

'Forget it, boss,' said Calamity speaking through the side of her mouth. 'I told you we were wasting our time. We should have gone for the squeaker in Penrhyncoch.'

'What's a squeaker?' asked Mrs Bwlchgwallter.

'Squeaker. That's what they call balloon-twisters –'

'As if she didn't know,' scoffed Calamity.

'W . . . who are you?'

'This is the Shirley Temple Kid, you remember her, don't you? Course you do. Best child star Cardiganshire ever produced. She's retired now, wants to give something back.'

'What about you?'

'All you need to know is who I work for.'

'Who do you work for?'

'The Man.'

Calamity picked up a tin ashtray and examined it with distaste. She chucked it down with a clatter. 'Hmm, *un problema muy grande*,' she said. 'It doesn't look like this lady likes nice things.'

'Not everyone likes money, you should know that.'

'I like money,' said Mrs Bwlchgwallter.

'So why spend your life making stinking gingerbread?' asked Calamity.

For a moment, the slur upon the gingerbread-making trade, in particular her little shop, stirred the spirit of rebellion in Mrs Bwlchgwallter. 'I'll have you know that shop has been in my family three generations . . .'

'How much do you make in a month?' said Calamity. 'Four-fifty? Four-ninety? Five maybe? I'd say five-ten tops.'

'But that's not the point is it?'

'Isn't it? You tell me, then, what is the point of spending your life turning sugar, eggs and flour into little brown homunculi? Because I'm damned if I can see it.'

'It's a service to the town . . .'

'It's a higher calling, isn't that right?' I asked.

'In a pig's valise,' said Calamity.

I gave her a puzzled look and she returned a scowl that said, That's what they say in Chicago; how come you don't know that?

'Mrs Bwlchgwallter,' I said, 'I'll be straight with you. I've seen your act. It's top drawer. I've seen a lot of acts, but it's not often I meet someone as gifted as you. At the moment you are burying it beneath all that crowd-pleasing blancmange. It's time to take the gloves off. The Kid here doesn't always express herself very nicely. That can happen. You spend too long in Acapulco, it can happen. Maybe to you as well. Tell her how many millions you made last year.'

'You know I can't count higher than nine,' said Calamity.

'That's what happens when you take them out of school to put them on the stage. She made fourteen million but only because of the three-month holiday in Acapulco. You ever been to Acapulco?'

'No, I –'

'Cancun is better. But how many months at a time can you spend in Cancun? Acapulco is the fall-back option. We can get you there.'

'But first you got to go Shrewsbury,' said Calamity.

'And before that you have to go to Ynys Greigiog. Just for an hour.'

'But what for?'

'Exposure. I need some newspaper headlines I can take to the Big Kahuna.'

'The deal is so simple, even you can do it,' said the Shirley Temple Kid. 'You know the farmer who saw the flying saucer? We want you to hypnotise him.'

'That used to be your thing didn't it? Part of your act back in the old days. Yes, I know all about you, I've done my homework. I've read the reviews: Borth Holiday Camp, Pwllheli Butlins, Barry Island . . . they say you were good. They say you were the best. The Kid says you're washed up, I've got five bucks that says you're not. First you have to go and speak to the farmer. Put him under and find out his story, then report back to us. We get you in the paper and from there it's a short step to the Shrewsbury Palladium. What do you say?'

'Well . . .'

I grabbed her hand and pumped. 'I knew I wasn't wrong about you. Throw the boots away, you don't need the props any more.' I handed her a business card, blank except for a telephone number. 'If you need to get in touch, call this number and ask for Louie Knight. The Kid will write down the farmer's address and give you the bus fare.'

We walked to the door.

'One more thing,' said Calamity. 'You need a better name. Something that won't make the neon sign-writer want to stick a gun in his mouth.'

Chapter 12

THE NEXT morning when I arrived at the office there was a note scribbled on the deskpad, from Calamity. She said she was going out to Borth with Jhoe, to have a picnic by the remains of the submerged forest. As directions go, you couldn't get much more specific than that. The phone rang; it was Mrs Bwlchgwallter.

'I can't stop,' she breathed, 'I've just popped out from the hypnotism. He's still under. He's been saying some terrible things. He says he murdered his brother.'

'I wouldn't pay any attention to –'

'Buried him in the cellar. And killed the dog.'

I picked a bottle of rum up off the floor next to my chair and tried to unscrew the cap one-handed. 'I shouldn't worry about it. Evidence from a trance is not admissible in court.'

'Shouldn't I tell the police?'

'What if he denies it?'

'They can dig up the cellar, can't they?'

I gripped the receiver between shoulder and ear and used both hands to open the bottle. I needed to refill my hip flask. 'The problem you've got there is, two things can happen. A, they don't find anything, in which case they throw you in the sneezer for wasting police time. B, they find something, in which case they start wondering how it is you know about it.'

'But I can tell them about the hypnotism.'

'Like I said, evidence like that isn't admissible in court. That's your alibi gone, you see? The farmer will deny it and you are all washed up high and dry on your lonesome. The cops, they don't greatly care who they pin it on, it's just paperwork to them.'

'Oh dear.'

I rested the bottle cap in my lap and began to decant the rum. 'My advice to you is finish the sitting and pump him about the flying saucer. We can think about contacting the police later.'

'But what about my conscience?'

'Conscience is a tricky thing, Mrs Bwlchgwallter. It has a rôle to play, but there are other voices in the mix that must be heard.'

Mrs Bwlchgwallter refused to listen to the other voices and persisted; an hysterical whine began to enter her voice. 'Yes, but the dog, the dog! I knew that dog, I . . . I gave him biscuits.'

'Mrs Bwlchgwallter, I want you to calm down. Are you calm?' There was a pause. I could hear her on the other end of the line taking deep breaths. 'Yes, I'm calm.'

'We're all sorry about the dog. But being sorry won't bring him back to life. It's a big bad, lousy, ugly world out there, Mrs Bwlchgwallter; some days I wake up with a taste on my tongue so bad it's like a badger crawled into my mouth in the night and died. Times like that the only thing to do is get up, brush your teeth and face the mirror. I say this to all my clients, so it's only right I say it to you: I can take you to Shrewsbury, but I can't promise you a rose garden.' I hung up.

I took a sip from my hip flask, screwed the top on and leant back. I closed my eyes; not even 9.30 and I was ready for a siesta. I dozed. Ten minutes later the phone rang. This time she sounded more distressed. 'It's getting very . . . racy!' she said. 'The angel wants him to . . . do it.'

'Do what?'

She swallowed audibly. 'I hardly like to say. You know . . . miscegenation.'

'What's that?'

'I suppose you would call it a form of inappropriate sexual congress.'

'Inappropriate?'

'Yes.'

'Who are the angels?'

'That's obviously what they are, isn't it? From the saucer. He says there are three of them. Two men and a woman. They are all blond and beautiful. Seraphim, I'd guess.'

'Why do they want to make love?'

'I haven't the foggiest.'

'OK, that's good. Now I want you to see if they told him anything about Iestyn Probert.'

I hung up and tried to sleep again.

Half an hour later she rang once more.

'He's got stuck.'

'What do you mean by stuck, Mrs Bwlchgwallter? Stuck in his chair? Stuck in a rut? Stuck in the middle with you?'

'Come again?'

'It's a song, don't worry about that.'

'I mean he's stuck like the needle in the groove of a gramophone record. He keeps saying the same thing over and over again.'

'What is that thing?'

'Something about a tin opener. What should I do?'

'Can't you give him some sort of a jolt? What about smelling salts?'

'That's terribly dangerous in the middle of a trance –'

'Why not give him a tin opener, see what happens?'

'That's a good idea.'

She hung up.

A minute later the phone rang again, but this time it was Eeyore. He asked me to meet him on the Prom, towards the castle. Normally you require more precise directions than that, but finding a man leading a train of donkeys is not so difficult. I picked up my hat but the phone rang again before I had time to put it on. I stared at the receiver, deliberating. If only it had rung just after I'd left. I answered.

'It worked.'

'What did?'

'The tin opener. He's talking again. He says they told him a lot about Iestyn Probert. One of their saucers crashed the same night as the raid on the Coliseum cinema. Skweeple – that's one of their people – got separated from the others and wandered off. He was hit by the getaway car and Iestyn Probert got out to help. He took Skweeple to the doctor's and not long after that Sheriff Preseli turned up and took Skweeple away. Two months later another saucer came looking for them and they resurrected Iestyn Probert to ask him what happened to Skweeple.'

'And what did happen?'

'I just told you, he went off with Sheriff Preseli.'

'I know, but what happened then?'

'I don't know.'

I paused. Then said with extra intensity, 'We're almost there, Mrs Bwlchgwallter, almost there. Can you feel the heat of those footlights on your face? Can you smell it? The greasepaint? The thick, dusty reek of those heavy velvet drapes at the Shrewsbury Palladium? Of course you can. We're in the home straight, just one little furlong left. Find out what happened after the sheriff arrested Skweeple.' I hung up.

Ten minutes later the phone rang again. This time it was Mrs Pugh, the farmer's wife. She was hysterical and told me to come right away; something terrible had happened.

Eeyore was standing at the railings at Castle Point, the train of donkeys happily idling. The wind had freshened and the surface of the sea was dancing with flame, green and silver like the verdigris patina of weathered copper, or the flecks in Miaow's irises.

He heard me coming, turned and smiled. 'I could stand here all day.'

'What's to stop you?'

He ran a hand along the mane of a donkey. 'New one, Silenus. Named after the tutor to the wine god Dionysus. He rode a donkey and could only be bound with a chain of flowers. Isn't that nice?'

I agreed it was.

'Just been speaking to that chap Raspiwtin. He says we are children born on a submarine who have never seen the sea. On the bridge there's a man looking into the periscope and he tells us what he sees: meadows and blue skies; white peacocks, avenues of wisteria; beautiful things. On and on we sail through this grey-green watery world; the sonar is our birdsong. Do you believe that?'

'I don't know, I've heard something similar.'

'From time to time, he says, a Wildman runs amok, tries to tell us it is all a lie, that there is nothing beyond the metal skin of the sub except the stuff that comes out of the tap. This is a prophet. They take him away to be burnt. What do you think he means?'

'I think he means our eyes and ears and noses send back electrical impulses and our mind turn them into images of a world outside, but it's not a true depiction of it. It's much better.'

Eeyore nodded. 'I'm happy with it.' He reached into the pocket of his raincoat and brought out a tube of rolled-up cardboard. He unrolled it like a scroll to reveal an old-style school photo; four tiers of children, thirty or forty abreast, the whole school assembled in front of the traditional schoolhouse. 'I found it while I was clearing out. Can you spot your dad?'

I studied the sea of bleary gray, stared through the lens of time at a lost world that stared back. The faces were indistinct blurs, smudges of tone; noses and mouths were lost, and eyes reduced to shadows, but strangely, by some process it was impossible to understand, each little chalky ball, balanced like a golf ball on a school-tie-shaped tee, somehow contained within its various smudges enough information to evoke a person's identity. Some faces were obliterated by filaments of spidery white where the thick gloss had cracked and creased. Finally I spotted a little boy who seemed to be the acorn from which my father had grown. I pointed with my thumb. He laughed. 'You think so? What about this one?' He pointed to a boy at the opposite end who also looked as if he had sprung from the same acorn. I flicked my eyes to and fro from the images. 'Have you got a twin brother you never told me about?'

He laughed again. 'They're both me. It's a trick, you see, we used to play in those days. To get the whole school in the shot, the camera moves, on a clockwork drive, and the shutter moves too, slowly across the plate. It means a naughty boy can jump down from the left end, run behind the chairs faster than the camera and then stand on a stool at the other end. You get in the same picture twice.' He grinned with pleasure at the recollection of the ancient transgression. 'I met a chap yesterday who asked about you,' he said.

I looked at him with interest.

'A felon from the old times. He mentioned you specifically.'

'Who was it, Dad?'

'One of the Richards brothers – the ones who took part in the raid on the Coliseum cinema. There's only one surviving now. The other died in a knife fight, I think.'

My interest quickened, but I knew it did no good to hurry Eeyore. He would get there at his own pace.

'He lives out at Taliesin.'

'How exactly did he mention me?'

'He heard you'd been asking about Iestyn. He wants to talk to you. That's all. Most mornings he sits alone in the pub at Taliesin, the one on the right as you drive past the water wheel.'

'I'll find him.'

'He'll ask you about Frankie. Frankie was some gangland boss he crossed in Swansea once who took a dislike to him many years ago. He's dead now, but that old fellah out at Taliesin won't accept it. He thinks it's a trick to catch him off his guard. Like those old Jap soldiers who refuse to come out of the jungle. Just thought I'd let you know.'

I took the road out of town and pondered the case. In one respect, it was baffling in a straightforward way. The Richards brothers raided the cinema and made their getaway. Somewhere out near Ystrad Meurig they ran someone over. Iestyn was kicked out of the car. He went to the aid of whoever it was they ran over and took him to the doctor's. Preseli turned up and Iestyn escaped. Preseli took the other boy away. He was never heard of again. Now, twenty-five years later, Preseli's brother is standing for mayor and he doesn't want any one looking too closely into certain incidents buried in the past. The doc probably knows more than he is letting on. Simple. All straightforward except for one thing: the kid was wearing a silver suit that they couldn't get off him. They say he was from a crashed saucer. Phooey.

I don't have a problem with the idea of aliens visiting us. The universe is either empty and we are just an astonishing accident, unintended, unlikely, pointless and terrifyingly unnecessary. Or we're not, in which case the place must be teeming with life. It doesn't really beggar my belief that they might pop over for a look. I just can't believe they crash. That's the trouble with these sorts of stories; the technology seems remarkably prone to the same problems that bedevil us. You'd think a being from another world would be in a position to tell us things that we had never seen before, things that we had never heard of, that we couldn't even begin to imagine. In the same way a man from Currys would appear as a demi-god to the first caveman. But it never works out like that. They always report things that seem straight out of a sci-fi B-movie: silver suits, goldfish-bowl helmets, consoles with flashing lights, dying races who, most improbably of all, need the seed of an earth-man to get them going again. And crashes. Prangs. Fender-benders.

So where did the kid in the silver suit come from? What is a silver suit, anyway? Do they mean like tinfoil? Or covered in sequins like the singer at Jezebels? Or a one-piece job made from one of those great alloys not found on Earth, the ones that were all the rage on Mars last spring? Did he have a goldfish-bowl helmet? Or was our atmosphere breathable for him? The odds are against it, but you sometimes get these lucky breaks when travelling in space. The same way sometimes the gravity is just right, like Goldilocks's porridge. A few extra clicks on the dial in either direction and it makes things really difficult. Either you are too jumpy, like a gazelle with spring-loaded hooves; or you carry a few hundred pounds on your shoulders making it hard just to stop imploding.

When you think of the endless variety of life on Earth, the mind-boggling permutations, you have to reflect that there's nothing special about the bipedal model; in fact it seems to be inferior in just about every department to other animals. Losing the fur was clearly a dubious idea; it means you have to get a job to pay for an inferior replacement made from stuff that isn't as warm, isn't as waterproof, doesn't fit so well or wear so well. We're covered in hide that cuts too easily and leaves purple welts where the cops interrogate you. Even on Earth our ascendancy seems to have been the fluke result of a pretty rare combination of circumstances. And yet the people from space seem to have followed the same improbable evolutionary path. They are bipedal and furless too, more or less. The areas in which they depart from the paradigm – pointy ears, slightly different eyes or different number of fingers . . . these things testify to the poverty of imagination of the beholder. Having hallucinated an alien that bears a remarkable resemblance to us, they add a few differences for good measure, but they take the first ones they think of. In the '50s, Beings from Outer Space came from Mars and had dials and knobs on their consoles. Nowadays, the term 'Outer Space' has fallen into disuse; it's passé and bespeaks a feeble grasp of the infinite possibilities of what lies beyond our planet. If we ask the farmer I'm sure he'll say the aliens had liquid-crystal displays. When we get something more advanced, they'll get it too. It seems in terms of technology we are always one step ahead of the aliens.

When Mrs Pugh opened the door to the farmhouse, her face was white and she was trembling. She looked at me with relief, but I don't know why.

'Thank God you've come,' she said. She led me into the sitting room, past a hall table on which the business card I had given to Mrs Bwlchgwallter stood propped against the phone. Huw Pugh was crouching in a foetal position on the floor in front of the fireplace. He was sobbing.

'There was a terrible scream,' said Mrs Pugh. 'And then Mrs

Bwlchgwallter ran out past me into the garden. I found him like this. He's been like it ever since. What should I do?'

I walked back to the phone in the hall and called an ambulance. At the same time, I slipped the business card into my pocket.

'They'll be here in a minute,' I said. 'There's nothing more I can do here. I'll go and look for Mrs Bwlchgwallter.'

She wasn't in the garden and wasn't on either of the main roads, the one that led to Ynyslas or the one that led to Tre'r-ddol, which meant she could have been anywhere. I decided the best option was to assume she would find her way home and look for her there. I drove to Borth to see Calamity and tell her what had transpired.

The ancient forest once belonged to the Iron Age kingdom of Cantref-y-Gwaelod, which, legend says, sank beneath the waters of Cardigan Bay. Geologists blame the Ice Age but folklore claims it was all down to some chap who got drunk at a party and left the gates to the dyke open. That was the end of the Welsh Atlantis. But we still have the tree stumps on the beach at Borth to remind us of the lost golden age. Even as I parked the car I could see Calamity and Jhoe at the water's edge.

I walked across the sand to the discoloration that looked from a distance like rocks and no doubt was taken as such by the casual observer. They were both sitting in camping chairs, staring out to sea. As I got closer the tree stumps resolved from the mass of brown colour. They were like dinosaur teeth embedded in the sand and flossed with seaweed.

Jhoe looked up and recited,

> *The big blue tube's just like Louise*
> *You get a thrill from every squeeze*
> *Burma-Shave*

Calamity said, 'He knows them all.'
Jhoe gave us another:

Don't lose your head to gain a minute
You need your head; your brains are in it.
Burma-Shave

'What are you up to?' I asked.

'Jhoe's been telling me about Noö. He says the rainy season lasts for two centuries, and I've shown him the sand dunes and the war memorial. He didn't like it. Too ingrokking.'

'Earth-man,' he said, turning to me, 'your violence appalls us. Sometimes, on this planet, I feel so ingrokked. So terribly ingrokked.'

Calamity tried to help him up. 'Please don't be unhappy. We can take you back to where you came from, if you like.'

'Such a thing would not be possible for many of your centuries.'

'Are you from a hospital, Jhoe?' I asked.

He shook his head. 'I am from Elysium, beneath the moons of Noö.'

'Why did you come to Aberystwyth?' I asked.

'As a penance. Once, many aeons ago, my people said the thing which was not. So here I must languish.'

'Are you sure you are not from a hospital, Jhoe?' Calamity asked. 'It doesn't matter if you are. We won't tell anyone, unless you want us to.'

'We have no hospitals, we have no need for them. I am so ingrokked.' He knelt down at the water's edge and put his hand on the seaweed mane that clung to the tree stump; he ran his fingers through it as gently as a mother stroking her daughter's hair.

'Because if you were from a hospital, we could take you back, couldn't we, Louie?'

'Yes, we would be happy to.'

'And we would come to visit you.'

Jhoe seemed not to be listening but stared out across the remains of the forest, lost in a reverie. 'I remember when all this was fields.'

Calamity looked at me in anguish. I put my arm on her shoulder and drew her to me for comfort. Who was Jhoe?

'Over there,' he said, 'is where I kissed a girl once. We used to come on holiday to Cantref-y-Gwaelod. If only you could see Earth as she was then. In the days when . . . she was a shepherdess, and all this vale where now the sea churns the sand was the home of her flock.' He looked round, his eyes filled with an intense longing. 'If only you could have seen it before . . . before all the bad stuff, when the earth was young. You would have been so grokked.'

I told Calamity to get the bus back to town and check out Mrs Bwlch-gwallter's shop in Bridge Street. I set off for Taliesin. The one surviving Richards brother was not difficult to find. He sat in the corner of the pub, his head slumped forward, chin on chest, like a marionette with a broken string. I put a pint down in front of him and he turned to look at me.

Saliva dribbled over his bottom lip. 'Did Frankie send you?'

'Frankie's dead.'

'If it's about the girl . . .'

'It's not about the girl.'

He heaved the sigh of a man for whom the act of inhaling is a chore. 'What's he doing these days? Still using the blowtorch is he?'

'I bought you a pint.'

'That's kind of you.' He took a deep draught. 'Why now? I mean, after all this time, all these years . . . I thought . . .' He stopped and shook his head. 'No, Frankie never forgets. I just wondered, that's all. Why did he never come sooner? I was waiting. I knew, after all the trouble . . .'

'Frankie's dead.'

'To tell you the truth,' he said, ignoring me, 'I'm happy. Happy that this day has finally arrived. A life spent looking over your shoulder is not a man's life, it's a dog's. I decided that long ago. When it came I would go quietly, and with dignity. Just make it quick, that's all.'

'Frankie's dead. I saw him die. His last words were of you. He asked me to tell you: Of all the blags you pulled, that one on the Coliseum was the best.'

The old con twisted his head to face me. 'He said that?'

'Those were his very words. The silly old bastard was proud of you. He just wasn't the kind to show it. He said, they don't make them like Old Richards any more; old school. That's what he said.'

He repeated the words in a reverential tone. 'Old school.'

'Caeriog and Siencyn, and Iestyn.'

He looked surprised. 'Iestyn? He didn't rate him, did he?'

'He mentioned him.'

'Iestyn was the reason I spent all those years inside sewing mail bags. Siencyn and me wouldn't have stopped, you see, but Iestyn was driving. He was soft. He was no good. He got out to see what we'd hit. I mean, what sort of robber stops during the getaway to take a pedestrian to the doctor's?'

'So you left them both?'

'I make no apologies for that. There was no other way. We was born on the wrong side of the tracks. They don't thank people like us for doing a good deed. One thing I've learned in this life, the folk at the top are every bit as rotten as we are. They just wear nicer hats.'

'I wouldn't disagree with that.'

'That doctor, spends all that time checking your heart, he should take a look at his own.'

'You're not wrong.'

'He thinks he's better than a man like me, but it isn't so. Things I could tell you about him, they'd soon wipe the smile off his face.' He turned to me. 'If you see Iestyn, tell him I'm sorry about what we did. There was no way we could stop.'

'I'll tell him.'

'They say he's back in town. He's been seen. Hard to believe. Just tell him. I'm too old for fighting battles.'

'I'll be glad to.'

'I'm not scared. The Lord could take me this afternoon and I wouldn't turn a hair. But, the thing is, I want to tell him. I want him to know, I'm not sorry for driving off like that because there was no way we could avoid it. But I am sorry that they hanged him and not us. That wasn't right. Normally there's nothing you can do about it.

But if he's alive, well, I could say to him, I'm sorry they hanged you. That would be something, wouldn't it?'

I touched his arm and squeezed. 'Yes, it would. The thing is, though, I need help to find him.'

'I'm no good to anybody any more. Drink my pint is about all I can do.'

'What do you know that would wipe the smile off the doc's face?'

'I never blab.'

'I know, and that makes you a true man in my book. But sometimes you have to make exceptions. I'm not trying to trick you, but is it right that your silence protects a man like that? What's he ever done for you? Tell me what you know, it may help me find Iestyn.'

His brow furrowed as he considered my words. After a while he seemed to make up his mind. 'We were working in the garage, me and my brother, in Llanfarian. This was before Iestyn arrived in town. The doc bought his fiancée a car from us, a 1963 Austin A35 in petrel grey. When she walked out on him some folk said he'd done her in; Sheriff Preseli started asking questions. Then we did the cinema job and were banged up. A year later she returned to Aberystwyth for a couple of days to collect some things. Driving the same car and all, so that put the wagging tongues to rest, and Preseli went round personally telling the gossips to give it a rest. He said he'd met the woman and so the rumours that the doc had murdered her should stop. And they did, mostly. Funny thing was, though, the engine was in the habit of over-heating so they left her car at our garage to have it checked out. My father told me about it. He said it was a different car. Almost identical, with the same number plate, but there were one or two differences only an expert would recognise. The car they originally bought from us had been a 1963 with a 1097-cc engine. But when she came back in 1966 the car was the 1962 with the 948-cc engine.'

I stared at him, wondering how much credence to give to his story. He sat, head still drooped forward.

'Maybe they just changed the engine.'

'Wouldn't have fit in the chassis; it was differently configured.'

'Or maybe your dad made a mistake.'

'But what sort of mistake? The number plate was the same, couldn't have been mistaken about that. The car was different. One thing my dad knew about was cars. I tell you, it wasn't the same car but someone had gone to a lot of trouble to make it look like it was. Don't you see? The woman who came back, who was she? Did anyone see her? Yes, I know, lots of people saw her from a distance, but who spoke to her? Who saw her up close? Only the doctor and Sheriff Preseli as far as I can tell. If he did kill her, and the rumours all got a bit too much, well this would be a way to stop them, wouldn't it? Easy to arrange: find a similar car, get a woman to dress the part, make sure no one meets her . . . you see what I mean?'

'Sheriff Preseli would need to be in on it.'

'That's right. And you'd need a woman to act the part. But no one else need know. I'm just saying, that's all.'

I thanked him and stood up to leave.

He put his hand on my arm. 'Is it true that Frankie's dead?'

'Yes, it's true. I saw it happen.'

'What were his last words?'

'He cried out for his mum.'

A look of wonder stole across the old man's face. He opened his mouth to speak but no words came. The image of Frankie Blowtorch on his deathbed, crying for his mum, robbed him of the power of speech.

Meici Jones was in my office when I got back. He stood up as I entered and raised his arms as if playing maracas, swivelled his hips to turn side-on to me and made a clicking sound with his tongue.

'New suit – got it from Fosters. The mayor says I will be doing some public engagements when the human cannonball starts so I'll need some new togs. What do you think?'

'It's very suave.'

'Yeah, I think so too. They've given me an account. No one else in my village has an account at Fosters. I got these, too.' He held out a small white paper bag. 'Gobstoppers. Take one.'

As if mesmerised, I reached into the bag and took one. 'Thanks, Meici,' I said. I put the gobstopper on the desk, next to the phone. 'I'll have it later, with my tea.'

He walked into the kitchenette and brought two tumblers from the drainer. I was surprised; I didn't think Meici drank. Before his mum was sent down for murder she oversaw every aspect of his life and was the sort of woman who would smell liquor on a man's breath from 50 yards away. People like that can smell it tomorrow through a crystal ball.

Meici put the tumblers down and took a small bottle from the inside pocket of his jacket. The bottle contained a chocolate-coloured liquid. He waved the bottle. 'It took me ages to find where she kept it.'

'What is it?'

He giggled. 'My mum's cough mixture.' He poured out two small measures, chinked the glasses and handed me one. 'Made by Auntie Pebim. It's got a special mushroom in it from the Amazon. Sospan uses it too in his under-the-counter ice cream.'

'I haven't got a cough.'

'Who's going to know?'

'What are we celebrating?'

The lines of his cheeks flickered, the corners of his mouth quivered as he tried to bottle the irrepressible excitement. 'You'll never guess what.'

'What?'

He reached under the table and brought out another Fosters suit, in a glistening polythene covering.

'That looks to me dangerously like the sort of clothes a man might wear at his wedding,' I said in genuine surprise.

He grinned. 'I asked Chastity to . . . marry me . . . She said yes!'

I was dumbfounded.

'What do you say to that, eh?'

'That's . . . that's tremendous.'

'*Okole maluna*!' He raised his glass. 'That's Hawaiian for cheers.'

'*Okole maluna*!' I replied. I held my glass up to try and sniff without it being obvious. It seemed inoffensive: mushrooms perhaps or a wooden box used to hold vegetables. I sipped. It was sweet, woody, mossy, but not unpleasant. Meici knocked his back in one and exhaled with satisfaction, slapping his chest in that strange ritual of the amateur drinker.

'When I was young,' he said, 'I sometimes used to pretend to have a cough even though I didn't. Those were the times when . . .' Two deep grooves formed at the bridge of his nose as he searched for the right word. 'I suppose you could say, I was . . . it was . . . I was . . .'

'Happy?'

His brow furrowed as he contemplated that possibility. Was it possible he had been happy once?

'When's the wedding?' I asked.

'Next week. I'm going to do my inaugural cannonball flight just before the service. We're doing it down at Plas Crug, going to invite the whole town.'

'Sounds like quite an affair.'

'I think so. I think Chastity deserves it, don't you?'

'Isn't it perhaps . . . oh, I don't know, a little bit much to do in one day – first human-cannonball jump and getting hitched?'

'What do you mean, Lou?'

'It would be a lot on anybody's plate.'

'I want to make her proud, Lou. Chastity hasn't had much of a life. I want to make it special for her.'

'I can understand that.'

'Birds, eh?' he said with the wry detachment of the man of the world.

'Yes,' I replied, 'birds!'

'I bought her a present. One of those "women's handkerchiefs". From the catalogue. Didn't have to hide it at the end of the lane neither. You should have seen the postman's face when I told him. "You can come right up to the house, now," I said, "mum's not here any more." Lord of the Manor he called me. Who'd have thought it? He says he might bring a lingerie catalogue next time. I'll invite you round. You wouldn't believe how brainy Chastity is. I think of all the birds I've had she is the best. She's nuts about you.'

'That's nice.'

'Always going on about you, she is.' A thought clouded his brow as he considered the implications of that. He blinked it away. 'I'm glad really because you are one of my best friends. She says we're lucky to have found each other, me 'n' you, Lou. Do you think that?'

'Yes, we're very lucky.'

'I never had a friend before you so Chas says it's incredible that I found such a good one. Thing is, Lou, I was wondering . . . I know we haven't known each other that long, but I haven't got any other friends, so I was wondering . . . will you be my best man?'

I froze and my grip tightened on the tumbler. Meici was so absorbed in the moment he didn't notice.

'Chas says we can all go on holiday together, to Caldey Island. I've always wanted to go there. I bet you've been, haven't you?'

'No, but I've had one or two clients who have.'

'Chas has been. She says the best thing is the gift shop. They make their own toffee. Chas says anyone's allowed to buy it.'

'That's what I've heard, too.'

Meici shook his head in wonder. 'Imagine if my mum heard about that! She'd say it was made by Satan; he makes loads of stuff.'

'How can it be made by Satan if it's made by monks?'

'I don't know. I'll ask Chas — she'll know; she knows loads of things. It's unbelievable really.' Meici refilled his glass; I put my hand over the top of my glass. The cough mixture seemed to be making him garrulous.

'You're probably right, you're not supposed to have too much of this stuff. Mum only let me have a spoonful just before bed. Auntie Pebim says, if you have a little bit it makes your cough go away and you see a funny shape in the distance but you don't know what it is. If you have more the shape gets closer and closer until eventually it's right in front of you and you see it's a drawbridge to a giant's castle. Then if you have more, you go across the bridge and Auntie Pebim says you see things on the other side that can really upset you. Sometimes you never come back. Do you believe that?'

'It's not how most cough mixtures work, but I guess it could be true.'

'I can't make up my mind whether I want to visit the castle. Sometimes I do and sometimes I'm scared to. Do you think we should try and help mum escape from prison?'

'Who's we?'

'Me 'n' you, Lou.'

'No, I don't think so.'

'Chas says she knows a way to do it. Look!' He pulled a paper from his pocket and unfolded it. The page had been torn from a children's picture book and showed a prisoner in a dungeon hanging by his hands from rings set in the wall above his head. An archetypal dungeon-keeper with a big spade-shaped beard and baggy stripy trousers sat at a table eating the prisoner's food, evidently tormenting him.

'It's Erik XIV of Sweden,' he said pointing at the wretch hanging by his wrists. Chas has been telling me about him. He was in prison for something and his wife used to send him food but the guards ate it all in front of his face and laughed. So he got her to make some pea soup with arsenic in it and the guards ate that and died and he escaped. We could do that. Chas says you can find arsenic everywhere, in apple pips and fly killer and stuff. We could bake mum a cake on her birthday. Chas says she knew someone once who ate arsenic and he nearly died. She says he vomited so much his stomach came out of his mouth.'

'Erik XIV?'

'Something like that. It used to happen all the time in the olden days.'

'What happens if the guards are nice and your mum eats the cake?'

'But guards are never nice, are they?'

'I think modern ones are usually OK. It's not like it is in books, it's more of a caring profession like social workers or something. Once upon a time it would have been a good plan, in the days when they had really big key rings and prisoners slept on straw, but the world has changed. Everyone eats in a refectory now and the meals are carefully planned according to the prisoners' calorific and dietary needs as worked out by a team of dieticians; the guards get plenty of food, too, so they don't have to steal from the prisoners.'

'You don't think it's a good plan, then?'

'Trust me, Meici, all that would happen is you would end up in gaol, too – for murdering your mum.'

He nodded solemnly. 'Thing is, Lou, it's quite lonely living in that house by myself. Do you know what I mean?'

'Yes, but once you are married all that will change.'

He seemed not to hear me, lost as he was in a world of his own. 'I sit there and think about things.' He narrowed his eyes as he recalled his lonely thoughts. 'You know, Lou, I don't think my mum ever really . . . really loved me.'

'I'm sure she did. Please don't call me Lou.'

'I never really saw much evidence of it.'

'Some people find it hard to show.'

He continued to knock back the cough mixture in single gulps while I pretended to drink mine.

'What did you want to see me about?'

'There's something I need to ask you, Lou. Man to man.'

'Yes?'

'I've been reading the manual, about conjugal duties.'

My innards froze. 'Meici, I'm not the best . . .'

'I didn't know who to ask, and then I thought of you.'

'Sometimes it's best to explore without too much formal advice.'

'It's the most important part of the whole thing, I don't want to mess it up. It's Chastity I'm thinking of, really. I don't know anything about it. So I thought I'd ask you, I thought old Lou will know what to do.'

'Meici, as long as you love each other that's all that matters. The rest is just, I don't know, just . . .'

'Just what, Lou?'

'Just like . . . just like shaking hands, Meici.'

He nodded as a load slowly lifted from his shoulders. 'So, there's nothing to it? Not a big deal, like?'

'No, not a big deal.'

'Will you do it then?'

'Do what?'

'Be my best man.'

I responded with a smile of bogus delight, but my soul squirmed.

Meici said, 'No, no, wait! Don't answer. Hang on.' He scooped the wedding suit up and ran to the kitchenette to change.

When he returned it was like witnessing a conjuring trick in which a stage magician sends a volunteer into a box and a different one comes out. The gauche ineptitude had gone, as if the outfit contained a built-in swagger the way corsets contain built-in stiffening.

'I wouldn't know you, Meici. I wouldn't have recognised you.'

His eyes sparkled as tears of joy welled up. He sat back at the table and continued to drink the cough mixture. He forgot to ask me again about being his best man; perhaps he thought the deal had now been clinched. His words slowed and he began to babble.

'Mum's really my aunt. My real mum died and left me, and her two sisters had to decide which one would take care of me. They played Pooh Sticks for me. Mum lost. Auntie Meinir left and went to Liverpool. She's got a fur coat and a chequebook and stuff. At Christmas we used to play Hansel and Gretel in the wood, but sometimes, it was funny, I would leave the trail of breadcrumbs and follow them but they led in the wrong direction. Once they went down the disused lead mine. Mum said the birds must have moved them. The woman from the social services asked me last week if I had any relations and I told her Auntie Pebim was sort of like an aunt and she told me to make regular visits to her. So I went round and she wouldn't let me past the garden gate. She said, "What do you want?" and I said I'd come to visit her, and she said "A likely story." ' He took another drink from the bottle.

'Are you sure you should be having so much?'

'Sss-all right.'

'I think your cough must be cured by now.'

'I can see the castle.'

'Maybe you should stop.'

'I was thinking, you and me, Lou, are mates. You live on your own, don't you?'

'Yes.'

'We could move in together. That would be good, wouldn't it?'

'Thing is, Meici . . .'

'Lou! I'm at the drawbridge!'

'Meici, stop!'

'They're raising the portcullis . . .'

'No! Meici!'

'Oh no!' He made a strangled, gurgling sound in his throat and slumped back limp and silent in the chair.

I dragged him out to the car and drove him home. He was still unconscious when we reached his house. I slapped his face gently to rouse him. He blinked up at me and scratched his head. 'I fell asleep,' he said unnecessarily. He sat there, making no attempt to move, looking groggy. 'Where are we?'

'I've brought you home.'

'Yes,' he said distantly. 'Yes. That's good.'

'You should go and lie down.'

He nodded. He looked down at his hand still holding the bag of gobstoppers. 'Tell you what, Lou. I want you to have these.' He reached forward and opened the glove compartment. A rag fell out and into his lap. It was a handkerchief. He stared at it in astonishment as if it were a religious relic. He stared and stared. It was Chastity's handkerchief. He turned to me with fire burning in his eyes. 'You dirty dirty double-crosser,' he hissed. 'You dirty double-crosser. You dirty dirty double-crosser.'

'Meici,' I said.

His hand reached to his side and fumbled with the door handle. He seemed to recoil from me, pressing himself against the door in his hurry to escape.

'Meici, it's not like you think . . .'

He opened the door and stepped out backwards, still staring at me in horror. 'Don't you say a damn word, Louie Knight, don't you say a damn thing. You've really done it this time, good and proper. You're in for it now, I can tell you. Just you wait and see what you get, you'll see! Dirty double-crosser.' He turned and walked up the path to the house, his right hand raised and twisted, pressed against his eye. I thought I should perhaps go in and see if he was OK, but even as I entertained the thought, I found my foot pressing down on the accelerator and my hands turning the wheel to leave.

Chapter 13

FOUR DAYS passed. Meici didn't reappear and didn't answer the phone when I called. I didn't greatly care. I was more worried about Mrs Bwlchgwallter, who hadn't been seen either. Calamity asked her neighbours each day, but they said she hadn't returned home. On the fifth morning I got a call from Calamity from the telephone kiosk across the road from Ginger Nutters in Bridge Street. She said she had forced the back door and found Mrs Bwlchgwallter, she'd been there all along, sitting in the dark. I said I'd come right away and she told me to steel myself.

I found Calamity standing in front of the shop, feigning interest in the window display. Normally it was crowded with gingerbread men – but now it was in darkness. A mouse nibbled at the remains of a confectionery foot. I pressed my face against the glass and looked in. Calamity walked down the alley at the side of the shop and I followed. The brick walls on either side glistened with moisture, our footsteps making sharp sandpapery rasps on the concrete. The alley led to a walled-in yard, barely big enough to hold the rig of a rotating washing line. The arms of Mrs Bwlchgwallter's laundry reached up like ghosts in a stick-up.

We walked into a dark kitchen. Burnished copper pans gleamed from the wall, a black iron oven like a steam engine filled half the kitchen but was cold as ash. We walked through across a floor that was sticky with discarded food. The sound of a TV was coming from above us. We climbed the creaking stairs up to a small sitting room. Mrs Bwlchgwallter sat in an armchair, facing the TV and watching the Test Card. A plate of half-eaten Heinz spaghetti sat on her lap, covered in green fur. On a side table next to the arm of the chair was an empty bottle of tablets, a cup of cold tea in a metal camping cup and an empty quarter bottle of gin.

'I think she's been here the whole time, working on that —' Calamity pointed at the fireplace. In the grate there was a full chamber pot and next to it, reaching almost to the ceiling, was a 7-foot gingerbread alien.

'It's a Grey,' whispered Calamity.

'Mrs Bwlchgwallter,' I said.

She turned her head slowly and focused her watery eyes. 'We're closed . . . Forever.'

'We didn't come for gingerbread,' I said.

'The time for gingerbread is passed.'

'You mustn't think that,' I said. 'None of us knows what lies in the womb of time.'

She narrowed her eyes, trying to comprehend. Then she parted her lips a fraction and breathed the words, 'The horror! The horror!'

'What was it?' asked Calamity. 'What did you discover in the hypnotism?'

Mrs Bwlchgwallter shook her head sadly and mouthed the word *horror*.

I threw the contents of her teacup into the chamber pot and filled the cup with rum from my hip flask. I held it out to her, but she was too enfeebled to grasp the cup. I pushed it towards her mouth, but the rum dribbled down her chin. I broke a finger off the gingerbread 'Grey', dipped the finger in the rum and used it as a makeshift teat. She sucked greedily and a fire was illumined in the depths of her eyes. It shone weakly from behind the wide panes of her spectacles like the pilot light on a stove. The frame of her glasses was made of semi-translucent pale blue plastic.

'Tell us what happened,' I said, withdrawing the gingerbread finger. She reached out feebly and I pushed her hand down. 'Let it go down first,' I said. 'Tell us about the horror.'

'I can't,' she whispered, 'I can't. Not for as long as I live.'

'Please, Mrs Bwlchgwallter,' said Calamity, 'we need to know; it's very important.'

Mrs Bwlchgwallter pointed at the gingerbread finger, using the last few dregs of her strength to drive a better bargain. I dipped the finger in the rum and gave it to her. She sucked greedily, making sounds like a coffee percolator.

'That's the last until you tell us what we need to know,' I said losing patience. She ignored me, continuing to suck. I dragged the rum-soaked finger away. 'OK, talkie talkie first, then drinkie drinkie.'

She took a deep breath, then said, slowly inserting an agonising pause between the syllables, 'The horror!'

'Come on now, Mrs Bwlchgwallter,' said Calamity. 'Just think of the applause at the Shrewsbury Palladium.'

I scowled at Calamity, indicating that this was not the time for the good agent/bad agent routine. She stared down at her feet.

I said, 'Fantastic idea! Barney and Betty Hill. How did it go again? It's the classic UFO contact from America in the early '60s. They were hypnotised by the military and –'

'How was I supposed to know this would happen?' said Calamity.

'That's what I keep asking myself.'

'What's that supposed to mean? When they hypnotised Barney and Betty Hill they drew a picture of the star system Zeta Reticuli. The aliens were puzzled by Barney's false teeth. Everyone was OK afterwards, they didn't curl up in a ball and cry or make giant ginger-bread aliens.' I could tell from her voice she was near to tears. 'How was I supposed to know?'

'I don't know. I told you it was a dumb idea.'

'You tell me all my ideas are dumb.'

'Most of them are.'

'Louie!' She shot me a look of appeal.

'We'll talk about it later.'

'Are we just going to leave her?'

'You want to bring her along?'

She shook her head. We walked down the stairs taking care for some reason not to make a noise. We walked out onto Bridge Street where the fresh air came as a relief, lifting our low spirits and leaving just a mild sense of guilt. Once we had put sufficient distance between us and the shop, around the top of Great Darkgate Street, we stopped and looked at each other.

'I think we should give up the case,' said Calamity.

'Me too.'

'I'm scared.'

'Me too.'

'Do you think Raspiwtin is really looking for Iestyn?'

'I don't know.'

'Do you think Iestyn is alive?'

'I don't know.'

'Do you think Raspiwtin is who he says he is?'

'He might well be since he hasn't really said who he is.'

'Has he paid us?'

'No.'

'Do you think he will?'

'No.'

'Why are we carrying on?'

'I don't know.'

'Don't you think we should stop?'

'Yes.'

'Will we?'

'Yes.'

'When?'

'I just need to do one thing first. Call an ambulance. Don't give your name, just tell them she's up there and hang up.'

'What are you going to do?'

'I'm going back to see the farmer.'

'According to Mrs Pugh, he's curled up like a baby.'

'I'll uncurl him.'

'What if he doesn't know anything?'

'I'll make him remember.'

Calamity grabbed my arm. 'Louie, I'm sorry about Barney and Betty Hill.'

I ran my hand over her brow and smoothed down her hair. 'I know. Don't worry about it.'

I drove and thought about Eeyore's school photo. There is something profoundly disturbing about that means of outwitting the universe. It violates our trust. Still photos record an instant, whatever an instant is, but this trick fuses two instants and makes them one. And that one fused moment becomes the truth, the official footprint left in the sands of time. I recalled the words of the old con out at the pub in Taliesin, about the woman who left in a 1963 Austin A35 and came back in a 1962 model with the same number plate. He could have been lying; most people who didn't know better would say you can't trust a word of a man like that. But the paradox is, you can. Precisely because he never spoke about it all these years. Normal people would have done nothing else but talk about it, but Caeriog Richards was a man who didn't blab. That didn't mean he didn't know things, it just meant in the absence of a compelling reason to do otherwise he wouldn't talk about them. That was the code by which he lived. It didn't indicate moral approval or disapproval. It was the code: you didn't speak about the things you knew.

I wondered about the pictures of Doc Digwyl's fiancée in the front room of his house. The picnic on the dunes. Behind, in the distance, the sea roars unchanging. The girl stands with one foot pointed slightly inward and her weight shifted a bit, to compensate for the shifting sand perhaps. The strand of hair across the eyes and the slight blur of the left hand that is about to make the journey up to brush it away. At her feet the picnic basket, on a tartan rug from the boot of the Austin. Was she the original Rhiannon? Or the one who came back in the wrong car? Where was the original one now? I saw a vision of the white bones, the skull filled with earth, lying in a shallow grave beneath the gorse on a hillside somewhere. That's how I would do it. In the middle of gorse bushes so thick no one, not even a dog fetching a stick, would venture there.

I ignored the turning to Borth this time and headed directly across the flat marshland towards Furnace and Ynys Greigiog. But you can never quite elude the calling sea. Away to my left, far but unmistakable, a long, thin line of silver sparkled on the horizon; forever glittering, forever restless.

Farmer Pugh was no longer curled up in a ball. He answered the door himself; he was unshaven and he looked tired, but otherwise seemed pretty normal. He was wearing his glasses too and looked at me with suspicion and without recognition.

'Yes? I'm not talking to the press.'

'I'm not the press. They'll be here tomorrow if you don't talk to me.'

'Cops?'

'They'll be here this afternoon. I'm private, I don't like cops and they don't have to know, that's up to you. I'm here to talk to you about the smell coming from the cellar in your old house. I haven't got much time and I need some information fast and you've got it. If you give it to me, nothing happens. If you don't we start digging up the concrete. I suggest you invite me in.'

He pulled the door open and I walked in.

'Shall I put the kettle on?'

'Not unless you can't go five minutes without a cup of tea. I want to know what went on in the hypnotism session with Mrs Bwlchgwallter.'

'But I don't know, I . . .'

'I know the story; you were found curled up in a ball gurgling like a little girl. You can't remember a thing. But I'm not buying it. I'm here to talk about your brother Rhys, whose head you smashed in with a spade because you caught him messing around with your sister; buried him in the cellar. Killed the dog too with a house brick. I'm a compassionate man, I don't see any reason any of this has to come out now, when it's all too late to change anything. I can see you've grieved in your own way over it, I can see the life you have lived since that day has been punishment enough. We can let it all lie, let those dogs, both sleeping and the one with the head all mushy like a smashed-in boiled egg, sleep. But I don't have to play it that way. It's up to you.'

'But, really, I have no idea what I said, really I don't.'

'You'd better start remembering quick, then.'

'How can I do that?'

'If you don't want to spend the rest of your life in gaol think of something.'

'Please, I can't remember.'

'Of course,' I said. 'Maybe it wasn't your brother messing around with your sister, maybe it was you. Maybe he caught you and you had to silence him. Was that how it happened?'

'No.'

'I can find her and ask.'

'You leave her out of this.'

'I want to, really I do, but I need you to help me.' I moved to the door.

'Stop!' His voice filled with anguish. 'Stop, please, don't tell my sister. Why don't you ask Mrs Bwlchgwallter?'

'Her memory isn't so good these days.'

'But the tape, she can play you the tape.'

'There's a tape?'

'She recorded it. She brought one of those portable tape recorders . . . it was in her handbag.'

I scrutinised his face for a second or two and then decided to believe him.

I drove back to town and went to see Doc Digwyl. I found him sitting in a dressing gown shivering next to an unlit fire in the front room of his house on Laura Place. He was eating beans on toast and listening to a 78-rpm gramophone record of the *Merry Widow*. Apart from the cold, the room was not greatly changed since the last time I'd been there when Mrs Lewis the housekeeper had been still alive. And yet everything was different; it seemed as if the doctor's life had imploded.

He stared past me, addressing his words to a fireless grate. 'Thirty years Mrs Lewis served me,' he said. 'Ministered to my every need, nursed me in sickness, comforted me, was my solace through the dark times, and in all that time I never said a pleasant word to her. I thought I despised her for her silly ways, all that endless demented polishing, the gossiping and perpetual insistence on seeing the bright side of things.' He snapped the fork down onto his plate with an air of point-less finality. 'Now look at me.'

'Do you think . . . is it possible that . . . that the mayor could have killed her?'

'And why would he do such a thing?'

'I don't know, it's just a suspicion . . . because she talked to me about that night in 1965 when the boys robbed the Coliseum cinema, when Iestyn Probert came round here with . . . with . . .'

'With an alien?'

'Wasn't it?'

'I don't know what it was. It was a boy in a strange silver suit.'

'Preseli took him away. What happened after that?'

'I don't know, how should I?'

'You must know. I need to know.'

He shrugged. 'I'm an empiricist. I can only tell you of the things I have seen with my own eyes.'

'You don't always need to see something to know it. The truth isn't like that. Truth is the wolf I have spent my life tracking.' I stood up and walked to the mantelpiece to look at the photos. 'You track with the heart, not the eyes. The eyes are easily deceived; easiest thing in the world to show something that isn't true and make people believe it. The truth is more elusive, but sometimes you know when you are in its presence. The first time I came here I knew there was something wrong about all these pictures.' I lined them up and arranged them, straightening some, moving others. There were no clues to indicate the chronological sequence; such clues had been carefully filtered out. But even so, they fell into two broad camps. In one group the woman was always shown too far away, so you couldn't recognise her. 'A man and woman fall in love, they plan to marry, but something goes wrong. She tries to walk out on him, but he doesn't want her to. Perhaps she has found another. Sometimes, when men are in love, they love so much they would rather no one has their love if they cannot. She left the neighbourhood, or so it seemed. And so the neighbours' tongues start wagging. In the meantime, the doctor helps the sheriff out with his own little difficulty. He agrees to keep quiet about the events of a strange night that some have called the Welsh Roswell. One good turn deserves another. So the following year the sheriff helps the doctor silence those wagging tongues. The missing fiancée returns for a week. There can be no doubt about it because the sheriff sees and speaks to her. But there's one funny thing about it. The car.' I placed two photos side by side. 'It was the same number plate, but the wrong model car.' I turned to look at him.

'You can't seriously be trying to blackmail me?'

'Where is she?'

He made a noise that was part chuckle and part sneer. The sound a man makes when there is nothing left in the world that he cares about.

'Tregaron Bog, where else? It's the customary place, I believe, to store the mistakes of one's youth. There's a map in the sideboard somewhere. I'll show you roughly where to look. I'll even lend you the spade.'

'I don't feel like digging myself. Maybe I'll just call the cops.'

'The phone's in the hall. Be my guest.'

'You really want to spend the remainder of your life in prison?'

He sneered again. 'Mr Knight, can't you see? I've been in prison since the day she . . . died.'

It was getting on for 9.00 when I parked in Patriarch Street and walked down to the office. They said it was a rounder's bat that he hit me with. It struck the back of my head, behind the ear. I fell forward, onto my knees. Another blow followed. The world began to spin, so now the night sky was beneath me, like the sea. I knelt, trying to rise, another blow fell, and a spot of blood dropped to the pavement where it spread out to form a starburst. I twisted round to hold up an arm in protection. Meici Jones stared down at me, his eyes bright and wide, like a frightened animal, and his teeth were clenched from the exertion. 'Dirty double-crosser,' he said.

He raised the arm holding the bat. I lay on the paving slab and noted details with the strange detachment that passengers in a car accident often report. The pavement was gritty and grimy, covered in spit and chewing gum and sweet wrappers.

'Dirty double-crosser,' he said again as the bat reached the acme of its swing.

'Please, Meici,' I said.

The slight clenching of his teeth indicated that his arm was about to fall.

A voice cried out in the night. 'No!' Miaow appeared from between the parked cars on the other side of the road. 'No, leave him, please, leave him.'

'Dirty double-crosser!' The bat came down. A shot rang out followed by the xylophonic chime of the bat hitting asphalt. Meici clutched his shoulder with a hand that turned red with blood. He fell to his knees and then onto his face. Miaow stood transfixed, holding a smoking gun. I slipped into unconsciousness.

Chapter 14

I OPENED my eyes and stared up into the face of Sauerkopp holding an ice cream. He smiled. I closed my eyes and waited. I opened them. He was still there, sitting on a grey-blue hospital chair, next to a grey-blue bedside table.

'Everything is grey-blue,' I said.

'They do it to be soothing on the eye,' he said.

'Blue and grey.'

'Soothing, you see? Sooooooooooothing.'

'Yes, I feel calm.'

> *O fervent eyelids letting through*
> *Those eyes the greenest of things blue*
> *The bluest of things grey.*

'That's lovely.'

'Swinburne. A much under-appreciated poet if you ask me.'

'You're eating ice cream. You're always eating ice cream.'

'I like it. Do you want one?'

'Not really. It's nice here, isn't it?'

'Yes. Such a shame you have to leave.'

'Do they need the bed?'

'No, but it might be a good idea for you to depart before they find out you are not Nathan Carolingus, which is the name we booked you in under, but Louie Knight, a small-time Aberystwyth shamus wanted for attempted murder.'

'I didn't attempt to kill anybody.'

'No, Louie Knight did. He shot a man called Meici Jones. Nathan Carolingus was just an innocent bystander.'

'How did Nathan get these bruises on the back of my head?'

'Meici put up a brave struggle and defended himself stoutly using a rounders bat until Louie Knight pulled out the gun and shot him in the shoulder. He's not on the critical list, but that was more due to luck than intent on the part of Louie. In the confusion Nathan Carolingus got hit by the bat.'

'I know Louie Knight, he wouldn't shoot anyone.'

'Someone shot Meici, and he says it was Louie. He said Louie attacked him for no reason outside his office.'

'Did they find the gun?'

'Not yet. It's probably in the river or somewhere. They usually are. Meici Jones works for the human cannonball —'

'I know who Meici Jones is. Why did you kill Mrs Lewis?'

'I didn't.'

'Who did, then?'

'I don't know.'

'I think it was you. I think you like killing people.'

'I've never killed anyone in my life, and if I had I certainly wouldn't have enjoyed it.' He stood up and removed his hat which had been hanging from my saline-drip dispenser. 'If I were you, I'd walk out of this room filled with furniture which you rightly point out is predominantly blue-grey; turn left outside the door and take the lift, which is situated at the midpoint of the corridor. You press G and emerge on the ground floor some seconds later and turn left and then straight ahead, and in less than a minute you are outside feeling the warm sun on your pallid face.'

'Then what?'

'I don't know; running might not be a bad plan. There's a cleaner's cubbyhole opposite the Gents, just before you get to the lift. There are some overalls in there. Take a clipboard, too. No one ever stops a man with a clipboard.'

'When I walk out carrying my clipboard, is that when I get arrested?'

'It's no trap. Why bother? If I wanted them to arrest you, I'd tell them now.'

'Why are you helping me?'

'You work for the Aviary. It's my job to look after people who work for us.'

'I don't work for the Aviary.'

'That's for us to decide.'

'You really going to let me go?'

'Yes.'

'Why?'

'I like you. We're on the same side.'

'No we're not.'

'You and I have got a lot in common. I know you don't think so, but that's because you have formed the wrong opinion of me.'

'Underneath it all you are just a cuddly toy, is that it?'

'No.'

'Everything you say is . . . is . . . a riddle wrapped in . . . how does it go?'

'A riddle wrapped in a mystery inside an enigma.'

'Yes, that's it. That was Winston Churchill, wasn't it?'

'Yes, indeed, talking about Russia.'

'You and Russia: a riddle wrapped in a mystery inside an enigma.'

'Except that I know what's inside the enigma.'

'You're doing it again.'

He winked.

'You said you and I are on the same side. What side is that?'

'The side where they don't put people's heads on sticks.' He tipped his hat, about to leave.

'No, wait. We're not on the same side. You think if you say it often enough it will come true and you won't have to feel so bad about yourself. But it's not true. For all my faults, I've got a heart. I can think and feel and love. Right now I'm hurting. What would you know about that? You who works for some shadowy organisation with the morals of a dungeon toad. You who slinks about in the shadows, looking at life through jaundiced eyes, a sour expression on your face. You and I are not the same because there are things that are sacred to me but you don't know anything about that. You wouldn't know what it means.'

He reached into his pocket and pulled out his wallet. He removed a photo. 'It's a nice speech, Peeper, but as I say, you are wrong about me. Sooner or later you'll realise it.' He held the picture out in front of me. It showed a little girl, maybe six or seven, playing on a rocking horse. 'This is my little girl. Her name is Johanna. She'll be eight on Sunday, only I won't be there to share it with her because she lives in Scotland with her mum, a woman who took such a dislike to me she doesn't want me near my little girl. They don't even have a phone, not because they can't afford one but just so I can't hear her voice. On Sunday she'll have lunch with her grandparents and I'll call. They'll give me five minutes if I'm lucky and that will be it until Christmas.' He put the photo back in the wallet and took out a five-pound note. 'I don't know if that counts as sacred in your book, maybe you set the bar higher than me. But those five minutes every year are all I have.' He put the five-pound note down on the bedside table. 'Here's your bus fare. Don't hang around, just do as I told you. Lift to the ground floor and turn left, not forgetting to drop by the cleaners' cubbyhole next to the Gents.'

I waited for a few minutes after he left and then followed his instructions. It didn't seem like there was much else to do.

The wind from the sea thudded incessantly against the wall of Miaow's caravan. She scraped takeaway Chinese food from their silver-foil containers onto three plates. In the background the TV news warned the public not to approach me.

'There's only one thing to be done,' said Miaow. 'I'll have to turn myself in.'

'That's a silly idea,' I said.

'But you didn't shoot him, I did.'

'We're not turning you in.'

'What else can we do?' She brought the plates over and set them down on the table.

'We'll think of something.'

There was a knock on the door and Calamity walked in without waiting for an answer. She struggled for a second or two to close the door in the gusting wind. She walked over and kissed me.

'How's the invalid?'

'Sore,' I said.

She nodded. 'We're lucky your head's made of wood.'

'I wish my heart was.'

She winced and hugged me. 'Oh Louie.'

'It's OK. It's not the first time I've been an outlaw. Where have you been?'

'Asking around. Mrs Bwlchgwallter went to stay with her sister in Trawscoed, but then she disappeared from there during the night. She hasn't been back to the shop, so I guess we can go and have a look round for the tape.'

'We'll go first thing in the morning.'

'Let's eat,' said Miaow. She poured wine into paper cups and we snapped apart the sets of wooden chopsticks.

Calamity raised the chopsticks holding a bail of twirled noodle clear of the sauce. 'The way I see it, all roads lead to the mayor. We need to get Meici to change his story. Meici works for the mayor. That human-cannonball job is the only decent thing he's got in his life; it would kill him to lose it. The mayor can take it away from him.'

'And the mayor's our friend; he would do that for us,' I said.

'Don't be like that, Louie. I hate it.'

'I'm wanted for attempted murder.'

'And I'm trying to help you. You've got to hear me out. All roads lead through the mayor. I agree that's not a great start, but we'll come to that. First we have to get Meici to change his story.'

'And tell them I did it,' said Miaow.

Calamity sighed with exasperation. 'No, the story is an unknown John Doe shot Meici. All Meici has to agree is it wasn't Louie. He was mistaken.'

'Meici was on TV a while back appealing to me to give myself up,' I said.

'That's where the mayor comes in. We get the mayor to lean on him. All roads lead through the mayor.'

'This is the mayor who chopped up my desk.'

'Yes, the mayor who chopped up your desk. It makes no difference; he's the one we have to work on. Why do you think Meici is doing this?'

'How many reasons do you need? He's a berk, he doesn't like me, and he found his bride's hanky in my car so he thinks he's Othello.'

'Those are all good reasons, but my guess is the mayor put him up to it. I can't see Meici having enough smarts to invent it himself.'

'Is it so very difficult?'

'Actually, I think it is,' said Calamity. 'I don't think it's an easy thing to do, especially for a bloke who has spent his life living with his mum and never doing anything of his own volition. Don't forget he was hanging out there in order to attack you. Because of that he would probably be too scared to tell a lie like this on his own.'

'I agree,' said Miaow.

'OK,' I said. 'Personally I think he is very capable of making it up himself, it seems just the sort of mean playground lie he would have learned to tell in school. But let's assume you are right. Let's suppose the mayor put him up to it.'

'This all started when Raspiwtin walked in with the Iestyn Probert case. There's something about it the mayor really doesn't want aired in public. We've got to find out what that something is. Don't you agree?'

'I agree,' said Miaow.

'In a sense,' I said. 'We already know. The kid in the silver suit.'

'The one from the flying saucer,' said Miaow.

'I'm not buying that part of it.'

'Who was he, then?' said Calamity.

'I don't know.'

'It was obvious he had to be from the saucer. Why else would he be wearing a silver suit they couldn't get off him? Why else would they suppress the information? Why else would the Aviary be involved?'

'I don't know the answers to these questions, but I'm sure there are some, somewhere.'

Calamity pulled a face.

The caravan door opened and Raspiwtin walked in holding a gun. It was pointed at me; they usually are. 'Poppet, are you all right?' he asked Miaow.

'Mr Raspiwtin, what are you doing?' she asked.

'He hasn't hurt you?'

'Of course not.'

'Thank God I came in time. Phone the police.'

'Don't be silly.'

'Do as I say, Poppet. This man is dangerous. He shot a man in cold blood.'

'No, he didn't, I did.'

'No, she didn't, I did.' I smiled. He looked confused.

'Look, Mr Raspiwtin –'

'Please try and call me Iolo Yefimovich.'

'Iolo Yefimovich, I know you are very keen on me, but that doesn't give you permission to enter my caravan uninvited.'

'But I came to save you!'

'I don't want to be saved.'

Calamity produced a length of connecting pipe from a camping-gas cylinder and pressed it into the base of Raspiwtin's skull. 'Drop the gun,' she said.

'I must advise you, I'm not afraid to die.'

'We're not afraid to kill you. Shoot him,' I said.

'Move out of the way first,' said Calamity. 'If you sit there you'll get some of his face in your eye like you did with that lollipop woman we shot.'

'Oh! Don't remind me!' I moved aside. 'I hate it when it goes septic.'

'Good Lord!' said Raspiwtin, appalled by the image conjured up.

Miaow grabbed the hand holding the gun, dragged it towards her and pressed the barrel into her stomach.

'Poppet!'

'Go on, shoot! I'm the one who shot Meici Jones.'

'Might be a good idea to drop the gun,' I said.

He loosened his grip and Miaow took the gun off him and handed it to me. I took out a handkerchief and wiped it, then held it still wrapped in the hanky.

'As I said, I'm not afraid to die,' said Raspiwtin. 'In a way I have died many times.'

'We don't have to kill you, we could just shoot you in the knee. I hear it is very painful and you can't bend your leg again for the rest of your life.'

'Yes, a shot to the kneecap is a terrible wound. I must implore you not to consider that option.'

'Tell me who you are.'

'Iolo Yefimovich Raspiwtin.'

'Who do you work for?'

'Humanity.'

'If he moves, shoot him,' I said to Calamity, who was still holding the copper pipe to his ear. I stood up lazily, took a step forward, then cracked the gun barrel on his kneecap. He howled and crumpled to the floor.

'Imagine how it must feel to get shot there.'

Tears welled up in his eyes. 'Can I have a drink?'

I nodded. Miaow poured some wine into a paper cup and handed it to him.

'And maybe some of your sweet-and-sour? I am very hungry.'

'Do you want to play Ludo as well?' I asked.

'You would regret that decision; I am a most formidable opponent across the Ludo board.'

'Sit at the table,' I told him.

Calamity slipped the pipe into her pocket and we took up positions at the table. I kept the gun trained on Raspiwtin. He began to eat.

'You are in a difficult position,' said Raspiwtin with a mouth full of half-chewed noodle. He took a gulp of wine. His spirits had been raised by the turn of events. 'Your hiding place here at this caravan has been revealed.'

'Who to?' I asked.

'Me, of course.'

'Anyone else?'

'Not yet.'

'Then it sounds to me like *you* are in a difficult position. It sounds like we might have to kill you after all.'

'If the police find out,' said Miaow, 'I will turn myself in.'

'Of course they will find out, where do you think we are? Outer Mongolia?'

I kicked Raspiwtin's knee. He winced. 'Don't get too cosy,' I reminded him. 'Now, suppose you pay for your supper by telling us the truth about who you are. The real story.'

'I have told you the real story. My name is —'

'Your name is Iolo Yefimovich Raspiwtin. We heard that bit.'

'I was born in the district of Ponterwyd, overlooking the Nant-y-Moch River in 1931.'

'I think you told us that last time.' I said.

Raspiwtin ignored me. 'My story really begins before that, many aeons ago, at the very dawn of time when there were just tribes wandering across the great empty savannahs; simple hairy folk who sought food and shelter and were spiritually at peace.'

'I'm not sure you need to go back quite so far,' I said. 'Maybe you could skip forward a few million years to somewhere around 1931 or possibly later.'

Raspiwtin scowled at me. 'I was a child of notable piety. Already in the womb, through careful listening, I learned the rudiments of the Lord's Prayer. As an infant I developed calluses on my knees from praying, and it is said I put aside my nurse's pap during Lent. I was brought up by my grandmother, who sent a few pennies every month to the Catholic church to help the orphanage in the Gilbert

Islands. She wrote a letter to the Vatican describing my precocious piety, and, to our great astonishment, I was offered an apprenticeship at the age of twelve in the Vatican laundry, under the tutelage of Father Theophrastus.'

'I think you told us about the laundry, too,' I said.

'Yes, but this is an important milestone in the development of my *apostasia*. You must understand, you see, the effect it had on my second day when I told the boys how I had been selected on account of my piety. "Oh really!" they laughed, "is that what you call it?" "Yes, yes," I said and told them about the scholarly essay I had submitted. How their mocking laughter echoed through the laundry! How my ears burned! How my eyes stung with tears! Those wicked imps! They told me that the clerics never looked at the essay, only at the photo which accompanied it. "Don't you see how pretty we all are?" they asked. "Didn't you wonder why they wanted a photo of you in your swimming costume?" Oh, those wicked boys!'

'I think he's playing for time,' said Calamity. 'Maybe he thinks the cops are coming.'

'He'll lose his kneecaps if they do.'

Raspiwtin continued unabashed. 'You asked me who I was. And what I have just laid out before you is a very, very small part of the story of what I am.'

'OK, what are you doing in Aberystwyth?'

'I was coming to that.'

'It didn't look like it.'

'I told you I was here because of a Burmese girl.'

'You told me about her, you said you were in love with her and she was murdered; this you found greatly upsetting. So much so that you burst into tears.'

'These are very tender feelings.'

'So is your kneecap. And by the way, I found a newspaper cutting with the same story, so I'm not convinced it really happened to you at all.'

He gave me an insouciant smile and continued. 'After the tragedy in Burma I was recalled to Rome, where my tutor took me into the postroom. In there they had a pile of letters from kind old widows all over the world who sent us postal orders to help with the orphanages. We searched for one from my own grandmother in Ponterwyd, cashed it at the Vatican post office, and spent the night drinking and whoring on the proceeds. During that night Father Theophrastus instructed me in the terrible truths of this world.'

'What does this have to do with anything?' I asked.

'Everything! You see, eventually I returned from this land of shadows . . .'

'Does it have anything to do with the Zed Notice?' asked Calamity.

He looked slightly taken aback. 'You know about the Zed Notice?' He paused, momentarily stuck for words. 'That is nothing to worry about.'

'Tell us what it is,' I said, aiming the gun at his knee and squinting along the top of the barrel. 'Then we'll decide whether it's anything to worry about.'

He made a dismissive gesture with his hands as if a Zed Notice was a parking ticket. 'It's just a piece of clerical work. For crimes of the level of Tower of Babel and above. Usually involves a simple razing of the town and then ploughing of the fields with salt. Tell me, have there been any deliveries of military-grade ploughs at the railway station that you know of?'

'Not that I have been informed,' I said.

'That's good,' said Raspiwtin. 'These things are hardly ever enacted. It's when the ploughs turn up that you have to worry.'

'I've got a great idea,' I said. 'Why don't you tell us again, in simple terms, what you think you are doing in Aberystwyth.'

Raspiwtin paused and beamed at us like a stage conjurer preparing his pièce de résistance. 'My goal in visiting Aberystwyth is nothing less than the emancipation of humanity from a prison it has been inhabiting, unaware, for ten thousand years.'

'You should see the camera obscura while you are here as well,' I said.

'Ah, you scoff! Because you think I am just a dreamer, a . . . a visionary. While you, Mr Knight, you think you are a cynic whose heart is steeped in the dark milk of disillusion, or so you fancy. But, in truth, you are wrong on both counts. When I say I mean to be the instrument of humanity's deliverance, I do not talk of some vague and abstract rarefied theoretical position but of things wholly definite and concrete. And you, dear Louie, are a stranger to the contents of your heart: it is not bitter gall that flows there, but love, yes! Love! Your heart is bruised but it is big, it contains multitudes, and it is for this reason alone that I have chosen you to aid me in my task.' He put the cup down on the table. 'Tell me, Louie, are you familiar with the Japanese word *koan*? It is the name of a type of conundrum upon which Zen monks meditate in order to achieve enlightenment. A well-known example is, "What is the sound of one hand clapping?" During my early years I discovered a *koan* of my own, one that turned my world on its head. It concerned the atom-bomb raid on Nagasaki at the end of the Second World War. Nagasaki was a Catholic city, you see, founded by the Portuguese in the sixteenth century and home to sixty thousand Catholics, including many orders of Holy Sisters. I read an article in *Life* magazine once about the military chaplain on Tinian Island in the Marianas, from where the bombing raid took off. On the day of the mission he said a prayer for the success of the raid and blessed the crew. The target they were to aim for was the Urekami Catholic cathedral in the centre of Nagasaki. The effect on me of this *koan* was quite, quite shattering.'

'Lots of people died, not just Catholics.'

'Of course, all civilian deaths were equally regrettable. And yet . . . surely if such a thing is possible, this is even more insane? Bombing ourselves? What greater insanity can be conceived of than this, that the priest blesses the mission that goes to bomb his own cathedral? I pondered this riddle for many years.' He stood up. 'And now I must leave it for you to ponder. Thank you for the excellent meal. It has all been charming.'

'Where do you think you're going?'

'I need to make some phone calls; I'll be back in a short while.'

'No, you won't,' I said, 'because you won't be going anywhere.'

'I really do have to go.'

'I'll shoot your knees out.'

He smiled and opened the door. 'No, you won't. You're too kind, Mr Knight. Any fool can see that.'

He was right. He walked out. Leaving just a scent of Parma Violets like a mauve ghost.

Chapter 15

THE NEXT morning there was a beautiful dawn. This was often the way: the gods played games with us. Under such a burning sky, pink and crimson, who could be unhappy? Even a condemned man waking on the morning of his execution to a sky like this would take extra care over the brushing of his teeth. Was it George Orwell who described a condemned man stepping aside to avoid a puddle on his way to the gallows?

I left Miaow still sleeping and drove at first light out to Penparcau to pick up Calamity. She was already standing on the pavement outside her auntie's house, yawning like a hippo. We drove to Ginger Nutters in Bridge Street and retraced our steps down the side alley to the back door. This time the TV was switched off. Mrs Bwlchgwallter was gone, but otherwise upstairs was the same as we had left it: the gingerbread alien, the brimming chamber pot, the room airless and smelling rank. We opened a few drawers, looked under a few cushions, but did so in a manner that said we thought the task of finding the tape was futile. As futile, perhaps, as our next mission: to go and see Meici and appeal to his better nature.

'Thing is,' said Calamity, 'if the portable tape recorder was in her handbag, then so is the tape, and she probably has her handbag with her.'

'Maybe she hid the tape.'

'If she did, it could be anywhere. It doesn't have to be here.'

I nodded.

'I wonder what the farmer said under hypnosis that made her scream.'

* * *

We gave up and drove to Machynlleth to kill time and to eat breakfast somewhere I was less likely to be recognised. We read the paper and drank coffee, and when it was coming up to 10.00 we drove to the caravan park at Clarach. Chastity was sitting on a kitchen stool at the water's edge. The day was starting to get hot. She had a forlorn air, her feet dangling in the bright water that reached her chair on each successive inflow. I coughed and she turned and looked up, squinting. Her spectacles were broken, and repaired with Sellotape; her left eye was half-closed, swollen and a mixture of yellow, green and mauve.

'Do you know the land where the lemon tree flowers?' she asked.

'All we've got is rhubarb. What happened to your eye?'

'I . . . I fell.'

'Really? How?'

'You know, I just fell . . . into a door.'

'Meici did it to you, didn't he?'

She pretended to be indignant. 'No! Of course not. Meici would never do a thing like that.'

'Yes, he would.'

'You don't know him, he's under so much strain with this new job. It was an accident. He just . . .'

'He just punched you in the eye. That's the sort of guy he is.'

'Don't you dare say anything bad about Meici, don't you dare!'

Calamity knelt down and put her arm around Chastity's shoulders. 'We don't want to upset you, we're your friends . . .'

'No, you're not. Meici said you would say bad things about him. He was right. I hate you both. I thought you were nice, but you're not. You're a murderer, Louie Knight, I saw you on the TV. Murderer!' She hid her face in her hands and wept. But it was the fake dry sobbing of a child throwing a tantrum. I waited until she stopped and peeked from behind her hands. She raised her face, sniffing inauthentically.

'Is he here?'

'Who?'

'Meici.'

'No,' she said, but her eyes betrayed her, darting for a fraction of a second towards the caravans parked on the grassy verge overlooking the beach.

I turned to look. 'Which one is it? The blue one?'

'No, I said he's not here.'

'You might as well say –'

Calamity nudged my arm. Meici Jones appeared walking down the road carrying a pint of milk. He entered one of the caravans. We followed.

He was standing in the kitchen area, reading a copy of the *Daily Mirror* propped up on the cooker while eating baked beans from a tin with a fork. When he saw us, he looked frightened.

'Hi Meici,' I said.

'Hi Louie,' he said with forced joviality. 'How are things?'

'Oh, not bad. How are the beans?'

He looked at them as if the answer to the question required deliberation. He became lost in thought. 'Good,' he said distantly. 'The beans are good, Lou.'

'You'll be getting married soon.'

'This afternoon, actually.'

'Chastity sure will look lovely in a white dress. Pity about that black eye.'

He feigned innocence. 'Which one's that?'

'The one you gave her.'

'Is that what she said?'

'She said she walked into a door.'

'That's right, that's what she did.' He forced a laugh. 'You should have seen it, Lou! She's so clumsy . . . I guess that's why I love her.'

'I need your help, Meici.'

'Sure, Louie, anything . . .'

'I'm wanted for attempted murder, did you know that?'

'Yes, I saw it on the TV.'

'I saw it on TV, too. I saw you on TV saying I was the murderer. Do you remember doing that?'

Meici didn't say anything. His eyes narrowed. Perhaps he realised being nice was not going to get him out of this one. 'Since you ask, Louie, I don't remember that.'

'I need to clear my name. Whatever quarrel you think you've got with me is . . .'

'You had her handkerchief.'

'Yes, her handkerchief was in my car. It doesn't mean anything.'

'You would say that.'

'It doesn't mean a thing. I gave her a lift.' I pulled out my hip flask and proffered it. 'Drink?'

He shook his head as if to say it was too late for such things. 'I trusted you, I thought you were my friend, you were nothing but a dirty double-crosser. You can't wriggle out of this one.'

'It's a serious charge, Meici.'

'You should have thought about that before you started messing about with my girl.'

'Will you withdraw your testimony?'

'I was brought up not to tell lies. I'll tell them exactly what happened. You shot me.'

'Meici, I know you've had a hard life –'

'What would you know about it?'

'Meici –'

'I'm sorry, Louie, I have a lot to do today.' He put the bean tin down on the hob.

I stared at him for a long while; he fidgeted, then picked the tin up again.

'OK,' I said. 'Nothing I say is going to make a difference.' I reached out my hand.

He jumped back. 'What are you going to do?'

'I'm going to shake your hand. What do you think I'm going to do?'

'You could do judo or something.'

I gave an exasperated sigh. He stared uneasily at my hand, the way a dog regards a stick that has been used to beat it in the past.

'I just wanted to congratulate you on your wedding.'

Confusion flooded his eyes.

'It's not a trick, for God's sake.'

He reached out his hand, gingerly, as if expecting an electric shock. We shook. His hand was pudgy and moist and childlike.

'Hope it goes well,' I said. 'I hope you and Chastity will be very happy together.'

His eyes misted, and he swallowed so hard he could hardly speak. 'Thanks, Lou, 'ppreciate it.'

'And thanks for asking me to be your best man. Sorry it didn't work out.'

He swallowed another lump. 'I got Ercwleff to do it.'

'He's a good choice. Dependable.'

Meici nodded. He opened his mouth to speak but the muscles quivered and his mouth assumed the shape of a figure-of-eight lying on its side.

'So long,' I said as I left.

'Bye Louie,' he squeaked, looking as shocked as a child waiting at the school gate for a mother who doesn't come. That's how it can happen sometimes. Just when you thought there was nothing left for Fortune to throw at you, she deals you a low blow. Kindness.

It rained in the afternoon. The day turned cold and squally with gusts of wind that turned umbrellas inside out and made the canvas doors of the marquee in Plas Crug slap together viciously. The ceremony was held in Llanbadarn church and afterwards there was a reception for two hundred in the marquee. I stood among the trees at the edge of the park watching, the ghost at the feast. After the toasts and speeches the crowd gathered outside in the rain to watch Meici's human-cannonball flight. He wore his silver space-cadet suit. A compère dressed as a circus ringmaster gave a running commentary through a public address system. He told us as Meici stepped out from the dressing tent and strode along the field of the great danger Meici was placing himself in. The crowd were dubious and it seemed many secretly hoped for a disaster. From white to black on the same day. No one had ever seen a human-cannonball wedding before; no one had ever seen a human-cannonball funeral. No one had seen both on the same day. Normally brides have to do a quick change of clothing into their going-away outfits but this would be something even more dramatic. No one liked Meici, and no one even knew Chastity, but everyone had to be there in case he entered the *Guinness Book of Records*.

Meici climbed up the stepladder and inserted himself in the cannon barrel, which pointed up and in the direction of a net for landing some twenty yards away. Chastity, in white rain-sodden taffeta, watched with eyes sparkling, half in fear, half in excitement. No man had ever done this for her before and would ever be likely to again. A recording of a drum rolled, the compère gave the countdown, the heavens opened. There was a pyrotechnic bang and flash from the fat end of the cannon and Meici sailed regally into the darkening sky, describing a gentle arc towards the net. The crowd held its breath. Meici held his arms out and landed neatly in the middle of the net. Chastity squealed with delight and the audience broke into spontaneous applause. A group of ushers helped Meici down and carried him shoulder high through the throng towards the bar; girls threw flowers and confetti over him. It was a moment of triumph and no one who had ever known Meici in his previous incarnation would ever have predicted it. A man who had known no friends, and no girls, who had lived for thirty-four years with his mum and been regularly beaten with a cane, had performed the most unlikely turnaround of fate. Later in the afternoon a hire car took the couple off to the mayor's holiday cottage in Aberdovey.

I spent the rest of the day walking in the rain. I was a fugitive; my description had been issued to all law-enforcement officers, along with the caveat that I was dangerous and caution should be used when approaching me. Anyone could have seen me, anyone could have reported me. I no longer cared. Sometimes you don't; it takes too much energy. I walked from the recreation field down Elm Tree Avenue, past the station to the harbour and from there along the Prom to Constitution Hill. I walked along North Road and up the steps to the top of Bryn Road and past the big red house that can be seen from every part of town. I walked up over the golf course and took the long route past the farms, the one that emerges at the top of Penglais Hill. And I walked across to Cefn Llan and down to Llanbadarn, and once I reached the recreation ground again, I did another circuit. It didn't stop raining. It was a good time to think about the human race. It's not something you would normally choose to join, a club full of snivellers, crybabies, back-stabbers, disapprovers, oafs and inquisitors, snoops and witch-burners, prigs, puritans, Pharisees, pardoners, pie-eaters, tell-tale tits, teacher's pets and curtain-twitchers. No, you wouldn't choose to join it, but once they cast you out from the fold, once they pass the writ of outlawry, there is no ache like the one in your heart to be allowed back in. It's one of the paradoxes for which this universe is famous.

I walked and walked because sometimes walking is slightly less painful than lying down. Given how low society sets the bar indicating who is allowed in, being deemed beyond the pale is a damning verdict. It's a bitter pill to swallow. All outlaws know this; don't believe the nonsense you read in the papers or from their twelfth-century counterparts, the balladeers. The romance is all phooey. Ten centuries of being sung about by troubadours in tights is not worth one night in a warm bed safe in the knowledge that no one will come and arrest you. In the movies Robin Hood and his men were always laughing in the face of misfortune, incorrigibly happy, sitting around the fire gnawing chicken and throwing the bones over their shoulders, cackling witlessly. You try sleeping in a tree in the rain. The outlaw doesn't steal because he wants to, but because he has to. He certainly doesn't do it to give to the poor. He doesn't give a damn. He steals from whoever's coming along the path and keeps it all. There is only one thing the outlaw wants: to go home, take his wet things off and drift asleep in front of the fire with a mug of cocoa. That's what I wanted to do. But home is the one place you can't go at times like this. They would definitely be watching the house and the office. In some ways, to be arrested as I walked through the afternoon drizzle would have been a blessing, but I couldn't bear to be taken at night, in my own bed. I shouldn't have slept at Miaow's either, but where else could I go? To sleep like an outlaw in the wood, on the wet ground, or in a cave so damp the whole hillside has rheumatism . . . no man is an island, no matter what he thinks. When the tough guys are gunned down in the street, with their last words they cry out for their mums. This is also true in battle, so they say; they lie dying on the field of slaughter and call out for the woman who brought them into this vale of tears. My heart couldn't bear, did not possess the strength, to sleep alone now. In the night, when the world hates you, it helps to sleep in the arms of someone who doesn't.

At the harbour end of the Prom the asphalt gives way to the wooden prosthetic of the jetty; this is where the outsiders park. Those people who have not renewed their membership of the human race. VW campers, old travelling library vans converted into homes, ancient ambulances from the days when they painted a red cross on the side so thick that no amount of painting over with white house paint will ever efface the outline. They don't paint red crosses on ambulances any more, it's one of those things that give the world its comforting familiarity and which they change without telling anyone. One day you wake up and notice all the ambulances are fluorescent green and yellow. They say it's safer, it enhances visibility, but they are wrong. In an ambulance you are never at risk from other traffic. There is only one danger to watch out for in an ambulance, and it was for this that the red crosses were painted on them: attack by dive bomber.

It must be odd sleeping in one; you would surely dream about all the people who didn't make it, who went to sleep permanently en route. You know you are in trouble if they switch off the siren. As long as you can still hear it, there's hope. For many of us it will be the last earthly sound we hear, the technological plash of Charon's oar. What thoughts rush through your mind as they carry you out through the front door of the house you will never return to? As they slam you into the back of the fluorescent funerary chariot, the eternal bread van? Do you know this will be the last time you see blue sky? What thoughts go through your head?

A man approached as I leant on the railings and watched the harbour lights glitter on the water. I thought he would ask for a cigarette, but it was Eeyore. He didn't say anything, just patted me on the shoulder, then leant on the railings next to me and stared out to sea. After a while, I said, 'The police are looking for me.'

'I know, I saw it on the news.'

'I'm tempted to go and give myself up. What should I do?'

'I don't know.'

'When you were a cop, how did you keep going?'

He thought for a while and said, 'I used to think about Big Nose George Parrott.'

'I've never heard of him.'

'Not many people have. Big Nose George Parrott was one of the people they never tell you about.'

'Tell me about him.'

'He was a cattle rustler from Wyoming at the end of the nineteenth century, with a $20,000 bounty on his head for killing a Union Pacific Railroad detective. They sentenced him to hang, but the townsfolk snatched him from the gaol and strung him up from a telegraph pole. After his death they sent his hide to the tannery, where they made it into a pair of shoes. The shoes were given to a fellow called John Eugene Osborne, a surgeon for the Union Pacific Railway, who wore them to the inaugural ball after being elected the first governor of Wyoming. I don't really know much more about him, but you don't really need to. I'm sure he was a swell fellow, a real darling. The first governor of Wyoming. I'm sure everywhere he went they loved him.'

'You say the man shot a detective?'

'A Pinkerton, I believe. It could have been you or me, I know, so it doesn't make sense that I should admire him.'

'It makes a sort of sense.'

'Sure, he never should have shot that Pinkerton, but it's not like he wanted to. He did it because he probably couldn't see any way out of things, and didn't have enough brains in his head to figure one out. They were hiding away in some bolt-hole, surrounded; their discovery was a surprise, I think. I'm sure if he'd had a choice he wouldn't have wanted to shoot that man. But people like Big Nose George Parrott never have a choice; they spend their lives in a corner with nowhere left to run, and the cards they hold are always twos and threes; it's the first governors of Wyoming who get the picture cards. The names change but the story never does. In 1950 builders doing alterations to the Rawlins National Bank across the road from the gaol found the shoes in a barrel. That's how it goes. People like that governor spend their lives walking all over the little guys. He just took it one stage further and made it literal.'

'Big Nose George Parrott, eh?'

'The thing about people like that first governor of Wyoming is they get all the breaks in life, sleep in a nice feather bed, go to the best schools, and it's easy for them; I don't mind that. It's the automatic sense of entitlement that goes with it that I despise. The presumption that they get all those good things because they are special people, that they are better than others. As far as I can see, there is only one difference between that governor in his fancy waistcoat and Big Nose George Parrott. He was luckier. That governor stuck his head out of the womb in a nicer room.' He turned to me and whispered, 'Son, all you can do sometimes is try and wipe the smile off their faces.'

Miaow held the door ajar on a safety chain that stretched across the bridge of her nose, her face twisted in the scowl of the householder disturbed late at night. She was wearing striped men's pyjamas: pink vertical bars sandwiching thinner lines of grey. There were three buttons on the jacket, the bottom one missing. Without the button the fabric parted, revealing the taut satin of her midriff. In the dim light it shone like antique amber.

'I'm worn out,' I said.

She put on a pair of spectacles and focused on my face.

'You're soaked through.'

I followed her in and sat at the Formica table. I placed my elbows on the tabletop and my head in my hands. Miaow slipped next to me and put her palms on my cheeks. Her hands were cool and soothing, like the hands of an alabaster saint. 'Poor you,' she whispered. I sat there and let myself be soothed. She moved her hands and pressed her head against mine. Her breathing took on the rhythm of the sea out in the darkness; the earth slowed, ceased its pointless celestial whirligig. She pressed her head closer, pulled tighter with her arms, but said nothing. Just breathed, like the ocean, with a hint of Jack Daniels.

'I just want to sleep.'

'You can.'

'They'll find me here.'

'If they do, I'll shoot them. I'll make some cocoa.' She stood up, moved over to the stove and began to boil milk. I went and stood next to her, slumped against the wall.

'Where did you get the gun?'

'It used to belong to my father.'

'What did he need it for?'

She smiled. 'He was an outlaw like you.'

'What sort of outlaw?'

'His name was Iestyn Probert.'

I looked at her in astonishment, mouth agape in the dark. 'Well, I'll be . . . all this time you . . . you've been . . . I don't know what to say.'

'I'm so sorry. I hated lying to you. I'm just a little kid, Louie. I don't think I'd be strong enough to stand on that battlement.'

I took her face in my hands and kissed her. 'You would, trust me.'

'Iestyn spent a week on the run before they caught him. My mother hid him in her cottage. Nine months later I was born.'

'And now you are looking for him?'

'Yes.'

'Even though they hanged him.'

'A lot of people say he's alive.'

She carried the two mugs of cocoa over to the table. I followed and sat down. She topped them up with Jack Daniels.

'And you are here in Aber now because you think he will come back because of the flying-saucer reports?'

'Yes. It's worth trying, isn't it? I want to see him. Wouldn't you want to see your father?'

'Yes, but –'

'I'm sure he would come if he could.'

'Do you know why Raspiwtin is here?'

'He's looking for Iestyn, too. He thinks I know where he is, so he watches me. But I don't. He's watching and waiting. What are you going to do now?'

'I don't know. I've run out of ideas.'

'You need to rest.'

Stupefied with tiredness, I followed her across the caravan to the bed. I slumped down and said, 'I'll be gone early tomorrow. I have something to do.'

'You said you'd run out of ideas.'

'I'm going to see Sauerkopp. Two days after Mrs Lewis was murdered he turned up in my office with a Polaroid of her body. His people must have been following me the night she was murdered. He must know who did it. He pretends he doesn't, but he must do. I'll ask him. If it was the mayor, I can use that to get him to make Meici drop the accusation against me. If it was Doc Digwyl, then that must have something to do with the mayor.'

'What makes you think he will help you?'

'I'll make him. I need to borrow the gun.'

She kissed me and said, 'OK.'

I watched through the obscuring gauze of my drooping eyelashes as she gently undressed me. Girl on the battlement; angel in pyjamas; her hands were cool and soothing like the apse of a church on a summer's day.

Chapter 16

I ROSE at first light, dragged from the depths of sleep by the first barely perceptible lightening of the curtains. It was damp outside and a sodden parcel lay on the metal step, addressed to me. It was from Chastity. Inside was a piece of wedding cake wrapped in a red napkin. Next to it, a letter written on lilac Basildon Bond notepaper that was almost certainly kept by her aunt in a zip-up leather case along with matching envelopes. Matching your letter paper and envelopes is like polishing the heels and toes of your shoes with equal dedication: not many people do it nowadays, but those who do would continue to do so even in the event of a nuclear war. The letter was neatly written in a childish variant of Victorian copperplate that hinted at many hours spent practising beneath the unflinching gaze of her aunt:

Dear Louie,

Please do not condemn Meici. I know this will be hard for you to believe in the circumstances but he loves you, more perhaps than you can imagine. In fact, we both do. This misunderstanding that has arisen has also driven a wedge through my own heart. We are both so happy now, together at last, and the only pall over our joy is the knowledge that fate prevented you from attending our wedding. Please be assured that I will labour ceaselessly in my efforts to repair this rift and effect the reconciliation of which I hope and pray. Until, then, please accept this enclosed sweetmeat as a token of the bond of love that joins us all eternally and as a harbinger of the good times that will come again.

Chaleureusement

Chastity

I fetched a coffee from the vending machine outside Reception and ate a makeshift breakfast of wedding cake and coffee as I drove east, towards Ystumtuen. The gun in my pocket felt as cold against my thigh as a linoleum floor in winter. Three wasps woke from their slumbers and buzzed repeatedly against the windscreen, seemingly looking back in dismay as Maelor Gawr caravan park receded in the distance. Once fully awake they transferred their energies to the cake. I drove one-handed and waved the cake erratically in a vain bid to fend them off. They ducked and weaved like First World War biplanes, darting in and out almost as if they were attached to my hand by elastic.

I wanted to call Sauerkopp but not from just anywhere. It needed to be a place with a telephone kiosk, place to park the car and a derelict house nearby. Iestyn's ruined house would do just fine. It began to rain and the drops whipped across the windscreen, overwhelming the feeble wipers to form a bleary and uniform opalescence. The gloom thickened; I drove in a trance.

The red telephone kiosk was situated at the junction of the main road and the lane that led up to Iestyn's old house. I parked the car in the lay-by further up and walked to the phone. The door squeaked like a frightened mouse; inside it smelled of urine and sheep dung; cold wind blew through a broken pane in the door. I called the number, hung up and returned to the car. Half an hour later a car arrived and parked opposite the kiosk. Sauerkopp spent some time looking round the telephone kiosk and then walked towards my car. He saw me, bent down to the window and found himself facing the gun. I got out, told him to turn around and put his hands on the roof of the car the way the cops did. He grinned as if it were the best joke he'd heard all week. I hit him over the back of the head with the gun, and he crumpled against the car, then slid to the ground.

When he regained consciousness fifteen minutes later, he was sitting against a wall in the abandoned croft, trussed up with gaffer tape. Staring at the gun. It took him a while to grasp all the details of the scene, but once he had he smiled and said, 'You've done well. I knew my faith in you wasn't misplaced.'

'Sorry I had to hit you.'

'It's OK, I'm used to it. If you're going to threaten to shoot me, I might as well tell you now, I won't believe you.'

'I'm not going to shoot you.' I eased the safety catch on and slipped the gun into my pocket. 'I just want to chat.'

'My door is always open.'

'I'm in trouble.'

'I know.'

'I'm wanted for murder; the only witness is Meici Jones, but he's lying. I think the mayor put him up to it. I don't know why, maybe because I poked my nose into his business and he didn't like it. It's something about this famous kid in the silver suit.'

'How can I help?'

'You told me at the hospital it was your job to look after people who worked for the Aviary.'

'I can't get them off a murder charge.'

'I didn't do it and you know it.'

'What I know doesn't count, it's what I can do that counts.'

'Your people were following me the night Mrs Lewis was killed. You must know what happened to her. I think it was the mayor who killed her. If I was sure of that, maybe I could get him to lean on Meici.'

'What if I don't want to tell you? Normally you need some sort of persuasion, and we both know you aren't going to shoot me in cold blood. You're too nice. I told you before, you and me are alike in many ways.'

I slipped my hand inside his jacket and pulled out his wallet. I took out the picture of his daughter. 'It's Sunday today, remember?'

He stared at me without expression.

'Remember that sacred five minutes? There's a phone 20 yards from here. How do you fancy staring at it for the rest of the day?'

He pulled a jokey face.

'It's going to be a very disappointed little girl not getting a call from her daddy this year. He never forgets. Maybe something terrible has happened to him.'

He shrugged. 'So she doesn't get a call from her daddy this year. She'll survive.'

'It seems like a good deal to me. The way I see it, you want to help me, you just don't like to do things the straightforward way. You like to have your fun first.'

'I like you, Louie, I really do. You remind me of a man I used to know, a friend of mine, he's dead now, he was just like you.'

'Who was he, your pimp?'

'My brother, sort of.'

'What you mean is, the man was you. The man you used to be before you lost your soul. It's a corny routine; I've seen it too many times before.'

'The reason you resist is, you know it's true.'

'One phone call away.'

'You've got me wrong. We're both fighting for the same thing. I told you before, heads on sticks, that's what it all comes down to.'

I shook my head. 'You're on the wrong side, the side of the bad guys.'

'And who are the good guys?'

'Man called Big Nose George Parrott. But that wouldn't mean anything to you. Big Nose George Parrott is one of the people they never tell you about.'

'They told me, he ended up as a pair of shoes. Is that what you want out of life? Your greatest ambition is to be a pair of shoes?'

'You would never understand.'

He began to slide sideways and shuffled his body to get upright again. 'You really going to leave me tied up here while my little girl waits for her daddy to call?'

I gave him a stony stare and he laughed. 'I love you, Louie, I really do. Only a man too decent for his own good could come up with a plan as crap as that. You need to be a tough guy, you see, but you're not a tough guy, so there's no point trying to play one when you've got a heart made of white chocolate candy.'

'You can push that button once too many times. I'm not *that* nice.'

'Let me tell you about Big Nose George Parrott. I spent ten years once living among the Big Nose George Parrotts. A long time ago I was a prison guard out at the Cardiganshire State Penitentiary at Tregaron Bog. You know that place?'

'Tregaron Pen? Who doesn't?'

'They've closed it now, but when it was still going it was a bad prison, full of terrible brutality. You think I'm no good, you should have seen the rest of the guards. Your old school games teacher was one of them.'

'Herod Jenkins?'

He laughed. 'They never told you that? Oh yes. He was in charge of the chain gang, sat all day on his horse, holding a shotgun. With a sour look on his face.'

'I know that look.'

'I have to say, building a place like that in the middle of Tregaron Bog was a nice touch; whoever thought of that knew what he was doing. There were a lot of shallow graves in that bog, and the people who had dug them were inside the prison.'

'They say criminals always return to the scene of the crime.'

'They do say that, don't they? What do they call that?'

'Ironic.'

'No, there's a word for it . . .'

'Living above the shop?'

'No, it's biological, like parasitical.'

'Symbiosis.'

'That's it!' He looked pleased, like someone completing the cross-word. 'Symbiosis.'

'I guess it would have made it hard to tunnel out. Prisoners are a superstitious lot.'

'That's true. They were happy to risk the gunshot from the man on the horse, but most of them drew the line at tunnelling through a bone yard.'

'Where does Big Nose George Parrott fit in?'

'Whole place was full of people like him. I was there the day they took over. Many of the inmates were in for terrible crimes, on multiple life sentences without possibility of parole. That means there was no hope, and without hope a man loses interest in behaving like a civilised person. It was a pressure cooker and one day it blew. There was a riot. The procedure in a situation like that was straightforward: we got out of there as fast as we could and locked it down. Leave them to have their fun and work off the excess energy. No hurry. Turn the electricity off, call up the national guard, and order the pizzas. You think you know me, but you don't know the half of it. You can't know until you know what I've seen. Any chance of a coffee?'

'Nix.'

'How about a cigarette – they're in my jacket pocket.' I nodded assent and fished a packet out of his pocket and a lighter. I put the cigarette between his lips and lit it. A moment of unsettling intimacy. He stared up at me, his face less than a foot away.

'Thanks,' he said, the cigarette still between his lips. I took it out for him and he carried on with his story.

'A few guards were trapped on the inside, but they were lucky. They died quickly. The ones who weren't so lucky were in the segregation wing. That was where we kept the prisoners who had to be protected from the others. Some of them were in on sexual charges, with minors, but many were there because they had given evidence against the other inmates at trial. Normally, they shouldn't have been in the same prison as the folks their testimony sent down, but this wasn't a normal sort of prison.' He stopped and I put the cigarette back between his lips. He took a couple of puffs and so we carried on.

'Once it all kicked off, the first thing everybody did was raid the infirmary. They drank the rubbing alcohol and filled their mouths with fistfuls of drugs, any drugs, it didn't matter. If it was pharmaceutical they took it. Soon they were insane. They knew the national guard would show up and retake the prison, but they also knew it would be a few days before that happened. In the meantime, they were going to let off some steam. The prison was laid out in concentric rings with the segregation block at the centre. We surrendered two rings but kept to the outer one, which had the towers. It gave us a ringside seat. So we sat up there eating pizza and watching. It's not something you would want to watch, but somehow you just can't tear your gaze away. Even if you did, you could still hear it and that was worse.' He paused and looked at me and it was as if the mask of facetiousness and irony slipped from his face and I saw fear.

'Crazed on alcohol and drugs and the pent-up fury that comes from years of brutal abuse in a prison which you are never going to leave save in a wooden box, they broke into the segregation block. It took a while because they had electrical central locking and the power was down. They were all carrying torches like in a medieval witch hunt. At first, all they could do was hurl abuse at the segregated prisoners. The block was one long corridor, with the cells arranged down one side, with floor-to-ceiling bars. So although they could see each other pretty good, the men couldn't get in to the cells. This went on for a while until one of the prisoners turned up with oxy-acetylene cutting gear they'd found somewhere. They started cutting. The bars in a place like that are toughened steel; it's not easy to cut. It takes a while. You've got to remember, the guys trying to get in knew the segregated prisoners personally. They saw them in court and they had seen them from a distance, sometimes, through a window, across a yard. They knew them. These were the men whose evidence had sent them down for life without parole. And now they were inches away. All they had to do was wait until the torch cut through the steel. Eventually it did, and the mob poured into the first cell. While this was all going on, the people in the other cells on the same corridor couldn't see anything, but they sure could hear it. They could hear what happened in that first cell. Then the mob moved on to the second cell. And the same thing would be repeated, and all the guys in the cells further down got to listen to it. A process like that takes time, but they all knew no rescue was going to happen, the cavalry were not going to show up that night. The men in the cells towards the far end had to listen to it all night; it took until dawn to do the whole block, they had to listen. When I lie awake at night I picture what goes through the mind of a man in a night like that. You know what's going to happen to you, you know there is no power on earth that is going to save you; all you have is hours and hours of listening and waiting your turn.' He paused and added simply, 'I knew one of the guys in the end cell.'

I put the cigarette back between his lips. He drew on it, then spoke with it still clenched between his lips. 'That's what the Big Nose George Parrotts will do to you given half the chance. I call them the heads-on-sticks guys. You're fighting the same battle against them as . . . I . . . am.'

The hesitation in his voice lasted no longer than the beat of a gnat's wing, a glint slipped across the waters of his eyes. I understood. I knew what was coming, but by the time the understanding had taken shape, four strong, hard hands emerging from the cuffs of combat jackets appeared and grabbed my arms. I had seen these hands before and I flinched as I recalled the slam into the hard basement wall. But it never came.

'I'm sorry, Peeper, I really am.'

'Don't be, I should have known you'd arrange to have me followed.'

'They were here before me. Once you turned off just before Ponterwyd it was pretty obvious where you were heading.' One of the soldiers cut through the gaffer tape that bound Sauerkopp. He walked over to me, massaging the circulation back into his wrists.

'So why the pantomime?' I asked.

'I needed to ask you for something.' He reached into my pocket and took out the gun. 'This.' He smiled again and told them to let me go.

I drove back to town. The downpour continued unabated. On the passenger seat the wedding cake lay forlorn; the wasps were asleep amid the rubble of crumbs, or maybe they were dead, chilled by the dropping temperatures. The roads became greasy, wet ribbons and I passed a man with a broken-down car on the Lovesgrove straight. The bonnet was raised and he was standing bent over looking at the engine. I pulled up and reached over to wind down the passenger window. The man walked over and peered in. We both gasped in shock. It was Herod Jenkins. He opened his mouth to speak, but no words came. We stared at each other, open-mouthed, gripped by the same paralysis. Eventually the bubble burst.

'You,' he said.

'Mr Jenkins.'

We both paused again in bafflement.

'Lovely weather for ducks,' he said.

'Let me give you a lift to the garage.'

'I couldn't possibly trouble you.'

'It's no trouble, Mr Jenkins. I'm going that way anyway. Can't leave you standing in the rain.'

He was torn. In one way accepting help from a boy he had so often reviled as a milksop was a blow to his pride, that pride whose fierce fire burns in the breast of every school games teacher. But the alternative was an afternoon of misery. I moved the cake to the shelf beneath the windscreen and brushed the wasps onto the floor. He climbed in.

'You strap yourself in, Mr Jenkins, can't have you falling out.' I released the clutch and pulled out onto the main road.

'It's very kind of you, Knight. I'm obliged to you.'

'Don't be silly. You keeping well?'

'Can't complain. How about yourself?' He looked at me and frowned. 'Hope you don't mind me saying, but you look a bit unwell.'

I shook my head. I was fine. Or was I? The truth was, I was becoming aware of a strange malaise rising through my body. 'I'm fine, just tired, that's all.'

He wouldn't be put off. 'Bit green about the gills if you ask me. You should take better care of yourself.'

'How's the mayoral campaign going?'

'Not too well, to tell the truth. A lot of people have complained about the suitability of my candidacy. They say I am a brutal man, a man with no conscience and no heart. Can you believe it?'

'Politics is a dirty business, Mr Jenkins. People make all sorts of things up.' My conscience grew two heads and battled in my heart.

This was the man who had sent Marty to his death on that cross-country run during the blizzard. Should I be giving him a lift? Should I be offering him succour? And yet . . . surely in the raging storm all men are brothers?

'They say I set out to humiliate and oppress my boys on the games field. They say that their suffering gave me pleasure, but it wasn't like that, it wasn't.'

'You mustn't let it get you down.'

'They don't understand how it was. You were there, Knight. You know.'

'Yes, but I have to admit, don't take this the wrong way, it did sometimes seem like . . . like you were . . . were enjoying our suffering.'

He turned in the seat to face me. He was not a tall man, but he was large-framed with the repressed power and top-heavy musculature of a gorilla. He was too big for my Wolseley Hornet, and squirmed in the confined space in a way that reminded me of those terrible images from the animal-cruelty charities of black bears in cages in China, daily harvested for their gall-bladder bile. He spread his hands out in supplication, and his big, prognathous head tilted to the side in a way that I had seen once before, somewhere long ago. I struggled to recall the provenance of the image that rose up to the surface of my mind. And suddenly I knew: it was that moment when King Kong, clinging to the top of the Empire State Building with one arm and holding Fay Wray gently in his meaty paw, brings her close to his eyes to peer in wonder. The moment when the blessed sacrament of love enters the dark heart of the beast. Herod's eyes shone in the gloom like two lanterns in the night. Across his wide face, confusion and uncertainty mingled with the ache to explain, to be redeemed. 'Don't you see, it had to be that way. You thought I was cruel and monstrous, but life is cruel and monstrous. Because of this, I had to hurt you in order to save you. I had to forgo your love in order that I might deserve it. In order to save you from the beast in man's heart, I had to give you the beast's cunning. Don't you see?' He shifted again and the safety belt across his huge shoulder became taut like a ship's hawser. 'I've been there, been to the nethermost cistern of man's heart. I've seen the hobgoblins that live there. Do you know what I did before I became a games teacher? I was in charge of the chain gang out at the Cardiganshire State Penitentiary at Tregaron. You remember that, don't you? When you were a kid, your dad must have taken you out there to see them, digging the peat in their hooped pyjamas. I saw the worst that man could do to his neighbour out there. I wish I could forget what I witnessed, but the horror of it will remain with me always. It was for that reason that I had to abjure the downy pillow, the grace and frivolity of the damasked path through the woods. Don't you see? I was saving you from the chain gang.'

'But what about the boys who died on that games field?'

'We must try and see death not as the end but as the beginning of the next journey, the true journey, the one home to our Father.'

'Is it right that they should start that journey so young?'

'No, it's not right. I had no control over these things. I did my best, but often my best wasn't enough. For that I seek no forgiveness; the sin was mine alone.'

I struggled with the alien phenomenon – my games teacher suing for exculpation. 'I don't know, it seems too easy to say that now.'

'Your problem, Knight, if you don't mind me saying, is that you cling too stubbornly to your own individuality. It's the *principium individuationis*, isn't it?'

I blinked in surprise. 'Is it?'

'I've been going to night school, you see. I didn't understand these things before, I saw through a glass darkly, but now I see more clearly. This life in which we are separated from each other through the process of individuation is an illusion; the separation is the cause of all our distress and we are so blind we mistake it for truth; after death we dissolve back into the continuum and become one, and this is supposed to be the real mode of being. This is Nirvana.'

'So you were leading us to Nirvana through the January snows?'

'Not like that.'

'How, then? I like my separateness; if you take it away you take away everything that I have.'

'But that is where you err. You are what Nietzsche called the Theoretical Man. You think you can access the truths of this world through the application of reason and the intellect, but this is a false belief. You worship at the shrine of Apollo and privilege the outward appearance of form over the chthonic and inchoate forces that lurk beneath . . .' He stopped as if overcome by the realisation that the task of explanation was hopeless.

I urged him to continue. 'Yes,' I said. 'Go on.' I could feel my limbs begin to shiver, and a strange confusion seeped into my brain, the same befuddlement I felt when I first drank cider in the afternoon as a teenager.

'The truth is Dionysian, the truth of this world is suffering, which we deny out of terror that it will crush our hearts. You always stood snootily on the touchline during the games of rugby; you cloaked yourself in a post-Socratic disdain for the dark, destructive forces which we sought to channel; for beneath the surface of artifice we find the universal Will, the collective bosom of man at his most primal. Rugby was the road to immersion in this primeval oneness.'

'Do you mean like in the bath after the game?'

'Yes, sort of. This way we could transcend for a while our separation, our existential homelessness. This is tragedy in which lives the essence of existence. *Tragos* is the Greek for goat, it means "song of the goat". In this respect the rugby team was the dithyramb through whose overwhelming ecstasy of music the *principium individuationis* was dissolved.'

'These are just words you use to spell away the death of Marty.'

'But don't you see how the duality of life and death is an illusion? For both are parts of the Atman. It's like Lord Krishna said to his disciple: "Arjuna, why do you mourn? For what purpose is this sorrowing and grieving? A true wise man mourns neither for the living nor for the dead. Never was there a time when I was not, nor thou, nor these men, nor will there ever be a time hereafter when we shall cease to be." You should read your *Bhagavad Gita*, then you'd see.'

'Thanks, I will.'

I dropped him off at the garage in Llanbadarn and carried on to the Prom, driven by some desire I could not account for to see the ocean. Perhaps it was the powerful, surging currents of dithyrambic wonder or maybe it was the dawning realisation that I was unwell. The befuddlement in my head was accompanied now by a headache and a racing heart.

I parked on the Prom and walked through the neon storm. I pulled my collar up against the flashing blue and pink, but it didn't help; each raindrop carried within its silver orb a miniature simulacrum of the signs: *Eats, Liquor, Motel, Big Chief, Pier, Whelks 24hrs, Toffee Apple, Oblivion*. Neon is the ink of heartache scribbled on the night sky. The glowing cursive script of tawdriness, of the meretricious things that make up the landscape of the night wanderer. Every sign has one broken letter fizzing like the out-of-control synapses of the callers to a late-night radio show. Neon flashes in the dark alley, poor man's lightning on the wet tarmac, it catches fire in the retinas of the cat curled beneath the fire escape. It seeps into your clothes, down your neck, into your eyes; it drenches you, turns your face orange and green; you try and brush it off, but it covers the hand you brush with. It's cartoon colour that you can't wash off. I no longer had the strength. I sat on a bench, my back to the iridescence, and stared at the blank wall of darkness beyond the railings, where the only light came from down the coast, across the water, the gentle stardust of Aberaeron and beyond.

The rain eased off and the wet scent of its passing filled the night. A man walking saw me and came over. It was Raspiwtin. He sat down. We turned to face each other, but it was as if we were both lost for words.

'We're almost there,' he said at last. 'I can feel his presence. He is close.'

'Why do you seek Iestyn?'

He considered for a moment. 'Tell me, Louie, did you contemplate the *koan*? About the bombing raid on Nagasaki?'

'I did, but all I could see was the book of puzzles from which you cribbed it and made it your own. Just as you probably took the Burmese story from a newspaper and almost certainly never spent even so much as a day in the Vatican laundry.'

'Is that what you think?'

'Everything you say sounds second-hand, like someone cobbling together a false biography.'

Raspiwtin turned and waved his finger at me. 'Even if what you say were true, what would it matter? The *koan* is still true. Men think, because they have been taught to think it, that this is the way the world is and no other way is possible. But it is an illusion. It could disappear with the swiftness of a soap bubble bursting. All it takes would be the discovery of an alien species – a humanoid, seemingly not all that different from us. The realisation that we were not alone, that instead of being composed of numerous warring and bickering tribes, we were really and truly the brotherhood of man . . . Who, having gained such knowledge, could continue to regard another human being as his enemy? What would be the purpose of armies? Humanity would wake from its trance and on that morning nothing would ever be the same again. War would be over. This is the quest that brought me to Aberystwyth. One alien we know escaped from the crashed saucer in December 1965, unaccounted for. Where is he? Could he be alive? Even the skeleton would be enough. The physical, undeniable evidence that we are not alone.'

'You don't want much for your £400, do you?'

He shrugged weakly and avoided my gaze.

'Normally my clients want me to spy on an errant spouse. Or trace a missing shoe. Once I saved Aberystwyth.'

'Now you can save Humanity.'

'So that's it? Four hundred pounds – including a down payment of two hundred which you seem to have forgotten about – and for that

I find Iestyn Probert so he can tell you where to find the body of the alien, assuming it's still here. And the shock revelation will cure humankind of its addiction to war. Millennia of barbarism wiped out in a trice?'

'It's easy to mock my plan, but in truth I think it is quite straight-forward and possesses a good likelihood of success. You see, I don't think humankind would have any other choice in the circumstances. The revelation would be overwhelming; they could not fail to feel a sudden upsurge of brotherhood. In your heart can you deny it?'

My head fell forward and I caught it in my palm.

'Are you all right?'

'Just feeling a little under the weather. It's probably something I ate.'

'You should get home out of the cold and damp.' He stood up.

Just something I ate. The image of the wedding cake surrounded by dead wasps rose before my inner vision and that was followed, as I uttered up a silent cry, by another image: Meici in my office telling me about the plan to spring his mum from gaol using a poisoning idea devised by Erik XIV of Sweden. Dirty double-crosser . . .

Raspiwtin wished me good night and walked off towards the public shelter leading to South Road.

Ten minutes later another man appeared, walking inverted in the rain-glazed pavement. It was the mayor. He seemed pleased to see me.

'Louie Knight!' he cried. 'Not out shooting people?'

I looked but didn't have the strength to answer.

'I must say, you don't look all that well, you look a bit peaky. Maybe you should get yourself a new job; all this running around playing cops and robbers . . . it's not good for a man of your age. You should get a nice desk job.'

'I'll look into it.'

'I've been finding out about you. It seems you are lucky to earn enough in a month to pay the rent on that crummy caravan you live in. Why do you even bother getting out of bed?'

'I do it because I like it. I can live happily in a caravan or anywhere else, it doesn't matter how lowly, whereas you can't be happy anywhere, because you can't look in the bathroom mirror without hating what you see.'

He forced a laugh. 'Is that so!'

'We both know it's true.'

'You couldn't be more wrong. I love myself.'

'On the surface you do, but deep down where it counts you don't and never can. And I know why too, and the why is what eats you up.'

'Is it that I am unkind to my dog?'

'A dog can give you what you want, but no man can. This is what gnaws away at you. Everything is easy for people like you. If you see something you want, you take it. But there's one thing that troubles you, and try as you might you can't get the worm out of your soul. It eats you up when you wake in the night without anyone there to comfort you, and you lie waiting for the first glimmer of light, counting the loveless days until they throw you unmourned into a hole. What eats you up is the knowledge that other men don't live their lives like you do. They resist the temptation to live by abusing other people. You cannot understand what it is in their hearts that makes them abjure riches and power. What do they get out of it apart from the easy conscience and the ability to look themselves in the eye in the mirror each day? You can't understand it. These men are admired, loved even, by other men for this quality of their character. People like you are feared but never loved, not even liked. Why should you give a damn? It's because this love is the one thing in the world you will never taste. Except when you give biscuits to your dog.' As I spoke I could feel the needle dropping slowly to empty. I was finished. The shivering had reached my teeth. Over the mayor's shoulder I could see Eeyore leading the donkeys on the last traverse. There was strength left for one last lie, to send the mayor in the wrong direction, away from my father on whose donkeys I could ride away. 'Please help me, my car is down by the Cliff Railway. Will you help me to it?'

He laughed and slapped his thigh. 'Of course I will.' He rose to his feet. 'I'll get a nice policeman to help you.' And off he went, as I knew he would, in the wrong direction. I waited a while, then stood up and stumbled to the railing. I walked along holding on until I reached Eeyore and fell into his arms.

The donkey that took me back to Miaow's was called Tampopo.

When I awoke I was in bed and Calamity was sitting watching me. Eeyore was standing by the door. I moved my eyes and took in the contours of the room. It was small with white-washed stone walls. I lay in a narrow bed with a crocheted cover. At the foot of the bed was a chair upon which my clothes had been neatly folded. It was dusk; soft yellow light could be seen outside the bedroom door, from the staircase. The sound of a TV could be faintly discerned. I went back to sleep.

When I opened my eyes again it was night. I was drenched in sweat and Calamity was dabbing my brow with a face towel. Eeyore stood sentinel at the door, unmoving, watching me intensely. Doc Digwyl came in and walked over to my bedside. My instinct was to recoil, for surely his presence meant the game was up? But I had no strength to do anything and Calamity seemed unperturbed by his appearance.

'Any change?' he asked.

Calamity shook her head. 'The fever still rages and he's been raving again, saying really crazy things.'

'Like what? I need to know.'

'He said we'd all misjudged Herod Jenkins and then some things about Erik XIV of Sweden.'

Doc Digwyl pressed his lips together in concentration, as if this was the final confirmation of what he had long suspected: Erik XIV poisoning. 'We have no choice,' he said and nodded at someone outside the door. 'We must use the Katabasis ice cream.'

Sospan walked in carrying a tray upon which there was a glass dish containing ice cream and wafers. The ice cream had green ripple. Sospan seemed to be wearing his Sunday-best ice-cream outfit. The white coat was crisply starched; he wore a tie and white gloves and bore a serious mien. He handed the tray ceremoniously to the doctor, who passed it to Calamity.

'Are you sure it's safe?' she asked.

'Of course not! All pharmaceutical interventions carry an inherent risk; I cannot conceal the truth so that you might sleep better. But in times such as this, we must be brave and trust to God. Please!' He jerked the tray towards her. She picked up a wafer and scooped some ice cream onto it, then brought it up gingerly to my lips.

'Go on, girl!' said the doc. 'Screw your courage to the sticking-post!'

She pushed the wafer between my parted lips. I closed my eyes again.

Chapter 17

I AWOKE encased from chin to toe in short-crust pastry. There were other men, lying next to me, each encased in a similar sarcophagus. The scullery maid moved along the row of human pasties dipping a brush into a bowl of egg yolk and coating the pastry. She sang a ditty about the ruination of a milkmaid who met a squire on the road to the fair. The pastry was still soft and malleable. I sat up. The maid shrieked and dropped the bowl of egg onto the stone flags, where it shattered into jagged shards. I wriggled like an escapologist and the front of my casing began to unzip. I pulled my arms free and pushed the pastry down like a sleeping bag with my hands and stepped out of it. The maid shrieked again. I walked past the other pasties; the faces stared up at me, blank and immobile, like prey that has been stunned by the sting of a giant spider and awaits its fate bound neatly with silk. They were the faces of my companions from the fourth-year rugby class. I jumped down from the tabletop onto a wooden stool, then let myself hang by my fingers from the edge of the stool and dropped to the floor. I rolled over and stood up. The maid continued to squeal. I looked round, searching for a means of escape; the door to the giant's counting house was ajar and I ran towards it, but the floor was vast, like many football pitches side by side, and I suddenly knew how a mouse feels running across the kitchen floor. Suddenly the giant loomed up in the doorway and howled with laughter at the sport before him. His feet formed a suede mountain range. The suede stopped at the knee in a big, floppy turnover, and beyond that twin pillars clad in green tights rose like gasometers to the leather jerkin, cincted at the waist with a thick iron-chain belt from which the heads of children hung, dripping gore.

High above this in a place where only eagles dare was his face, cloven by the horizontal crease we children of the damned had learned to call a smile. It was Herod Jenkins, my former school games teacher. He spat out a chewed-up bag of bone and gristle and indigestible rugby jersey and roared with laughter; he jabbed out with a foot in an attempt to stamp on me. Fortunately the dim-witted maid had not bothered to take away my belongings before encasing me in pastry. I still had my leather purse. I tugged at the strings and pulled out a talisman, a piece of paper. I held it out towards the giant. 'I've got a note from my mam!' I cried. 'I've got a cold.' But Herod Jenkins just laughed and told me boys with colds were even more delicious. The magic had failed. I turned and fled. The giant came in pursuit, trying to stamp on me as I zig-zagged wildly across the stone floor. Up ahead the maid swatted down with a sweeping brush and now my way was blocked by the hem of her skirt, which lay in folds on the ground. I lifted them and climbed in. She screamed again, but the sound was muffled now in the pitch-black, strangely warm bell chamber in which I found myself. I ran blindly and blundered into a foot; it lifted as she began to hop. I clung on to her shoe and climbed up, using the walls of her sock as rigging to get out of harm's way. The hopping became wilder, each jolt stunning my consciousness and threatening to dislodge me, but I held on. I reached the knee, which was raised high so that the thigh was horizontal to the ground. Daylight flooded the cathedral of underlinen; the giant had lifted her skirt and was peering up now from the floor and laughing. Just above the knee the flesh was encircled by an elasticised rope thicker than a man's waist and from it folds of cloth ballooned upwards like the sails of a galleon. Except this galleon had perhaps belonged to the Flying Dutchman or the Ancient Mariner: the cloth was grey and mottled with the overlapping smudges of ancient stains. It did not seem that maid washed her drawers more than annually. The giant's hand swooped in and grabbed me as easily as a butcher grabs a rabbit from a hook and drew me out into the air. The maid screamed once more. The giant held me aloft, gripped by his tree-like fingers. He peered at me quizzically and I stared with dread and terror and grisly fascination into the twin dark eyes. They say that the way to fend off shark attack is to punch the shark's nose, and I considered this possibility now. Before I could decide whether it would only madden the giant further, he opened his mouth and I found myself plummeting down a manhole without end.

I fell through the darkness, tumbling slowly, biffed and butted by half-chewed tomatoes and boulders of Rice Crispies which rained down like a meteor shower. It came as no surprise to me to discover that my former games teacher bolted his food, but the revelation that he ate Rice Crispies in the afternoon was a dagger to my heart. Down and down I fell into the abyss. Then there was a splash and for a while I was unconscious.

I woke up on the shore of an inland sea, washed up like a Robinson Crusoe, above my head a domed, cavernous roof. The water lapped gently, rocking me back and forth; the surface sparkled like a moonlit lake. I crawled up the beach, which had the texture and polished, bulbous surface of lamb kidney. I struggled to my feet. Up ahead I saw a light flickering and moved towards it. The noise of conversation reached me, the light began to dance and resolve into flames. A group of women were gathered round a fire, three old crones with Punch-and-Judy hooked noses and hair wilder than the quills of a porcupine. They were stirring a cauldron set on a tripod over a fire of brushwood. The flashes from the fire revealed in brief half-glimpses sparkling pac-a-mac coats above blue suede orthopaedic boots. They were singing:

> You can burn my house, you can steal my car
> Drink my liquor from an old fruit jar
> But don't you step on my blue suede 'paedies . . .

As I approached they stopped stirring their cauldron and turned to me.

'Hssst! He comes!'

FIRST CRONE

All hail, Louie Knight, Thane of a caravan in Ynyslas.

SECOND CRONE

All hail, Louie Knight, Thane of Stryd-y-Popty.

THIRD CRONE

All hail, Louie Knight, Mayor of Aberystwyth.

LOUIE

What nonsense you talk, weird sisters. Aberystwyth already has a mayor.

FIRST CRONE

Has yes, and soon will have anew.
More to the point, 'twill be you.

LOUIE

It is an honour that I dream not of.

SECOND CRONE

Oh yes, that's what they all say.

ALL (Singing)

You should have been a chimney sweeper,
Your bottom warmed by fire.
Instead you were a dirty peeper
With a halo and lyre.

The fire went out, and suddenly there was silence, except for the far-off din of the giant's heartbeat.

'Tarry a while, midnight hags!' I said. 'I would talk with you.' But the only answer was the echo of my own voice returning to me from the white cliffs of rib.

I continued walking. My eyes grew accustomed to the dark and I came upon a hall and in the centre of the room a vast round table; around it were seated boys in the decaying cobwebs that had once been school uniforms; their arms were wires of pale flesh poking like coat hangers through the torn shirts. Their eyes had the stare of dead fish. All of them were there, all those boys whose notes from their mums had been rejected over the years, preserved at the age they'd been when they'd run out across the threshold of this world. A boy put a gentle hand on mine. I looked round. It was Marty.

'Hello, Louie,' he said.

'Marty!' My voice rasped with awe.

'I told them you would come, but they didn't believe me.'

'Where are we?'

'With friends.'

'I dreamed I was eaten by Herod Jenkins.'

'It was no dream, Louie.'

'What's the table for?'

'We are the Counsel of the Swallowed. You mustn't fret. It's not so bad here.'

'What do you do?'

'We do what we can, Louie.'

One of the wraiths, his face half-obscured by the black webs of his decaying school cap, piped up, 'We have found a way to give him indigestion.'

I backed away and walked off to the far corner of the room, where an arched door led onto a spiral staircase of stone slabs. I began to climb. It led to another great hall where I met Doc Digwyl wearing a nightshirt and carrying a candle. He greeted me excitedly and told me to follow him. The steps stretched high up into the blackness. He climbed and I followed, higher and higher. Occasionally he would stop and turn and beckon as if we were pressed for time. Higher and higher we climbed; the air got thinner and a wind whistled past. A faint disk of light appeared above our heads, like the moon through thick cloud. We reached a landing and a door opened leading onto a chamber. Miaow, wearing a pointy Rapunzel hat and carrying a suitcase, ran out and gasped when she saw me. 'Louie!'

'Come, there is no time,' said Doc Digwyl, 'the fight is about to begin.' He grabbed my arm and pulled.

'Oh Louie, I'm sorry,' said Miaow. 'Everything's turned out wrong, I'm so sorry.'

'You're leaving?'

'I have to, Louie. I've explained it all in the letter. It's on the table, next to the Jack Daniels. I knew you would find it there.' She pointed behind her to a writing bureau.

The doc pulled more vigorously and I found myself following him but looking back in dismay, yearning to return to Miaow and the letter.

'Don't forget,' cried Miaow waving. 'On the desk.'

'Read it later!' shouted the doc, 'We must hurry.'

We continued to climb. The light above our heads grew stronger and acquired an outline in the shape of a disk; the disk became more distinct and turned into a cave entrance. I followed the doctor in. We found ourselves in a cavern the colour of seaside rock, made from pink, translucent flesh; the walls were smooth and curved in giant whorls like those of a satanic cockleshell. The walls spiralled up to a hole in the roof from which daylight streamed. Water dripped from the walls making discordant sounds like a kitten dancing on a xylophone.

I looked up and around at the cavern walls.

'What do you think?' he asked in a reverential whisper.

'It's . . . it's eerie.'

'Yes, precisely. That's where we are: in the giant's ear.'

'Why have you brought me here?'

'Follow me!' He took me by the hand and dragged me into the cavern. In front of us on a raised dais there was a hospital bed upon which lay a girl in a wedding dress being attended by anxious nurses.

The bride groaned and a nurse placed a compress on her brow. She looked at me and waved feebly. It was Chastity. 'I didn't see you at the wedding, Louie.'

'I was at the back, in the trees.'

'Did you enjoy it?'

'It was beautiful.'

She emitted a groan and the doctor rushed forward; the baby's head appeared from beneath the white taffeta and was drawn out by a nurse, who handed it to Doc Digwyl. The baby was silent, regarding the room through wide, unblinking eyes colder than a fish's. It wore a little suit, with short trousers and a jacket, and all was sodden and slicked with natal slime.

'Looks just like Meici,' I said.

Chastity grinned.

Doc Digwyl tied the umbilical cord, then fished out a pair of wall-paper scissors and cut. Chastity applauded: 'Bravo!'

The baby turned to me and said, 'Remember, Louie, the giant is wrong: the community must make sacrifices for the weaklings, not the other way round.'

The nurses wheeled the hospital bed away as Chastity waved like the Queen in the back of a golden coach.

'It was nice knowing you, Louie.'

'It was nice knowing you, Chastity.'

'Come!' said the doctor. 'There is no time to lose. I just heard the bell.' He clambered forward over boulders of wax up to the hole. I followed and stood beside him in the earhole. Cool air streamed through. Doc Digwyl nudged me. 'You see, the cochlea is the seat of our sense of balance; we are well-placed. I've got money on Herod Jenkins to go down in the second.'

We looked out onto a boxing ring. Ercwleff, in silk shorts, sat on the stool in the red corner. The referee turned towards us, reached down and hoisted Herod Jenkins's gloved fist up past us. 'In the blue corner, all the way from Talybont, the tracksuited Torquemada, scourge of our school days and mocker of our manhood –' boos rang out and dough-nuts were hurled onto the canvas. 'The only full-time professional Jungian archetype of horror, the dimly demonic and sincerely satanic, half-man half-troll, the hairy, the scary, don't ever call him a fairy, ladies and gentlemen, it's your friend but not mine, school games teacher and honorary Neanderthal, Herod Jenkins!' Boos rained down and the seating thundered with a thousand stamping feet. The referee held up Ercwleff's hand. 'And in the red, the ponderous pachyderm from Pont-rhydyfendigiad, the gormless, grinning, gaping, gurning, goofing, suet-souled, swede-faced *Über*-dumpling, one of God's children but thankfully not one of mine . . . Ercwleff!' Cheers filled the arena, the bell rang, and Herod Jenkins stepped forward and punched Ercwleff on the nose. There was a split second as the world waited to see what Ercwleff would do. The crowd held its breath. And then he slowly turned the other cheek.

'Looks like I've lost my bet,' said the doctor.

Chapter 18

THE TREES and grass glittered and dripped beneath a sky dyed a deep and perfect indigo. The morning glistened like a chick emerging from the fragments of its shell, its feathers still wet with albumen. It was how I felt too as I ate my boiled egg and drank the coffee that Calamity had made. She talked as I ate. 'You were in the Giant's Castle for two days.'

'I thought the game was up when I saw Doc Digwyl.'

'Eeyore went to fetch him. He said he was delighted and couldn't wait to make you well again so he could shake your hand. "I want to shake the hand of my deliverer," he said.'

'What did I deliver him from?'

'Servitude or something. He has had one of those conversions like the bloke on the road to Damascus. He said he'd been in prison all these years and you released him.' She refilled my coffee.

'And how did I do that?'

'After the hypnotism, Mrs Bwlchgwallter went to stay with her sister –'

'I know, and then she disappeared.'

'Still hasn't been found. Tore off all her clothes and ran into the woods, they say. She told her sister about Farmer Pugh murdering his own brother and burying him in Tregaron Bog. So the sister told the police and they started looking for the body. The doc saw them and thought you'd told them about his missing fiancée and they were looking for her. For a moment he panicked, but then he realised the prospect of being able to tell the truth brought him joy. It was a terrible weight off his mind, he said. He wrote a confession and was going to post it to the police. I don't know whether he has or not.'

I spread butter over another piece of toast. It was hungry work being in the Giant's Castle. 'What else has happened?'

'I had a brainwave about the missing tape. I worked out where Mrs Bwlchgwallter must have hidden it.'

I gave her an expectant look.

'In the gingerbread alien. I went round to see, but the alien had been broken in half. I think someone beat us to it. There's something else, but I'll wait till you finish your breakfast.'

I could sense repressed excitement. 'Just say what's on your mind, Calamity. I can listen and eat at the same time.'

'Not until you finish your breakfast.'

'If you don't tell me, I won't finish.' I put the egg-covered soldier down on my side plate.

'OK,' said Calamity. 'I think I've found a way to get Meici to drop the charge.'

'Get the mayor to lean on him.'

'Right.'

'But we don't know how.'

'I think we do. Iestyn has been spotted. He's been seen up by his old house; lots of people have seen him. And there were reports of lights in the sky two nights ago up there. He's up there, Louie. If we can find him he can tell us what happened to Skweeple after Preseli took him into custody. The boxing match is this afternoon. There's still time.'

'How on earth are we going to find him by this afternoon?'

'We smoke him out. Iestyn is from the Denunciationists' community, right? Ran away to become a mechanic. So we use bait. We use a piece of technology that no self-respecting Denunciationist could possibly resist. Something so wonderful it's like pornography to him.'

'And what's that? The Devil's Bridge train?'

'Better than that. Sospan's ice-cream van.'

I stared at her wide-eyed.

'Remember you telling me he's got an emergency van hidden away in Bow Street? We take that and drive up to where the sightings are and play the tune. What do you think?'

I grinned in delight. 'I think it's so daft it might even work.' I paused and added, 'As long as Sospan doesn't mind.'

'He doesn't mind, as long as . . .'

'Yes?'

'He said as long as you don't object to him writing about you and the Katabasis ice cream in the autumn issue of *The Iceman Cometh*.'

Half an hour later we were in Bow Street lifting the garage door. The concrete counterweight gave off a dull, scraping roar. Inside, the beast glimmered mystically in the dark like a fish in an enchanted pond. We reversed out of the garage and headed first for Clarach to fill up at the petrol station. As we did so, Calamity sitting beside me in the cab put a hand on my arm in surprise. Up ahead was a woman walking towards us, down the centre of the road. She wavered from side to side and had the air of a sleepwalker or someone in a trance. She was wearing a wedding dress that was muddy and torn. I stopped and we jumped out.

'Chastity,' Calamity cried and dodged into her path with arms outstretched to catch her. 'What on earth has happened?'

Chastity struggled to speak through sobs. Her hair was wild like candy floss and a few tresses fell untidily from a broken hair slide into her face. She had lost her broken spectacles and stared at us myopically. She snivelled, and snot dribbled down over her top lip. I observed through eyes narrowed with scepticism, wondering if this was just more playacting. 'Thanks for the cake,' I said.

She gasped softly. 'Oh dear, you're angry with me, aren't you? I knew you would be. I said to Meici you'd be upset about the cake.'

'Not at all, it was very nice. It was kind of you to think of me.'

'Everything has turned out horrible. Everyone has been complaining; they've all been sick. I told Meici we should have bought a cake from a shop, but he said he knew how to make one. Damn and bother.'

'You mean,' said Calamity with eyes widening in surprise, 'everyone else was sick too?'

Chastity nodded and squeezed her eyes tight shut as more tears threatened to brim over. 'He ran out of sultanas so he used some shellfish he found. I'm so sorry.'

Calamity turned green at the thought.

'Where is your aunt?' I asked.

'She's gone home to Shawbury. She was very unhappy about me marrying Meici.'

'Where is Meici now?' I asked.

She wrung her hands. 'I don't know. For two days he was sick and all the while he was so upset about you; after you shook his hand like that he cried and said you were the best friend he had ever had. Yesterday he called the mayor and said he didn't want to lie any more and send you to prison. The truth is, he doesn't know who shot him, he didn't see. The mayor was really angry. He said he would fire Meici from the human-cannonball job. So last night Meici drove up to see him; he took his human-cannonball uniform to hand back, he was going to quit. But he hasn't come home.'

We put Chastity in the cab, squeezed in between me and Calamity. Each time I changed gear my hand rustled past the muddy silken cloth of her wedding dress. We turned the van round and headed for Capel Bangor. Before we could make the long cross-country trek to Ystumtuen we had to head south first, to Ystrad Meurig, where the mayor lived. It was probably the only time an ice-cream van ventured so far into those badlands.

The house stood at the interstice of dry-stone walls which held the hill in a net of rock. With its neat white-washed walls the place looked like a piece of cotton wool caught in a spider's web. The hills had the dry, faded green that betokened a wiry coarseness of grass in the deep country, one that paralleled the lives of those who walked across it. It was a world where compassion was atrophied by the bitter wind that never seemed to stop keening. The lane to the farm narrowed to a single track and dropped beneath the level of the fields till it was almost a groove; on either side, spiky yellow grass scratched against the sides of the van, and above our head curious sheep looked down imperiously from behind wire fences. We drove over a cattle grid and onto the muddy expanse of cleared ground before the house. Away to the right at the foot of a stone wall Ercwleff was digging.

We made Chastity stay in the van, got out and walked over to him. He seemed not to have heard the van arrive and carried on digging, oblivious. A pile of clothes lay at his feet.

We coughed and he stopped and turned.

'Hello Louie and Miss Calamity,' he said. He looked pleased to see us.

'Hi Ercwleff, are you having fun?' I asked.

He grinned.

'Not chopping desks up today?'

'That was a good game, wasn't it?' he asked.

'Yes, I really enjoyed it, didn't I, Calamity?'

'You sure did. I'm really sorry I missed that game.'

'We're playing a hiding game today,' said Ercwleff.

'Wow!' said Calamity. 'You're so lucky. You're burying clothes.'

Ercwleff made an enthusiastic hurr-hurr sound. He pushed the pile at his feet into the hole. As it tumbled in we saw that it was a human-cannonball outfit, together with a white, blood-stained shirt. 'Meici had a nosebleed,' said Ercwleff, 'and ruined Preseli's shirt.'

'Where is Meici?' I asked.

'He's sleeping. Preseli has taken him to the lake where we took the angel.'

'Do you remember the angel, Ercwleff?' asked Calamity. 'It was a long time ago.'

'Yes, Preseli brought him here and let me play with him . . . but he went to sleep.'

'When do you expect your brother back?' I asked.

'I don't know. It's a long way to the lake. It's up at Cader Idris. They are going to send a car for me later for the boxing match. We've got a special plan to win, but you mustn't tell anyone because it's a secret.'

'Oh, we won't,' said Calamity, 'we cross our hearts and hope to die, if we tell a lie.'

'I mustn't hit him. Preseli says if I don't fight I will win. Do you want to play the hiding game?'

'No, we . . . er . . . have to go now. We need to borrow the shirt.'

Ercwleff's brow clouded. He looked confused.

'Your brother asked us to fetch it,' I said. 'He changed his mind about the hiding game.'

'Yes,' said Calamity. 'He's got a new game now, he said the hiding game is boring. And he told us to get the shirt and give you some ice cream.'

At the phrase *ice cream* his eyes lit up.

'Yes!' said Calamity pointing. 'It's an ice-cream van.'

Ercwleff looked in wonder.

'Have you seen one before?'

'No.'

'Listen!' said Calamity. She darted off back to the van and climbed in the cab. A moment later the ice-cream tune started playing, tinny and anaemic, but still the only sound for miles around except the occasional bleating of sheep.

Ercwleff gasped. He looked at me; I nodded encouragement. He ran up to the van. I picked up the blood-stained shirt.

We left Chastity with Calamity's auntie in Capel Bangor and drove up into the wilds of Ystumtuen. The hills, worn smooth by the wind, have the knobbled surface of dough and are smudged with conifers that were planted long ago to replace the forests denuded by the First World War. In their shadow lie the remains of lead mines abandoned after there was no longer any need for bullets and church roofs.

The grass coating of the hills is torn and scuffed, like old shoes, and the crofts and farmsteads are tenanted by sheep and brambles. The Mr Whippy song rang out across the hills, causing the sheep to temporarily abandon the urgent business of their lives. Even the birds stopped calling and listened for a while. We pulled into a passing place on the road overlooking the valley in which Iestyn's house was situated and waited. Sheep bleated, the wind sighed, and Mr Whippy tinkled cheerily. And then the miracle happened. A man appeared from out of the woods, walking towards the van with a rapt expression as if indeed Calamity had been right; no man from the Denunciationists' community could possibly withstand the lure of this symbol of forbidden technological fruit. It was Jhoe. He was Iestyn Probert. And I had never seen him look more grokked.

Ercwleff and Herod Jenkins walked round the ring, arms raised, wearing silk dressing gowns; a cassette player played the 'Dambusters March'; the crowd roared. The ref drew the two fighters into the centre of the ring, holding each by the wrist. 'Ladies and gentlemen of Aberystwyth,' he began. 'It behooves me now in accordance with the powers invested in me to present two new aspirants to that most sacred of offices – Mayor of Aberystwyth.'

The crowd cheered. I scanned the ranks of people, mostly the usual familiar faces of the burghers of Aberystwyth, in holiday mood. But interspersed among them were faces I did not recognise: hardened, tough-looking types from the farms in the hinterlands. They looked like hired men, hired for a purpose that almost certainly wasn't good. Were they the mayor's men? Here to cause trouble? They made me uneasy. The people on either side of them looked intimidated.

The ref continued his speech. 'In performing this duty I am mindful of the centuries of tradition that weigh down upon me; countless generations of men before me have stood on this spot and presided over the sacred rite by which we elect our mayors.' The crowd grew restless and called for the fight to begin. 'Other lesser, meaner, towns,' the ref continued, 'prefer the lowly ballot box, but as you all know, a ballot is no measure of a man's true worth, whereas no one can fake the test of mettle that derives from the crucible of the boxing ring.'

The contestants slipped off their dressing gowns. Herod Jenkins flexed his biceps and splayed his back to the cheering crowd. The ref recited the thesaurus: 'All the way from Talybont, the tracksuited Torquemada, scourge of our school days and mocker of our manhood . . .' Boos rang out and doughnuts rained down on the canvas. It all unfolded as it had done in my dream of the Giant's

Castle: '. . . the goofing, suet-souled, swede-faced, *Über*-dump-ling . . . Ercwleff!'

The bell dinged and the fight began. Herod Jenkins stepped forward, punched Ercwleff on the nose. He didn't follow up with a second blow, but stopped and looked puzzled. Why didn't Ercwleff attempt to fight back? The pause lengthened, the crowd grew restless; slowly, Ercwleff turned his other cheek and presented it to his opponent. The crowd gasped, and a strange thing happened: men and women began to cross themselves. Whispers passed through the assembled ranks like a breeze through ears of corn. 'He turned the other cheek!' they said. 'Holy Lamb of God, he turned the other cheek!' At various points in the crowd the people who stood in the vicinity of the hired tough guys began to drop to one knee in a clumsy pantomime of a people struck by the presence of the Holy Spirit. They had the demeanour of players following a script, but not one they liked.

'People of Aberystwyth,' the ref said, 'we find ourselves in the presence of a miracle. Witness the shining example that has been set to us. This day marks a new departure for our beloved town, a new opportunity.' Silence descended. 'Today it is given to us to turn our backs on the curse of violence and take a different road, the one that leads towards the sunlit uplands. Today we have the chance to elect, not a fighter, but a man of peace. A lamb of God, not a lion. You all saw just now how pure and gentle was his heart – so much so that he forbore to raise his hand in violence but offered instead his other cheek in accordance with the example given to us in the blessed beatitudes of the Lord. In recommending Ercwleff to you I ask you to recall to mind the words of our Lord. For did he not say, "Whosoever will save his life shall lose it; but whosoever shall lose his life for my sake and the gospel's, the same shall save it"? As it was in Judaea, so let it be on the Prom. Ladies and gentlemen, I give you the new mayor of Aberystwyth, the loser who by losing wins, the man with the lion's strength but the lamb's heart, Er-coooooooooooo-leff!'

The crowd cheered but the celebration was short-lived, cut short by an astonishing sight: the appearance of a wild, haggard woman, naked except for the twigs and leaves that were matted into her unkempt hair. 'Stop!' she cried. 'Stop this at once!' It was Mrs Bwlchgwallter, former lead singer of the Ginger Nutjobs, and one-time paragon of Welsh gingerbread-baking. She pointed at Ercwleff. 'This man is not fit to be mayor of Aberystwyth.' The crowd turned reluctantly towards her, anger beginning to well up at the unwanted interruption. Someone threw a doughnut at her. Voices cried out to disparage her.

'Go away!'

'Put some clothes on.'

'Mind your own business!'

Mrs Bwlchgwallter's eyes glittered with insanity, or fury, or both. 'I will not be silent,' she cried. 'I will not stand by and watch the name of my beloved town sullied by the election of a degenerate mayor. This man is sin-blackened, more steeped in obliquity than any of you can imagine. This man has committed a crime of such baseness that the Lord will never forgive us if we elect him to the highest office in our town.' The crowd grew quiet, the imprecations grew fewer as the people harkened to what she had to say. 'I tell you he has committed an act abominated by all civilised peoples. He has defiled an angel!'

The crowd looked aghast.

'The angel's name was Skweeple. The poor little mite was visiting our world and was involved in a car accident. This information was given to me by Farmer Pugh under hypnosis. Iestyn Probert took Skweeple to Doc Digwyl's. Then the mayor came and arrested the little angel and took him away. He left him with Ercwleff guarding him and Ercwleff used a tin opener to get his little silver suit off.' She paused. The people in the crowd looked at her in horror. 'And then he violated him! He used him cruelly after the fashion of the men of Sodom!'

Anger and disappointment swept through the crowd. 'No!' they cried. 'No!' But it was not a 'no' of disbelief but one of dismay and dejection of spirit. Ercwleff looked queasy, aware perhaps that it was still not too late for the police to come and take him away; the ref was robbed of the power of speech. I caught sight of Raspiwtin in the crowd; he saw me and, remembering the outstanding debt he owed me, turned to escape. On finding his way blocked, he pointed at me and cried out, 'Seize that man! He is a fugitive from the law. Wanted for the attempted murder of Meici Jones!' Voices in the crowd joined in the call: 'It's Louie Knight, the fugitive!' Hands reached out to grab me. I was manhandled forward and pushed up into the ring. People began to boo and a doughnut flew past my ear. I was still holding the blood-covered shirt. I found myself face to face with Herod Jenkins. He looked at me, as surprised to see me as I was to see him.

'I need to talk to them,' I said. 'I need to speak. They must listen.'

Herod considered for a brief moment, perhaps remembering the kindness I had recently done him during the storm. He nodded. He stepped forward, twisted the microphone out of the ref's hand and pushed him roughly aside. He addressed the crowd and waved a hand over their heads. 'Everybody shut up, now!' he cried. 'Shut up the lot of you or you will have me to deal with, and you know what that means.' Evidently they did and the Prom became as silent as a church. 'You all know me as a plain-dealing man. You all know me to be a man of few words, but the words I utter I weigh carefully first. Is there anyone here who would dispute that?' There wasn't. 'You all know I have had my differences with Louie Knight over the years. For most of those years you could have said he was my enemy; certainly there was no love lost between us. So when I say to you I know this man, you can bet your bottom dollar I know what I am talking about. Is there anyone who disagrees with me on that?' There was no one. 'And so I can tell you, Louie Knight is not a murderer. He is not a fugitive. He is a good and noble man who spends his life fighting for justice on your behalf. Is this how you thank him? You turn against him the moment some villain makes an accusation? Well, in this town, for all its faults, we do not condemn a man without first hearing what he has to say for himself. Louie is going to speak and you lot are damn well going to listen and if I catch anyone not listening I will give him a belting so hard he will wake up in the middle of next week.' He handed me the mike.

I looked out at the crowd and saw Calamity with Jhoe at the front. She gave me a thumbs-up sign, and something in her expression told me plainly that this was not the time for mealy-mouthed sentiments nor Socratic appeals to reason. This was the time for the tactics of the demagogue and the fire-breathing preacher. I thrust my hand into the air holding up the blood-stained clothing. 'People of Aberystwyth!' I cried. 'Hear my words and weep! Meici Jones lies dead!' Gasps. 'Our human cannonball lies now in the dust, slain, but not by my hand, for I never raised a hand in anger to Meici. His flightless wings are now broken and forever glued to the unforgiving paving slab. No more will he soar into the blue sky with our dreams on his back, no more will he gild the mountain tops with his golden sandals! No more will he gather the clouds in his arms and bring their softness down to our hard Prom. Weep for him, I say!'

'Who?' they cried. 'Who did this to Meici?'

I silenced them with an imperiously upraised hand. 'Oh no! Do not ask me that. Do not force me to break your hearts anew. You are only men. The flesh of a man's heart was never made to withstand such a cruel blow as that.' My eyes met Calamity's again and she made an O of her thumb and index finger and gently raised it to convey her appreciation of my performance. Encouraged, I continued.

'Tell us!' they cried. 'We demand to know who took our Meici!'

'I cannot say, nay I will not! The man who did this is a man dear to your hearts. A darling of Aberystwyth. Is it right that I turn him away from the doorstep of your bosom? Is it right that I set you upon him in this frenzied hour? Is it meet that you would pluck out his beard and dash his brains against the rocks beneath the pier?'

'Yes,' they cried. 'Yes!' And from the left, at the front, the man from the twenty-four-hour sweet shop shouted, 'Be he my own grandfather I will dash him!'

The anguish was etched deep into their faces, the pain of losing Meici too great to bear, even though up until this moment not one of them had liked him.

I told them once more that I could never tell them the identity of

Meici's murderer, and then I told them. Words heard on a school trip to watch a Shakespeare play many years ago came to me across the years. 'The man whose purple hands still reek and smoke with Meici's blood is none other than our former mayor! But an hour ago he wore this shirt and would have buried it too if we had not stopped him. Look at it! See the crimson drops that Meici spilt! The man who did this was Preseli Watkins.' Gasps of horror and disbelief rang out. 'I would never have harmed a hair of Meici's head. It's true we had our disagreements, we didn't always see eye to eye.' I paused. The crowd gazed at me, mesmerised, hanging on every syllable. I remembered Meici and felt for the first time the true anguish and injustice of his death. 'Meici did not have many friends, but he chose me to be one. He regarded me as a brother and no man can give a more precious gift than that. It may be that I did not appreciate it . . .'

One or two cries of 'No' rose from the assembled crowd.

'Yes, yes, I confess it freely. If I have committed any crime, it is simply this: that I did not love him as he deserved. I don't ask you to believe this, I ask only that you fetch the police so I may tell them what I know.'

Whispers ran through the crowd: 'I think Louie has been much wronged in this matter.' 'It's true,' another said. 'Louie would never hurt Meici, they were old friends.' 'He loved him like a brother, did you hear that? How then could he have attacked him?'

'Please!' I called out. 'Call them now, bring the police here to this spot and deliver me into their keeping. That's all I ask!' A muttering realisation passed through the crowd; they acted as one, like a shoal of fish, and turned towards Raspiwtin with fury in their hearts. Fear appeared in his countenance, the fear not just of the cornered beast but of the man of the world who knows, and has probably seen, how terrible the rage of a mob can be once its collective heart has been stirred to vengeance. But Raspiwtin had the cunning of a cornered beast. A moment passed, only a fraction of a second but one of those rare splinters of time that are drawn out far longer for those who participate in the drama of the moment; his fate hung precariously in the balance as the mob bent on mischief turned towards him. He pointed at me and shouted, 'Let us have Louie Knight for our mayor!' The suggestion fell like a flaming match onto dry bracken in a parched summer. The passion of the mob switched direction again. The chant 'Louie for Mayor' tore through the ranks of people and, with each iteration it gained in volume. 'Louie for Mayor! Louie for Mayor!' I raised a voice in protest, but the torrent of their desire could not be dammed. My pleas went unheard, and so, swept forward on the irresistible tide of history, I became mayor of Aberystwyth.

Chapter 19

PRESELI MUST have got wind of what happened at the boxing match and decided not to return to town. The police duly alerted all ports and airports. They also began a search of Tal-y-Llyn Lake. It's deep and cold and lonely up there, lying in the shadow of Cader Idris mountain. It's the sort of lake that contains many secrets, including, so they say, a crashed Heinkel bomber. Meici Jones will be down there now sitting in the cockpit and, not far away, perhaps in the gun turret, will be Skweeple – one of those unfortunate visitors to town who have their holiday spoiled by an accident on the road. These things happen. The police were also keen to interview the former mayor about the murder of Mrs Lewis, and a search of his house turned up a gun among his possessions. Ballistics analysis matched it to the one that had shot Meici Jones, the one that Sauerkopp had taken from me the day of my ill-fated attempt to kidnap him. I don't know how he managed to magic the gun into the mayor's possessions, but it got me off the hook and the charge was dropped. Chastity went back to her auntie in Shropshire to sit in a rocking chair and listen to Frank Sinatra LPs every Sunday evening after church. One day, maybe in the not too distant future, her auntie will pass away and it will be just Chastity and Frankie. She will listen to him croon 'You're Nobody till Somebody Loves You' as she sifts through the memories, trying to make sense of it all, a summer holiday by the sea, a love affair with a human cannonball who flew too close the sun.

Jhoe, we learned from other sources, had recently escaped from a psychiatric hospital after reading newspaper reports about flying saucers. He had spent the previous twenty-five years in various such institutions, never receiving visits from anyone except a benefactor who took great care to see that he was well provided for. The benefactor wore black and turned up each time in a black 1947 Buick. No one knew who he was, but I did: it was Sauerkopp. The fact that Jhoe was Iestyn Probert meant that Miaow was his daughter, and arrangements were underway to have Jhoe discharged so that he could return with Miaow to the Denunciationist community in Cwmnewidion Isaf. If all this was true, if the aliens really had resurrected Iestyn, it left two unanswered questions burning in my mind. What had made him lose his sanity? And why had Sauerkopp gone to such lengths to protect him?

Preseli's absence meant that he was unable to complete the traditional handover of mayoral responsibilities. As a result, I was obliged to spend some time attending to such matters and it was three days later before I got round to Maelor Gawr caravan park.

In Reception, behind the desk, the same fat man sat, still not caring less. He was eating cake. I asked him about Miaow. He didn't take the cake out of his mouth, but mumbled through the crumbs a story I didn't catch. She didn't owe rent, which was unusual and one more reason not to care. But I cared. I was tired, too. And during the past week or so I had forgotten my manners, so when I asked him for the key to her caravan and he didn't jump to the task I stepped sharply round the desk, grabbed the back of his swivel chair and twisted him round. Then I placed my palm on the back of his head and rammed it into the filing cabinet. After that, he gave me the key. He slid it across the desk and held his handkerchief to his nose, and for a while took a break from not caring.

The curtains were drawn and the inside of the caravan was warm and stale, still heavy with the smell of takeaway Chinese food. A wasp buzzed indolently at one of the windows. I drew one curtain aside to let in some light and surveyed the scene. There was nothing in the wardrobe, nothing on the bed, no letter on the table and none in the bin. On the drainer in the kitchenette there was an empty bottle of Jack Daniels and a tumbler that had been rinsed. I picked it up and sniffed – it smelled of Parma Violets. Raspiwtin was the only man in Aberystwyth who ate them. I let the wasp out and followed.

I walked back to the office. At the stairwell to my office I smelt the Parma Violets once more. He was sitting in the client's chair much as he had done the day he'd first walked into my life. He smiled. 'She left you. It serves you right, really, for betraying me.'

'I didn't betray you. There was nothing in our arrangement about her.'

'It looks to me like you gave her your heart. That wasn't what we agreed. I should dock some funds for that.'

'Since you haven't paid me a bean, that won't be easy.'

'Why should I pay you? You haven't produced Iestyn. Our arrangement –'

'The arrangement was two hundred up front, and two hundred if I succeeded. I admit I never found him. For that I apologise, but you still owe me the first two hundred.'

He raised an upturned palm to the heavens. 'He slipped through your fingers. You are not a very good private detective.'

I shrugged in what I hoped was a convincing show of contrition. 'No, I'm not a very good detective.'

Raspiwtin smiled the smile of a man who sees through your lies. 'No, no, I happen to believe you are a very good detective. Iestyn did not slip through your fingers at all. You just fell in love with the girl and now you pretend you couldn't find him. That is what I believe. However, it no longer matters. I wanted you to find Iestyn so that I could find Skweeple. I have been making some inquiries of my own. It appears police frogmen are at this very moment searching Tal-y-Llyn Lake.'

'For Meici Jones.'

'Yes, but my information is that there may be someone else down in those bitter-cold depths: Skweeple.'

'Humanity may yet be saved. Give me the letter.'

'There was no letter.'

'Sure, and there was no Jack Daniels either.'

He reached into his jacket and took something out. 'There was no letter, just this. A photo. She left this for you on the table. That's why

I came round – to give it to you.' He slid it across the table. 'And now I shall write you a cheque for the £200. The church is a poor institution, but I am a man of integrity.'

'Both of those statements are false.' I picked up the photograph.

'Ah yes, my friend,' said Raspiwtin. 'What exquisite agony it is to look at a photograph of someone we loved and who is now lost to us. The photo is a record of a now that is past, a now that is then, like all nows; but what is a now? Who can say? It is impossible to grasp the fish of now, because even as we try it has slipped away. They rush past us so fast, these nows, they contain such detail, that we miss so much, alas! We dip our cup into the Niagara Falls of time and bring it up empty except for a few meagre droplets of memory. But a photograph! Ah that is different! A photograph is a net in which we catch it, that slippery fish of now, a record of a truth that eluded us at the time it was made. A photograph is a slide under the microscope of time, a grain of the past recovered from the bottom of the hourglass.'

I looked up and stared at him over the photo. 'Why don't you catch the slippery fish of now and write the cheque.'

'Perhaps if we were to bait the hook,' he said slyly.

I shook my head. 'You drank a whole bottle of bait at the caravan. There's no more.'

'A small libation to toast your ascendancy to the post of mayor. You will make a very fine mayor, I am sure.'

I gave in, fetched two glasses from the drainer and filled them from my hip flask. 'Don't think for one moment I have forgotten how you turned the mob on me at the boxing match.'

He ignored that and returned his attention to the photo and the vivisection of my former joy. 'Two lovers sit under a tree and squint into the bright sky, the shadow of the man holding the camera rakes the ground. I have many such photos myself . . . The wind blows her hair across her face, the man's leg moves, becomes a slight blur . . . There are plates and somewhere too the ants maybe, yes, there are always ants on such occasions. You don't notice them at the time, but later when you take out your photograph . . . my advice to you is secrete it well in a drawer you never intend to open. Then one day it will ambush your heart with such a torrent of sweet remembrance that you will be slain by the exquisiteness.' He took out a chequebook and scribbled me a cheque; he pushed it across the desk. I put the flat of my hand down on it. He drained the glass in one gulp, wished me luck and left without another word.

Chapter 20

U P BEYOND the summit of Constitution Hill, past the place where the Cliff Railway ends and past the wooden hut that serves teas, past the post embedded in concrete that holds the coin-operated telescope that ends as suddenly as life, there's a track that leads across the cliffs to Clarach. And up there too is a small radar station, unmanned but with a small place for parking off a track that leads past the many farms that dot the hills overlooking Aberystwyth. The wind never stops blowing up there, even in the depths of summer, and the grass is yellow and spiked and long and never stops dancing. This was where Sauerkopp had parked his car one afternoon at the end of May.

The old wooden carriage of the Cliff Railway creaked and groaned. From under my feet the trundle of the cable vibrated through the wooden floor. Like the brass weights of a clock, the two cars swapped places six times a day. This was the heartbeat of Aberystwyth. The up car ticks, the down car tocks . . . The town fanned out in the rear window, tiny and remote; the respiration of the sea was suspended. The car shuddered and groaned, emitting a bellow like a cow at dusk to signal arrival at the summit. I clambered out onto the inclined platform and struggled into the wind. Up here you could discern the curvature of the earth so clearly; one big circle, a globe, a planet.

Sauerkopp was sitting at the wooden picnic table outside the café, drinking tea from a styrofoam cup. There was one there for me too. He was dressed in black: black suit, black tie, black silk handkerchief peeping out of his jacket pocket, black pigskin gloves and black shoes.

He had a charcoal fedora with a black band on the table and wore a black flower in his buttonhole.

I sat down.

He looked up and smiled. 'I bought a tea for the new mayor.'

I picked up the styrofoam cup slowly, twirled it between my palms and enjoyed the stinging heat.

'So Jhoe is Iestyn,' I said. 'We finally find him and are still none the wiser because he can't tell us anything apart from weather reports from Noö. Apparently the rain has stopped.'

Sauerkopp chuckled. 'It looks like the rainy season is over, at least for another three hundred years.'

'Yes, now would be a good time to visit.'

Sauerkopp stared out to sea; in the wind his eyes narrowed and glittered.

'So, is it true?' I asked. 'The revelation that drove Mrs Bwlchgwallter nuts? Did Ercwleff violate Skweeple?'

He shrugged. 'Who knows? Preseli left Ercwleff to watch over him and he got the silver suit off with a tin opener. Maybe he was just being friendly. Either way it looks like Skweeple didn't survive the ordeal, so they threw him in the lake.'

'So he never made it back to Noö.'

'I don't know that either. The aliens came back and resurrected Iestyn to ask him what happened. I don't know if they found Skweeple again. Maybe they did: if they could resurrect Iestyn then I don't see why they couldn't do the same for their own kind. Unless too much time had passed. Maybe he's still in the lake. Who knows?'

I bowed my head into the steamy warmth of the tea. 'Calamity believes it all happened just like you say, but I'm not so sure.'

'She's a smart kid, smarter than you.'

'Someone once told me the Aviary disseminates disinformation.'

'It's true.'

'And one way they do that is forge the truth in order to discredit it. It seems to me,' I said, 'that if there really were such things as genuine contactees and the organisation you work for wanted to prevent anyone taking them seriously, if you wanted to somehow suppress the truth like Raspiwtin says . . .' I paused.

He looked at me. 'Go on.'

'A good way to do that would be to spread stories like this. Maybe even arrange for the contactee to be hypnotised and claim later that he disgorged all manner of nonsense. After all, a person under hypnosis would have no way of knowing afterwards whether it was true or not.'

'No way at all,' said Sauerkopp.

'You could claim he said anything you liked.'

'Yes, it would be like someone claiming you talk in your sleep. How could you dispute it?'

'The poor bloke coming out with a story like that would be mocked.'

'What you describe is a classic disinformation campaign. But that's not what happened with the farmer. What he described in the hypnosis with Mrs Bwlchgwallter really happened. And now, a quarter of a century later, they came back to see Iestyn.'

'For old time's sake, I suppose?'

'Why not?'

We both sat hunched over, anchoring the styrofoam cups with our hands lest the wind tipped them over.

'And yet,' I said. 'And yet . . .'

'The "and yet" is always the interesting bit.'

'If there was nothing to hide, why would you be here hiding it?'

Sauerkopp looked up and over my shoulder into the distance. 'Out there somewhere in the far reaches of our universe there is a planet identical to ours in every detail except that the two men sitting here on the summit of Constitutional Hill this afternoon are drinking rum.'

I took out my hip flask and poured rum into the tea. 'Where does Raspiwtin fit into all this?'

'Officially he's an ecclesiastical policeman from the monastery on Caldey Island, investigating the rumours about Skweeple. If he finds out it's true that Ercwleff violated Skweeple, he'll put a Zed Notice on the town. Have it razed and ploughed into the ground. But he'll never find any evidence. Old Sauerkopp is too smart for him.'

'What about unofficially? What is he really up to?'

'What did he tell you?'

'Lots of things. He told me about his time in Burma, and in the Vatican laundry, but mostly he said he was here to save humankind from making war. He said if he could prove there were aliens out there we would all stop killing each other. Was that all moonshine he was telling me?'

'No, I think he's serious.'

'It sounds like quite a noble plan.'

'It is. The trouble is, it wouldn't work out the way he thinks. It would be a catastrophe. That's what my job is all about. Keeping well-meaning fools like him in check.'

'Why? If there are aliens, why are we not allowed to know?'

He looked at me as if the answer was obvious.

'Why?' I asked again.

He sighed. 'Yes, I know. People think the revelation that we are being visited by aliens would be just so wonderful for Planet Earth; but the truth is, it would be a disaster. Do you own stock?'

'Couple of share certificates in the Rock Factory left to me by my aunt. That's about it.'

He forced a smile. 'How much do you think they would be worth the day after the aliens landed at Cardiff Arms Park? Believe me, the reaction from the mob wouldn't be pretty. I don't care greatly for religion, but I'm not sure I'd want to wake up the day all those billions of people who had devoted their lives to it suddenly found out it wasn't true. For a lot of them it is the bedrock of morality, the reason they don't kill or steal or violate your daughter. Would you like to be around when they find out they've been duped? The ultimate sanction, the penalty you pay in the next life, is no longer valid? Goodbye governance, law and order, goodbye everything. We'll all be finished, including you.'

'Don't humanity deserve to know the truth?'

'Of course they don't, you stupid fool. That's just idealistic nonsense. You know that in your heart. Even if you thought they deserved it, would you want to be the one who told them? The world might be in a mess at the moment, but it's a familiar sort of mess, it's a mess that works, and we get by after a fashion. If the President of the United States addressed the people of the world tomorrow and told them aliens were official, it would be as cataclysmic as a comet hitting the Pacific Ocean and generating a tsunami 5 miles high. It would be like the end of the dinosaurs. They'll have to disclose it one day, but I sure as hell don't want to be around when they do.'

'Of course, because once people find out the government have known for forty years and not told them, they might not be too happy about it.'

'For sure! But trust me, Louie, your head will be the first on a stick. People like you and me will be the first to get that honour because we are the stupid ones who will put up a fight when the mob arrive. When they turn up with their torches flickering in the night, the same ones who used to leave flaming crosses as their calling cards, you'll be there saying, "This is my house, no one crosses this threshold, you'll have to kill me first," and they'll be happy to oblige you. You and me are in the same business, you just don't want to believe it.'

'I don't think so.'

'You wage your war every day against the heads-on-sticks guys, the cross-burners. You get paid peanuts, risk your life for people who don't deserve it, you get banged over the head with tyre irons . . . You don't realise how close we are to the sharpened sticks. The only thing holding back the tide is the cops. You'll say they are venal and corrupt, and I wouldn't disagree, but they do the job that someone has to do. However bad they get, they will never be as bad as what happens if they don't show up to work tomorrow. And this is the golden uplands as far as humanity is concerned. In the past it was much worse. It wouldn't take much for us to regress a few centuries. That charlatan Raspiwtin says we are all in thrall, imprisoned in a cage of our own imagining, bars of delusion that we could blink away if we awoke from our trance. He's right, mostly. We are all held in thrall, but the magic spell is the delusion that the status quo I just described is robust. The head-on-sticks guys keep a low profile, they lurk in the shadows, but really, what's stopping them taking over? Almost nothing. It's just a realisation away. Have you seen how little it takes for them to take to the street and start looting? That's always where it starts. Sure, we conceal the truth. But only because we are not in the slightest doubt about what would happen if it ever got out.'

'Maybe there would be anarchy for a while, but humanity would be better off in the long run.'

'I'm sure you are right, but we've only got one life. It's like planting a tree that won't fruit in your lifetime. What's the point?'

'So you are saying it would be like that here? Aberystwyth would be like the inside of that locked-down prison you told me about?'

'Not Aberystwyth, Louie, the whole world.'

I drained my tea, crushed the cup into a ball and put it to rest on the ashtray. A puff of wind blew it away.

'The letter Raspiwtin gave me, the interdepartmental Aviary memo. I took it to a kid, a forensic linguist. He said it was a fake. But according to you it told the truth?'

'Exactly! The investigation into the story of Iestyn, the discovery that he had been resurrected, was true. So we faked the account of it.'

'In order to discredit the truth. And the Buick?'

'The Buick and the Men in Black are just a little hocus-pocus we do to blow smoke in the eyes of the masses. After all, if a man has an alien contact some people will believe him. But who's going to believe that man when he reports visits from the Men in Black and nonsense like that? Jhoe dresses like one because he is delusional. I'm the genuine article. I've got the car, the hat and the suit. I wear it to funerals too, and get to charge it on expenses. It's one of the perks of working for the Aviary.'

'Mrs Bwlchgwallter made a tape of the hypnotism. How come you are not worried about it? Shouldn't you suppress that too?'

'I'm not worried because I already know where it is. In the boot of my car.'

'Calamity guessed it was hidden in the gingerbread alien, but someone got there first. Was it you?'

'No, it was Miaow, while you were sick. She offered to trade: she would give me the tape in return for me getting you off the charge of attempted murder. I was going to anyway, but it suited my purpose to agree. That's how the gun ended up in the mayor's possessions.'

I absorbed the information. It made sense. 'There are two things I don't get. You must have kept Iestyn's whereabouts concealed from the Aviary all these years. Why do you protect him? Your job should be to deliver him up to them.'

He looked at me and became serious. 'I guess you could call it atonement. You remember me telling you once I've never killed anyone? It's true, but I was once responsible for a man's death. A very cruel death. He was from the Denunciationists out at Cwmnewidion Isaf, and he got arrested for stealing a tractor. They put him in the penitentiary at Tregaron Bog, just in transit. It was only for a few days, and we were heaving at the seams, so I put him in the segregation block. It was the weekend the riot broke out. He was the one I told you about in the end cell.'

I let out a soft gasp as the horror of that sank in.

'Besides, I've grown quite fond of Jhoe over the years.' He looked at his watch and said, 'Time, I think, to drive Jhoe and Miaow home to Cwmnewidion Isaf.'

I placed my hand on his arm. 'What made him go like this in the first place? What made him lose his sanity, do you know?'

He grinned as if he'd been hoping I would ask the question. 'The aliens showed him something . . . something wonderful . . . too wonderful. A thing not of this earth, a thing so beautiful, so glorious it blew his mind the way a 40-watt light bulb pops when you put too much current through it.'

'Am I supposed to know what it was?'

'They showed him the engine to the flying saucer.'

And then Calamity appeared over the brow of the hill, walking with the gentle gait of one for whom many of the mysteries of the world are slowly being resolved. She held her arms folded tightly in front to keep her parka closed in the fierce wind, and hobbled at a half-trot half-walk up to meet me. She grinned, and the hair blew across her gentle face.

'I've seen the Buick,' she said, eyes sparkling with excitement. 'It's amazing. You must come. It's on the track over the hill.' She took me by the hand.

Viewed from behind, the car in the lay-by had the streamlined profile of a crouching hare: bulbous, muscular thighs swelled out on either side above the rear wheels, and a tiny rear window was inset like a porthole. The panels of metal were painted in deep, lustrous black like the lacquered lid of a Steinway concert grand. They don't paint cars that way any more, they don't make anything like that any more. It was an old car, hailing from a time when every part had to flair or swoop or shine, and the nose had to grin like a chromium shark. It was the sort of car that had spent its youth at drive-in movies beneath the huge, flickering, popcorn-scented faces of Humphrey Bogart and Katharine Hepburn. You wouldn't hitch a caravan to a car like this, that would be heresy; instead you would choose one of those beautiful silver zeppelins, the Airstream trailers, made from aluminium skin and riveted like the fuselage of an aircraft. Together you would make the pilgrimage to the Promised Land along Route 66, the Mother Road, the one Steinbeck called the Road to the Great Second Chance, where Burma-Shave signs flickered along the way. Or you might, as today, make a different journey along the B4576 to Cwmnewidion Isaf. It was a beautiful old glossy black American car and looked about as unobtrusive on the verge of the road on top of Constitution Hill as Flash Gordon's rocket. They say you never forget your first sight of a black 1947 Buick.

Two people were standing next to it. Jhoe and Miaow. Jhoe came running up to us like a fawn, while Miaow held back shyly. Jhoe took my hand and shook it warmly. 'I have a daughter . . . she's taking me home,' he said. 'Home with my daughter. I'm so . . . so . . .'

'Grokked?' I offered.

His eyes filled with tears. 'Yes, so very grokked.'

'Jhoe says we can go and visit him in Cwmnewidion Isaf whenever we like,' said Calamity.

'That would be great,' I said. My words drifted as my gaze sought Miaow in the background.

Jhoe stood aside. 'Go and talk to her.'

I struggled into the wind. She stood on the summit, outlined against the sky, much as I had imagined her in the night club: hair wild and blowing freely in the wind, her gaze scanning the horizon for that sail. She flung herself into my arms and hugged me. We broke off and kissed, and then she pulled away and looked down.

'When I found your caravan empty, I thought you were going to leave without saying goodbye.'

'I was, but I changed my mind.'

'Why not change it again and stay?' I asked.

'You know I can't.'

'Why?'

She looked at me and shook her head gently. 'I'm going back to Cwmnewidion Isaf, to be with my people. I'm going to look after my dad.'

I stared into her eyes, trying to think of things to say.

'I don't fit in here in this town, Louie, I was just visiting. I'm a bit like Skweeple.'

'Maybe you should stay a bit longer.'

'I want to look after my dad. I've never had a dad.'

'I could move to Cwmnewidion Isaf. Do they allow caravans?'

'Only horse-drawn ones.' She smiled.

'I don't want you to go.'

The smile faded. 'You would never fit in among us Denunciationists.'

'I could try. They allow stills. We could make gin.'

'I wouldn't want you to. It wouldn't be you. A rabbit and a fish can fall in love, Louie. But where will they build a home?'

'Couldn't we build a dam, like beavers?'

'They might turn us into hats.'

'As long as we were the same hat, I would be happy.'

She shook her head, kissed me sadly and prepared to climb into the back of the Buick. She paused, and said, 'I think it's great that you're the mayor now.'

I smiled. 'It feels strange.'

'You'll get used to it. When is the human-cannonball flight?'

'One day,' I said. 'One fine day.'

'On that day I'll come back.' She climbed into the car and sat next to Jhoe.

Sauerkopp shook our hands and wished me well with the new job. He parted from us with the heavy heart of one who knows our paths will not cross again and feels regret for it, but knows too that there is no remedy because there are many things in this world that must be borne and cannot be helped. I put my arm round Calamity's shoulder and drew her close to me as we watched the white-walled tyres grip the turf and the great car turn with regal ease. As it drove off, two faces peered through the small porthole of a back window and we watched until they shrank to dots and passed over the hill. Calamity looked up at me. 'Please don't be ingrokked about Miaow.'

I hugged her and told her how glad I was that, despite the truly terrifying odds thrown up by the universe, Calamity and I happened to be sharing the same planet, the same epoch and, best of all, the same office. And in a region of the solar system where the rain seldom lasts for more than a week. She pressed her face against me and spoke into the folds of my trenchcoat, saying how grokked she was that I was the new mayor. I laughed, and together we walked slowly off into the wind that never stops blowing.

Acknowledgements

I would like to thank my agent Rachel, and Helen and Erica and the rest of the team at Bloomsbury.

A NOTE ON THE TYPE

The text of this book is set in Fournier. Fournier is derived from the *romain du roi*, which was created towards the end of the seventeenth century for the exclusive use of the Imprimerie Royale from designs made by a committee of the Académie of Sciences. The original Fournier types were cut by the famous Paris founder Pierre Simon Fournier in about 1742. These types were some of the most influential designs of the eight and are counted among the earliest examples of the 'transitional' style of typeface. This Monotype version dates from 1924. Fournier is a light, clear face whose distinctive features are capital letters that are quite tall and bold in relation to the lower-case letters, and decorative italics, which show the influence of the calligraphy of Fournier's time.

ABERYSTWYTH MON AMOUR

'Spot on. This rollicking black comedy should be ludicrous but isn't. Huge fun'
Arena

Schoolboys are disappearing all over Aberystwyth and nobody knows why. Louie Knight, the town's private investigator, soon realises that it is going to take more than a double ripple from Sospan, the philosopher cum ice-cream seller, to help find out what is happening to these boys and whether or not Lovespoon, the Welsh teacher, Grand Wizard of the Druids and controller of the town, is more than just a sinister bully. And just who was Gwenno Guevara?

LAST TANGO IN ABERYSTWYTH

'Combines Monty Python absurdity with tenderness for the twisted world of noir ... Add a clown, a brain in a box and an endearing gallery of grotesques and stir maliciously. Priceless' *Guardian*

To the girls who came to make it big in the town's 'What the Butler Saw' movie industry, Aberystwyth was the town of broken dreams. To Dean Morgan who taught at the Faculty of Undertaking, it was just a place to get course materials. But both worlds collide when the Dean checks into the notorious bed and breakfast ghetto and mistakenly receives a suitcase intended for a ruthless druid assassin. Soon he is running for his life, lost in a dark labyrinth of druid speakeasies and toffee apple dens, where every spinning wheel tells the story of a broken heart, and where the Dean's own heart is hopelessly in thrall to a porn star known as Judy Juice.

B L O O M S B U R Y

THE UNBEARABLE LIGHTNESS OF BEING IN ABERYSTWYTH

'Malcolm Pryce is the king of Welsh noir . . . he dishes up a dastardly mix of gothic comedy where Edgar Allen Poe meets *Phoenix Nights* in a flurry of blood-stained absurdity' *Sunday Telegraph*

There is nothing unusual about the barrel-organ man who walks into private detective Louie Knight's office. Apart from the fact that he has lost his memory. And his monkey is a former astronaut. And he is carrying a suitcase that he is too terrified to open. And he wants a murder investigated. The only thing unusual about the murder is that it took place a hundred years ago. And needs solving by the following week. Louie is too smart to take on such a case but also too broke to turn it down. Soon he is lost in a maze of intrigue and terror, tormented at every turn by a gallery of mad nuns, gangsters and waifs, and haunted by the loss of his girlfriend, Myfanwy, who has disappeared after being fed drugged raspberry ripple . . .

DON'T CRY FOR ME ABERYSTWYTH

'Inventive, funny and dark, Pryce packs more style into a sentence than most authors could hope for in volumes' *Big Issue*

It's Christmas in Aberystwyth and a man wearing a red-and-white robe is found brutally murdered in a Chinatown alley. A single word is scrawled in his blood on the pavement: 'Hoffmann'. But who is Hoffmann? This time, Aberystwyth's celebrated crime-fighter, Louie Knight, finds himself caught up in a brilliant pastiche of a cold-war spy thriller. From Patagonia to Aberystwyth, Louie trails a legendary stolen document said to contain an astonishing revelation about the ultimate fate of Butch Cassidy and the Sundance Kid, but he's not the only one who wants it. A bewildering array of silver-haired spies has descended on Aberystwyth, all lured out of retirement by one tantalising rumour: Hoffmann has come in from the Cold. Louie Knight, who still hasn't wrapped up his presents, just wishes he could have waited until after the holiday.

BLOOMSBURY

FROM ABERYSTWYTH WITH LOVE

'Effortless and hilarious . . . Pryce is in a league of his own' *Time Out*

It is a sweltering August in Aberystwyth. A man wearing a Soviet museum curator's uniform walks into Louie Knight's office and spins a wild and impossible tale of love, death, madness and betrayal.

Sure, Louie had heard about Hughesovka, the legendary replica of Aberystwyth built in the Ukraine by some crazy nineteenth-century czar. But he hadn't believed that it really existed until he met Uncle Vanya. Now the old man's story catapults him into the neon-drenched wilderness of Aberystwyth Prom in search of a girl who mysteriously disappeared thirty years ago. Soon Louie finds his fate depending on two most unlikely talismans – a ticket to Hughesovka and a Russian cosmonaut's sock.

ORDER BY PHONE: +44 (0)1256 302 699; BY EMAIL: DIRECT@MACMILLAN.CO.UK

DELIVERY IS USUALLY 3–5 WORKING DAYS. POSTAGE AND PACKAGING WILL BE CHARGED.

ONLINE: WWW.BLOOMSBURY.COM/BOOKSHOP

FREE POSTAGE AND PACKAGING FOR ORDERS OVER £20.

PRICES AND AVAILABILITY SUBJECT TO CHANGE WITHOUT NOTICE.

WWW.BLOOMSBURY.COM/MALCOLMPRYCE

B L O O M S B U R Y